A REGIMENT OF SLAVES

The 4th United States Colored Infantry,
1863–1866

Edward G. Longacre

STACKPOLE
BOOKS

Published by
STACKPOLE BOOKS
5067 Ritter Road
Mechanicsburg, PA 17055
www.stackpolebooks.com

Printed in the United States of America

10 9 8 7 6 5 4 3 2 1

FIRST EDITION

Library of Congress Cataloging-in-Publication Data

Longacre, Edward G., 1946-
  Regiment of slaves : the 4th United States Colored Infantry, 1863-1866
/ by Edward G. Longacre.
      p. cm.
Includes bibliographical references and index.
  ISBN 0-8117-0012-7
1. United States. Army. Colored Infantry Regiment, 4th (1863-1866) 2.
United States—History—Civil War, 1861-1865—Regimental histories. 3.
United States—History—Civil War, 1861-1865—Participation, African
American. 4. African American soldiers—History—19th century. 5.
United States—History—Civil War, 1861-1865—Campaigns. I. Title.
  E492.94 4th .L66 2003
  975.004'9755—dc21

                                                              2002008079

for

RUSSELL F. WEIGLEY,

mentor and friend

CONTENTS

Acknowledgments   vii

Preface   ix

One   **For Freedom and Union**   1

Two   **Off to the Wars**   21

Three   **Willing Hearts and Strong Hands**   39

Four   **Errands of Destruction**   57

Five   **Error and Redemption**   76

Six   **Heat! Dust! Flies!**   93

Seven   **"Boys, Save the Colors!"**   108

Eight   **Seaside Excursion**   124

Nine   **Like Lords and Conquerors**   144

Ten   **The Last Long Year**   161

Notes   181

Bibliography   204

Index   217

ACKNOWLEDGMENTS

I BEGIN BY THANKING THOSE DESCENDANTS OF MEMBERS OF THE 4TH United States Colored Infantry who shared with me the war experiences of their great-great-great-grandfathers: Raymond Bantum, Baltimore (Pvt. Perry Bantum, Company K); Darlene M. Dorman, Baltimore (Pvt. Jarrett Morgan, Company F); Stephen M. Hilton, Baltimore (Sgt. Alfred B. Hilton, Company H); and Tanya Jones-Sullivan, New York (Pvt. Daniel Eastard, Company A).

Several others made critical contributions to this work. For assistance in obtaining wartime writings by officers and men of the regiment, I am greatly indebted to Andy Trudeau of Washington, D.C. Dr. T. Adrian Wheat (Colonel, USA, Retired), the acknowledged expert on Civil War–era Yorktown, Virginia, helped me locate the 1863–64 camp of the 4th outside that historic town. Chris Fonvielle, Wilmington, North Carolina, gave me a guided tour of the regiment's position during the January 1865 attack on Fort Fisher. Bryce A. Suderow of Washington, D.C., and Noel Yetter of Arlington, Virginia, provided more general research assistance.

Others who assisted in one way or another include Jill Abraham, DeAnne Blanton, and Mike Musick of the National Archives, Washington, D.C.; Agnes Kane Callum, Baltimore; Susan Cornett of the Bateman Library, Langley Air Force Base, Virginia; Paul Dangel, Berwyn, Pennsylvania; Kathleen Gillikin of the Enoch Pratt Free Library, Baltimore; Bill Godfrey, Hampton, Virginia; Elizabeth Hamlin-Morin of the New Hampshire Historical Society, Concord; Randy Hackenberg and Richard J. Sommers of the U.S. Army Military History Institute, Carlisle Barracks, Pennsylvania; Mary E. Herbert and Emily Hubbard of the Maryland Historical Society, Baltimore; Ida E. Jones, Clifford L. Muse, Jr., and Robin Van Fleet of the Moorland-Spingarn Research Center, Howard University, Washington, D.C.; Bruce Kirby of the Manuscript Division, Library of Congress, Washington, D.C.; Robert E. L. Krick of the Richmond National Battlefield

Park; Barbara L. Krieger of the Dartmouth College Library, Hanover, New Hampshire; and Paul O'Neill of the Baltimore Civil War Museum.

Finally, I thank the women most responsible for keeping me writing: my editor, Leigh Ann Berry, and my wife, Melody Ann Longacre.

PREFACE

ALTHOUGH THE CONTRIBUTIONS OF AFRICAN-AMERICAN SOLDIERS WERE largely neglected for more than a century following the Civil War, several attempts to rectify the situation have been made over the past thirty years. Most of these efforts have taken place during the last decade or so, a period that saw the publication of such general works as Joseph T. Glatthaar's *Forged in Battle: The Civil War Alliance of Black Soldiers and White Officers* (1990) and Noah Andre Trudeau's *Like Men of War: Black Troops in the Civil War, 1862–1865* (1998). These and other wide-ranging studies have augmented and amplified such earlier, groundbreaking works as Dudley T. Cornish's *The Sable Arm: Negro Troops in the Union Army, 1861–1865* (1956) and Benjamin Quarles's *The Negro in the Civil War* (1953).

A more recent trend is the publication of histories of individual African-American regiments. This trend is encouraging, for the microcosmic perspective afforded by the unit history can be quite illuminating. The regiment was the basic building block—organizationally, tactically, and in matters of morale and unit identity—of every Civil War army. Also encouraging is the attention that historians recently have devoted to units of United States Colored Troops (USCT). The 54th Massachusetts, the first black regiment to take the field, has long enjoyed the lion's share of the attention devoted to African-American units, even receiving Hollywood treatment in *Glory,* a highly dramatized account of the outfit's service, released in 1989. Yet the 54th was atypical of African-American service in the Civil War. More than 90 percent of the blacks who fought for the Union served not in state-affiliated regiments, but in the USC outfits supervised, armed, equipped, and maintained by the Federal government.

Even those few works that have chronicled the USCT have overlooked a critical aspect of the African-American experience. Most have covered regiments that were recruited and organized in the Northern states, the overwhelming majority of whose members were freemen, many of whom enjoyed social, economic, and educational advantages denied to the majority of their race. As its title implies, *A Regiment of Slaves* is one of the first works to study an outfit raised in a border state (Maryland), one that featured an intriguing mix of free blacks and fugitive and liberated chattels.

Many of the earlier USCT histories have suffered from limited scholarship. While each has been based to some extent on primary sources, they include few personal accounts—published or unpublished—by the rank and file. Perhaps understandably, they have relied on the more abundant and more available writings of the units' white officers, thereby presenting a skewed perspective on regimental life. *A Regiment of Slaves* attempts to redress this imbalance by telling the story of the 4th United States Colored Infantry (USCI) as much as possible through the eyes, and in the words, of its enlisted force.

That story is a record of service and sacrifice, of hardships endured and obstacles overcome, one that closely parallels the record of the larger Union effort in the East during the latter half of the conflict. Organized in Baltimore and surrounding counties in the summer of 1863, the 4th USCI spent its first several months in the field on occupation duty in Yorktown, a strategic rear-guard position on the Virginia Peninsula. As the 1864 campaign got under way, the outfit became an integral part of Maj. Gen. Benjamin F. Butler's Army of the James, whose primary objective was the capture of the enemy capital at Richmond. As an element of the all-black 3rd Division, XVIII Army Corps, the 4th saw its first field service that May during the Bermuda Hundred campaign. Its baptism of fire came on May 18, 1864, when the 4th repulsed an attack on an earthwork it had helped build at Spring Hill, along the south bank of the Appomattox River. Six weeks later, it participated in the initial assault on Petersburg, Virginia, suffering heavily in the fighting at Baylor's Farm and rendering valuable service when attacking the outer works of the city.

Months of siege duty outside Petersburg involved the 4th in numerous skirmishes and engagements and gave it a supporting role during the July 30 battle of the Crater. Further siege duty was capped by the regiment's involvement at New Market Heights, where it penetrated the first line of defense south of Richmond. In that bloody attack on September 29, the regiment absorbed almost 180 casualties but exhibited such gallantry that three enlisted men were later awarded Medals of Honor, joining an officer of the 4th who had won the same distinction not only for New Market Heights, but also for an earlier battle. No other USCT outfit boasted more Medal of Honor recipients.

The survivors of September 29 served on the siege lines outside Richmond, after December 1864 as members of the XXV Corps, the only

American army corps composed exclusively of black units. That month and again in January 1865, the 4th USCI was sent on expedition to Wilmington, North Carolina. There it protected the rear of a Union assault force, making possible the capture of Fort Fisher, a massive earthwork that blocked land and water access to the last operational seaport of value to the Confederacy. In later weeks, the regiment played an active role in the capture of Wilmington itself. It then endured months of monotonous occupation duty that stretched beyond the formal end of hostilities, before being transferred to the defenses of Washington. Unlike most of the white units in its army, the 4th remained on duty until May 1866, more than a year after Robert E. Lee's surrender at Appomattox Court House.

By all indications, the 4th—freemen and ex-slaves alike—comported itself well, and often gallantly, until the end of its prolonged term of service. Its conduct in camp and field, and especially the manner in which its disparate elements came together to form an effective tool in the fight to preserve the Union and eradicate slavery, is a story that has been left untold for too long.

Head Quarters 4th U.S.C.T.
In the Field, July 23rd/64

[Maj. Gen. Benjamin F. Butler]:

I have the honor to state that the 4th Regt U.S.C.T. was recruited in the State of Maryland in the months of July, August, and September 1863, and that about one half of the men were Slave and one half free. . . .

—Lt. Col. George Rogers, 4th USCT

CHAPTER 1

For Freedom and Union

ON THE OVERCAST MORNING OF SATURDAY, JUNE 20, 1863, CHRISTIAN Abraham Fleetwood, a free black resident of Baltimore, left his house at 48 Tyson Street, in the southwestern corner of the city, to visit the Holliday Street home of his friend and business associate James Jordan. The walk took the twenty-one-year-old through parts of the city in which white residents predominated. As he traversed these neighborhoods, he maintained a carefully controlled pace, neither fast enough nor slow enough to attract unwanted attention.

Fleetwood was well advised to be cautious. Although Baltimore boasted the largest population of free blacks of any city in the war-torn nation, it also lay in the midst of a slave state that had long straddled the boundary between North and South. Since April 1861, when some of the earliest shots of civil war had sounded in the streets of its largest city, Maryland had maintained an uneasy neutrality. The majority of its people professed allegiance to the Federal government, but many who did so were slaveholders. Moreover, a majority of nonslaveholding Unionists appeared to support or at least condone the "peculiar institution." Conservative attitudes toward race relations held sway in Baltimore, where discrimination against African-Americans was a fact of life. Thus black residents trod lightly—literally and figuratively—when negotiating streets that lay outside their own neighborhoods.[1]

Not even a man as remarkably gifted as Christian Fleetwood could afford to make himself conspicuous in the city's white districts. Freeborn, like both of his parents, he had grown to maturity in the home of one of the city's most prominent businessmen, John C. Brune, chairman of Baltimore's chamber of commerce. Fleetwood's father, Charles, was the majordomo of the Brune household, and in early youth, Christian had been groomed to take over the position. The course of his life had changed, however, when the matron of the childless family "took a great fancy to

Christian A. Fleetwood,
circa 1863 LIBRARY OF CONGRESS

the boy and treated him almost as her own." An older acquaintance recalled meeting Christian as "a child of four or five years, elegantly dressed in embroidered jacket and silken hose, the pet and pride of the household, sitting with Mrs. Brune at the parlour window, on bright days, playing with the children of aristocratic parents in the neighborhood."

Mrs. Brune took a special interest in the boy's education. With or without her husband's approval, she taught Christian to read and write, thereby introducing him to a world of learning denied to all but a select few of his race. The youngster, "all unconscious of the unique position which he occupied, was [soon] disporting himself in the big library among the many rare and elegant books, reading romance, history, travel and poetry and laying in that fund of knowledge" that would make him one of the best educated members of black society.[2]

As a teenager, Christian could read and write so fluently that it was decided he should receive both a practical and an academic education, upon completion of which he would assume a position in John Brune's sugar refining business. Because the family's wealth depended on the raw cane that abounded in West Africa, Charles Fleetwood's son was groomed to serve as the Brunes' chief agent in the sugar-rich republic of Liberia. That newly independent nation, which had been colonized by former slaves from the American South, enjoyed diplomatic as well as economic ties with the United States. To provide the youngster with the necessary experience, in 1856 John Brune sent him on a sea voyage to Africa, which included excursions to every seaport in Liberia as well as to Sierra Leone and other countries that exported sugar to America.

Upon his return to Baltimore, the seventeen-year-old was placed in the offices of the American Colonization Society. There, under the guidance of Dr. James Hall, the organization's secretary, he was exposed to bookkeeping, accounting, and other business practices that would aid him in his future employment. Then, in the fall of 1857, the Brune family sent him to Philadelphia to begin a three-year course at the Ashmun Institute (later Lincoln University), an academy of higher learning founded by a prominent figure in the colonization movement. At the institute, Fleetwood shouldered a heavy and varied curriculum, laden with courses in Greek, Latin, and the other classical studies that buttressed every institute of higher education in that day. "All of the students, excepting myself," he recalled, "were preparing for the Ministry and followed the curriculum. I was taking a business course preparatory to an expected mercantile life in Liberia and so substituted book-keeping, French and Spanish for Theology, Greek and Latin, but had to do my turn at all of the English branches, arithmetic, algebra, grammar, geography, geometry, history and elemental philosophy." Rather than concentrate on the narrow focus that "mercantile life" demanded, he demonstrated such a wide-ranging mastery of his studies that, in June 1860, he graduated as the valedictorian of his class.[3]

Even as a college graduate, Fleetwood was not considered sufficiently prepared to enter the Brune family concern. On July 1, 1860, he began a three-year apprenticeship with the Baltimore firm of G. W. S. Hall & Company, shipping and commission merchants trading with Liberia and Liverpool. Not until the fall of 1863 did he expect to take up his "life work in Liberia." In the interim, he mixed his business responsibilities with literary and journalistic pursuits. He became one of the leading lights of a literary society known as the Galbraith Lyceum and in the spring of 1863 helped found the journal of the organization, the *Lyceum Observer*. This weekly newspaper, which Fleetwood coedited with four other residents of Baltimore including two of his best friends, Jim Jordan and A. Ward Handy, became the first journal south of the Mason-Dixon line to be owned and published by and for African-Americans. Reflecting the tastes of its editorial board, the *Observer* blended topical stories, such as an appraisal of borderland politics, with fiction, verse, and essays on topics including "The Beauty of Virtue" and "The Importance of a National Literature."[4]

However, as Fleetwood made his way uptown on this cloudy, late-spring Saturday, his thoughts were not of prose and poetry, but of events military and political. The war between the sections, which had been raging at white heat for so many months, appeared to be approaching a crisis stage. On the third of this month, the Confederate forces of Robert E. Lee had begun to depart the Fredericksburg, Virginia, vicinity, heading north. The movement marked the start of Lee's second invasion of what was considered to be Northern soil, the first having been turned back the previous September following a day of horrific carnage near Sharpsburg, in Maryland's western reaches.[5]

There seemed little doubt that the new invasion would return Lee's Army of Northern Virginia, almost 78,000 strong, to Maryland. Once in the Old Line State, the army could again supply itself from farmlands that had felt the hand of war only lightly in contrast to the ravaged Virginia countryside. There, too, Lee might recruit his depleted ranks in the state's central and eastern regions, which were regarded as fertile sources of Rebel manpower. In fact, rumor had it that Lee's second invasion would pass through Baltimore and its surrounding counties.

Even before Lee's march got under way, this view of things had stoked the fears of the local commander, Maj. Gen. Robert Cumming Schenck, who, from Baltimore, administered the military domain known as the Middle Military Department. Schenck's fiefdom was garrisoned by the VIII Army Corps, composed of about 33,000 officers and men. But the department was so vast—it took in portions of five states, stretching as far west as the Ohio River—that it could not be properly defended by so few troops, many of whom were administrative rather than combat units. Lee's natural opponent was the 93,500-man Army of the Potomac of Maj. Gen. Joseph Hooker, stationed across the Rappahannock River from Fredericksburg. But early in May, Hooker had been defeated by Lee's smaller but better-led command in the battle of Chancellorsville. Many within and outside the Army of the Potomac—perhaps including President Abraham Lincoln himself—feared that "Fighting Joe" had been so demoralized at Chancellorsville that he would never again effectively oppose his nemesis.

For his part, Schenck was concerned that even if Hooker staged a rapid pursuit, the Rebels would beat him to Maryland. If Lee did not move on Baltimore with his entire army, surely he would send a large portion of it—perhaps the greater part of his cavalry, under Maj. Gen. J. E. B. Stuart—on a raid through the Maryland countryside. Before this could happen, Schenck applied to Washington for help, only to be told he must make do with his force on hand; reinforcements were unavailable.[6]

Left to his own devices, as early as mid-May Schenck had begun to strengthen the fortifications that defended Baltimore, including Fort McHenry, whose repulse of a British attack in September 1814 had inspired Francis Scott Key to write a patriotic ode. Because most of the troops who occupied the city had been posted to the existing defenses or were patrolling outlying areas such as those crossed by the strategic Baltimore and Ohio Railroad, Schenck depended on the voluntary efforts of civilians, white and black, to improve his defenses. In some instances, these men were augmented by slaves hired from local masters.

By June 20, Schenck had decided that volunteers were insufficient to meet the job at hand. As he had feared, Lee had indeed stolen a march on Hooker, breaking Union communication lines in the Shenandoah Valley and securing the approaches to the Blue Ridge Mountains. One of Lee's three infantry corps had already crossed the Potomac River into lower Pennsylvania, while the rest of his army was poised to advance in any of several directions. Unknown even to Robert Schenck, in a matter of days Lee would consider a suggestion from Stuart that his hard-riding troopers cut loose from the main army to raid east and then north via Washington, D.C. Schenck's understrength garrison appeared to be in grave and imminent danger.[7]

Driven to desperation, on the twentieth Schenck resorted to barricading the streets of Baltimore and impressing military laborers. In theory, any citizen was fair game for the bands of city policemen, marshals, and various extralegal elements that began to scour the city. In practice, however, free blacks were singled out for detainment. Thus Christian Fleetwood, minding his own business and "thinking no evil," had advanced only a few blocks from his home when he found himself pursued by a group of "poor white trash . . . running, chasing, catching and impressing every 'likely negro' they could lay eyes on in the house or out of doors." For a time he avoided being overtaken, but in front of a theater well short of his destination, he was accosted by a group of white youngsters who attempted to "take [him] down by force."

Although Fleetwood was interested in military affairs, as indicated by the martial allusions with which he described his adventures this day, and despite his strong sense of civic duty, he was determined to avoid involuntary servitude. "Not recognizing their authority," he broke away from his pursuers and "executed a flank movement" up Lexington Street and then along North Street, which skirted the upper limits of the city. Despite his speedy maneuver, his tormentors "hung on [his] flank and rear and raised promiscuous Cain." They matched him nearly stride for stride as he veered south along Saratoga Street, heading toward the city's commercial district.

Once on that heavily populated thoroughfare, the would-be captors "reared and yelled for guard and police, but none came," said Fleetwood, "only another boy taller than myself." The boy rushed ahead of Fleetwood in an effort to head him off. Undaunted, Fleetwood shouted a warning so intimidating that the youth took to his heels. Thereafter, the black man accelerated his pace and outdistanced his pursuers.

Eventually he slowed down, caught his breath, and prepared to double back toward his destination. But before he could resume his journey, he met another African-American who had escaped from white pursuers. The man advised Fleetwood to return home and stay there until the streets were clear. Holding in check his desire to assert his rights and to oppose mob rule, Fleetwood turned back to Tyson Street, which he reached without "further molestation." But he could not leave well enough alone. After remaining indoors for a few hours, he took to the streets once again, determined to reach his friend's house.

Although he made better progress in his second attempt, it too ended short of success. This time he reached Holliday Street, but before he could gain his destination, he was set upon by four rough-looking whites, whom he took for Irishmen. They "charged at me from the rear and left flank simultaneously. To escape by the front was impossible, by the rear ditto, by the left flank ditto. I executed another strategic movement of my entire column by the right flank at a double quick step through the [Baltimore and Ohio] depot into North St." En route, he outmaneuvered a fifth Irishman who, having heard the commotion, dove at him from a North Street doorway. Making "a rapid change of base," Fleetwood, "after a forced march of about a mile, succeeded in running the blockade, passing the barricade, and occupying Fort 48 on Tyson Heights."

He "remained in garrison" throughout the following day, the Sabbath, not daring to venture forth to attend Bethel African Methodist Episcopal Church, where he taught Sunday School. By now the policemen and press gangs scouring his neighborhood had become more insistent and persistent. They hammered on every door; if denied entrance, they would break into any home where African-Americans were thought to be living. They passed by 48 Tyson Street only because a female neighbor swore that Fleetwood was out of town.

Fleetwood remained quiet and nearly immobile until Monday morning. By then his close confinement so infuriated him that he decided he "would rather go out and work on the fortifications than spend another such day . . . in the house." At length he sent a message across town to his employer, describing his plight and requesting procurement of a pass that would exempt him from the labor details. After much delay and difficulty, Mr. Hall obtained the certificate. "His statement that I was his only assistant . . . saved me," Fleetwood recalled.

By Monday afternoon, his frustration had abated. Fleeing his prison, he strolled to his place of employment. He took pleasure in displaying his pass to all who tried to bar his path: "It was amazing to see the looks of astonishment with which everyone regarded me as I passed, walking in my usual free and easy style, but with a little extra <u>set</u> to my hat, just for the fun of it." He encountered no further harassment, although he later learned that Jim Jordan and several other friends and acquaintances, including William H. Brown, a fellow editor of the *Observer*, were apprehended and put to work on the fortifications being erected on the southwestern side of the city.[8]

In the end, the labor went for naught. En route to its showdown against the Army of the Potomac in south-central Pennsylvania, Lee's main body passed through the western corner of Maryland. Stuart's cavalry ranged farther afield, but it too gave Baltimore a wide berth, passing more than twenty miles west of the city. Following its bloody defeat at Gettysburg on July 1–3, the Army of Northern Virginia went home via the same roads it had taken north. The city on the Patapsco River had worried in vain about invasion and attack. Even so, neither General Schenck nor the local citizenry breathed easily until the last Rebel had returned to the "sacred soil of Virginia."[9]

Although many African-Americans avoided service on the city's defenses or dug ditches and built revetments only under duress, hundreds of others had willingly joined the labor gangs to work alongside the white volunteers. When the invasion scare abated, many of these men expressed a willingness to continue to serve their city and their nation in a military or quasimilitary capacity. Their spirit impressed Schenck, who sought ways to harness it, not only to aid the war effort, but also to make points with his superiors in Washington. On June 30, he wrote directly to Abraham Lincoln, claiming that upward of 2,000 free black residents of the city would be willing to "fight for the Government" and that he believed "one or two regiments for the war could be raised out of the good material" available to him. As if uncertain of the strength of the martial impulse that Lee's invasion had activated, Schenck advised the president, if he wished to add these men to the army, to "authorize it . . . while the humor is on them."[10]

A year or so earlier, Schenck's suggestion would have been considered audacious, impolitic, even revolutionary; most likely, it would have been rejected out of hand. For the first two years of the war, the U.S. government in general and the War Department in particular had treated the free black population of the North with studied neglect. Two and a half centuries after the first African slaves set foot on American soil, blacks continued to be regarded as intellectually, culturally, and socially inferior to the white majority that ruled the land. From 1861 on, little attention, at least on the national level, had been paid to the notion that the race had something to contribute to the task of restoring the Union. On both sides of the Mason-Dixon line, the war that would decide the fate of the American experiment in democracy was viewed strictly as a white man's fight.

A prolonged war, especially a civil war, can exert tremendous pressure on a nation's political and social institutions. In the months following the firing on Fort Sumter, the government's thinking on the subject of black soldiers had changed, albeit with glacial slowness. By mid-1863, so many men in blue had been removed from the firing lines by death, wounds, and sickness that in many sections of the Union the manpower pool was running precariously shallow. The Federal government was about to resort to conscription—that dreaded expedient to volunteerism—on a large scale for the first time in the war (in the Confederacy, a rigidly enforced draft had been in operation for more than a year). State officials feared their constituents' reaction to the draft, but months of Union military setbacks and the specter of ultimate defeat appeared to leave the War Department little choice.[11]

Inevitably, perhaps, the government began to scrutinize a hitherto-untapped source of manpower. Free blacks in the North and in those parts of the Confederacy under military occupation numbered in the millions, and precedents existed for using them as soldiers. Individual African-Americans had served in various regiments—as they had, in smaller numbers, in the Confederate armies—since the war's earliest days. Many had done so by disguising their race; others served in defiance of legal prohibitions, often with the complicity of their officers. Moreover, beginning in early 1862, units of African-Americans had been formed in various war zones. Most of these organizations, however, had enjoyed a short life.

The door to recruiting black soldiers had first been opened by a politician-general from Massachusetts, Benjamin Franklin Butler. In the spring of 1861, Butler had given refuge to slaves who had fled to his headquarters at Fort Monroe, on the tip of the Virginia Peninsula. When a representative of their owner demanded the slaves' return, Butler, a shrewd lawyer who had made a reputation defending Irish mill workers and other members of society's underclass, refused. Having learned that the chattels had been forced to erect Confederate fortifications just beyond his lines, Butler declared them "contraband of war" and put them to work, instead, on his own defenses.[12]

Until this point, the return of fugitive slaves—regardless of whether their masters were friendly or antagonistic toward the U.S. government—

had been the unspoken policy of the occupation army. Now, however, the War Department not only upheld Butler's action, but called on other Union commanders to furnish escaped slaves with protection, sustenance, and employment. At first these benefits were limited to those who had been forced to support enemy military operations, but by early 1862, Union commanders had extended them to all fugitive slaves. Soon these commanders were also employing free blacks as laborers, stevedores, and teamsters. The theory behind the practice was simple: It freed white soldiers from rear-guard details and put them where most needed—on the firing lines.[13]

The transition of the African-American from laborer to combat soldier was an inevitable process. In October 1861, the government authorized Brig. Gen. Thomas West Sherman, commanding the land forces involved in an amphibious expedition against Port Royal, South Carolina, to use African-Americans, including escaped slaves, as "ordinary employees, or, if special circumstances seem to require it, in any other capacity." Sherman's orders left him much latitude, but he failed to exploit it; he preferred to restrict the able-bodied blacks in his department to support duties. However, his successor at Port Royal, Maj. Gen. David Hunter, a Virginia-born abolitionist, tested the limits of his authority by recruiting—in some cases, dragooning—local slaves into his command. The result was the 1st South Carolina Volunteers, a regiment composed of black enlisted men and white officers.

Although radical politicians across the North applauded Hunter's farsightedness, he had moved too precipitately for more cautious officials, including Lincoln and his secretary of war, Edwin McMasters Stanton; both disavowed the general's action. At their insistence, Hunter eventually disbanded the 1st South Carolina and made no further effort to enlist blacks.[14]

If Hunter had moved too far too fast, his timing was off by only a few months. By the fall of 1862, Lincoln had come to see that the war had forever changed the political and social fabric of American life. In this dynamic climate, he felt able to add a new objective to the war effort. On September 24, one week after Lee's retreat from western Maryland gave Lincoln the political capital he needed, the president issued a preliminary Emancipation Proclamation. Under its terms, every slave living in those parts of the country still in rebellion against the Federal government as of January 1, 1863, would be considered "forever free."[15]

Lincoln's edict, despite its limited application and uncertain enforceability, exerted a long-lasting influence on the country and the conflict. One of its more immediate effects was to open fully the door to enlisting black troops. Within weeks of its issuance, General Butler, who had been transferred to the command of occupation forces in captured New Orleans, formed three regiments of African-Americans, mainly free men with pre-war militia experience. A unique feature of these organizations was that they included black officers, one of whom was given field rank. The regiments survived Butler's relief from command in Louisiana at the end of 1862, although his successor, Maj. Gen. Nathaniel P. Banks, a more conservative political general, purged them of their black officers.[16]

Soon after Butler formed his regiments, other African-American units, commanded by white officers, sprang up in Kansas as well as on the occupied Sea Islands of South Carolina. Early in 1863, after the Emancipation Proclamation took effect, the governors of three New England states recruited black regiments, including the soon-to-be-famous 54th Massachusetts. Still other governors expressed an interest in forming units of black volunteers, not only to help defend the Union, but also to lower their states' quota of troops to be raised by conscription.[17]

Although Washington allowed the governors to fill their draft quotas with black men, it did not trust the states to administer the units thus created. Enlistment policies, as well as the manner in which units were assembled, clothed, equipped, armed, officered, and trained, varied widely from state to state. Only the U.S. government appeared able to impose uniform standards on black mobilization, ensuring that the recruits were used where, when, and how they would most benefit the war effort. As a result, on May 22, 1863, a federally controlled Bureau of Colored Troops was organized under the supervision of Maj. Charles W. Foster.

Because it was preferable to organize units from compact geographic areas, cities and states would be permitted to handle their recruiting. Once enough enlistees were on hand to satisfy the manpower standards—approximately 1,000 men for a ten-company infantry regiment, 1,200 for a twelve-company regiment of cavalry—the government would furnish them with uniforms, arms, and equipment, while also appointing their officers, all of whom, with the possible exception of chaplains, would be white. For governors, the policy represented a trade-off: While their states could avoid conscription by enlisting blacks, the officials were denied the political patronage inherent in awarding field-rank commissions.[18]

Days after the Bureau of Colored Troops began operation, the revolutionary experiment at its core appeared to prove its value. On May 27, 1863, African-American troops for the first time experienced combat on a large scale when Banks's Army of the Gulf, in remote support of Maj. Gen. Ulysses S. Grant's operations against Vicksburg, Mississippi, attacked the Confederate garrison at Port Hudson, Louisiana. Although the larger offensive failed, the blacks gave such a strong account of themselves that their supporters were greatly encouraged. Subsequent actions, such as the gallant but futile assault by the 54th Massachusetts on Battery Wagner, outside Charleston, on July 18, served to change the attitude of many white soldiers who had been aghast at the thought of fighting alongside free blacks and ex-slaves.[19]

Conversely, the African-Americans' introduction to combat incensed and alarmed their enemy. The Confederate government officially condemned the arming of black men and declared that any captured in battle, regardless of his legal status, would be treated not as a prisoner of war but as a fugitive slave. Subsequently, the Confederate Congress passed legislation that held captured white officers liable to summary execution. In attempting to raise the stakes involved, however, these policies appear to have backfired on those who promulgated them. They merely hardened the resolve of black soldiers and their leaders to fight to the last, preferring death in battle to the ignominy of the gallows or the firing squad.[20]

His earlier appeals to Washington having gone unheeded, on Independence Day 1863 General Schenck again wrote Abraham Lincoln "to suggest that somebody be sent here authorized to accept the services of, and organize, these blacks, who are now willing to be enrolled." With Baltimore no longer in danger of attack, in a couple of days Schenck would be compelled to discharge from emergency service the thousands of African-Americans who had helped bolster his defenses. More than 200 others, residents of Maryland's Eastern Shore, had tendered their services to the city and the state. Schenck pointed out that if these men were "not accepted and organized while this spirit prevails among them it will be difficult to get them hereafter."[21]

This latest communiqué had the desired effect. Although ever wary of promoting policies that might upset the neutrality of the border states, Lincoln realized that Maryland, like his native Kentucky, was a fertile source of black manpower. If recruiting could be handled deftly enough to avoid antagonizing conservative Unionists, it might bind Maryland more firmly to the war effort.

Once the president made up his mind, he acted swiftly. At his behest, on July 5 Secretary Stanton sent a telegram, via Maj. Gen. John Gray Foster, commanding the Department of Virginia and North Carolina at Fort Monroe, to Col. William Birney of the 2nd United States Colored Infantry. The son of celebrated abolitionist and presidential candidate James Gillespie Birney of Alabama, William Birney was a zealous libertarian who had long agitated for the enlistment and employment of African-American

Col. William Birney
PHOTOGRAPHIC HISTORY
OF THE CIVIL WAR

soldiers. He had recently been transferred from northern Virginia, where his own regiment had been forming, to Norfolk, a part of Foster's department, to help complete the organization of Col. John H. Holman's 1st USCI. Now Birney was informed that his services were more urgently required at Baltimore. He was directed to report to Schenck's headquarters as soon as possible, while "leaving needful directions for the work going on at Norfolk." The following day, Stanton advised Schenck of Birney's coming and informed him that a regiment would be recruited in and near Baltimore under the auspices of the Bureau of Colored Troops. Because a third USCT outfit would soon begin forming in Philadelphia, the one to be raised in Maryland would be known as the 4th United States Colored Infantry.[22]

Birney threw himself into his new assignment. Leaving Fort Monroe by boat on the evening of the fifth, he was in Baltimore, conferring with Schenck, the following morning. From the start, he exuded enthusiasm and optimism. To Stanton as well as Schenck, he predicted that if a requisite number of assistants—two officers, a drummer and fifer, and twenty picked men of the 1st USCI—were sent to him in Baltimore, he could "raise a Regiment in less than ten days."[23]

Birney's timetable would prove unrealistic. By the thirteenth, the colonel had opened a rendezvous for black recruits on Camden Street, not far from the local B & O depot. At about the same time, an enlistment office specific to the 4th USCI began operating at the corner of Baltimore and Holliday Streets, in the eastern part of the city. Recruiting began briskly, but it soon became apparent that to fill an entire regiment, Birney would have to draw on areas outside the city, where enrollment agents licensed by the government augmented his own efforts. Many of the city's black residents were reluctant to enlist—perhaps because so many had been dragooned into service by Schenck. They could not be certain that the Bureau of Colored Troops would be less inclined to violate their rights.

Another obstacle to enlistment was the knowledge that blacks would be discriminated against from the day they took the oath of enlistment. Whereas private soldiers in white regiments were paid $13 per month, most African-Americans of like rank would receive $10, of which $3 could be held back to cover clothing expenses. There was a legal basis for this inequity: Whereas the white units had been raised under 1861 laws governing the recruitment of volunteers, the only statutes applicable to USCT were militia laws that mandated the smaller compensation. Even so, the discrepancy was difficult to explain to men who were being asked to make the same sacrifices as their better-paid comrades.[24]

Discrimination also colored the payment of bounties, enlistment bonuses offered by states, counties, and municipalities, principally as a means of assisting dependents whom the recruits left behind. At first the men of the 4th USCI were deemed ineligible to receive any bounty at all. Finally, in the winter of 1863–64—with the regiment already in the field—the Maryland General Assembly voted the payment of bounties averaging about $100 per recruit. The enabling legislation, however, was so weak, and the validity of retroactive payments so murky, that many months passed before the men of the 4th saw any bonus money. By then many were dead of wounds or disease, and more than a few fatherless families had virtually disintegrated under the crushing weight of poverty.[25]

Even those disposed to overlook such inequities in their desire to fight for the Union and the liberation of their race hesitated to report to Birney's offices. Only days after evading Schenck's press gangs, Christian Fleetwood had seriously considered enlisting. Before June was out, he was seeking the counsel of parents, friends, and employers. Most of those he spoke to, including his father, Charles, advised him not to enlist, although the basis of their objections remains unknown.

On July 7, the still-undecided Fleetwood gained an interview with Birney himself. Undoubtedly the colonel was impressed by the young man's education, social standing, and interest in things military. At this first meeting, he may well have promised Fleetwood the rank of sergeant major, the highest position any enlisted man—therefore, any African-American—could attain. Even so, the following morning, Fleetwood resolved not to enlist until he could give the matter further thought. Later that day, he accompanied his friend A. Ward Handy to Birney's office for another audience with the officer who was now referring to himself, in official correspondence, as the commander of the 4th USCI. Their host's opinion that Handy was also noncommissioned officer material may have prompted Fleetwood to reconsider his course, but neither he nor Handy committed himself at this time.[26]

While Fleetwood and his friend held back, others made the decision to fight for freedom and Union. Recruits began to trickle into Baltimore soon after Birney's recruiting offices opened. Within a week or so, larger groups were flowing in from outlying areas to enlist as a body. On July 28, a steamboat hove to at the city's wharves, carrying ninety-three recruits from Dorchester County, on Maryland's Eastern Shore. At once they were sworn into Federal service and conveyed to the 4th's newly established rendezvous at Camp Belger, on the western edge of the city.

The recruits kept coming. By the first of August, one hundred African-Americans whom Birney's agents had recruited in Carroll County, in north-central Maryland, had joined the others at Camp Belger. Later that month, almost forty black residents of Talbot County, also on the Eastern Shore, took a steamer up the Chesapeake Bay to Baltimore, where all but two were found physically qualified to join the 4th. And in early September, Washington County, in the far western corner of the state, furnished another forty recruits, including several with musical talent, the nucleus of a regimental band.[27]

From the first, Birney had intended to augment freeborn recruits with fugitive or liberated slaves. Many of these he assisted in escaping from their masters; others he and his officers forcibly removed from farms, plantations, and slave pens. On July 27, Schenck granted Birney the authority to liberate the inmates of a slave prison in downtown Baltimore and enlist every able-bodied male of military age who was owned by an avowed Confederate or a Rebel sympathizer. Many of the prisoners were known to be the property not of Marylanders, but of residents of the District of Columbia. Congress having abolished slavery in the district in April 1862, these masters had transferred their chattels to Baltimore for safekeeping.

When he arrived at Camlin's Slave Pen, Birney was revolted by the conditions he found there. Fifty-six inmates, half of them women, several of them children, were living in squalor and filth. Most of the men, and

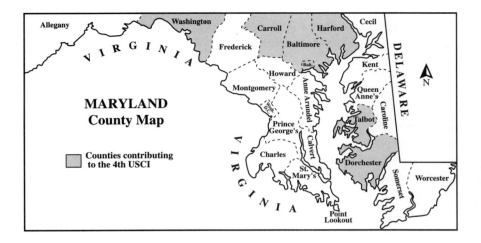

some of the women, were kept in chains twenty-four hours a day. Although not all were the property of enemies of the U.S. government, Birney freed the entire lot. When he offered the men the chance to enlist in the 4th USCI, everyone accepted. At once the colonel marched them to his headquarters, where he swore them into service, then escorted them to Camp Belger.

He also attempted to find accommodations for the women and children. Federal authorities informed him, however, that they must be released to their masters, none of whom was known to be a Confederate soldier or sympathizer. Against the colonel's protests, every slaveowner who reported at his office, produced papers of ownership, and swore his allegiance to the government was permitted to reclaim his chattels. Still, no slave who had been mustered into the 4th was removed from Camp Belger and returned to his master.[28]

When Birney extended slave recruitment to areas outside Baltimore, he encountered much difficulty. In mid-August, one of his ablest subordinates, Col. J. P. Creager, was arrested in western Maryland by local authorities responding to the protests of loyal slaveholders, whose chattels Creager had tried to lure into the army. According to Birney, in this manner 200 prospective recruits were denied to the 4th USCI. In other areas of the state, slaves who had voiced their intention to flee their masters and enlist were arrested at the behest of opponents of black recruitment. Local officials also jailed freemen who had entered into contracts with white employers, to prevent them from enlisting and reneging on their legal obligations.[29]

Although hundreds of liberated or runaway slaves eventually entered the ranks of the 4th USCI, the difficulties Birney and his agents met in enrolling them resulted in a temporary shift toward recruiting freemen. But this practice also encountered resistance when nonslaveholders loyal to the Union began to complain of discrimination. Birney's recruiters were so zealous that by late summer, the pool of free blacks on which many non-slaveowning farmers depended for labor was drying up. At exorbitant rates, employers were forced to hire workers from their slaveholding neighbors, many of whom were openly or privately hostile to the government.[30]

The perceived unfairness of the situation, coupled with Lincoln's reluctance to antagonize border-state loyalists, led to a decrease in black recruitment and a renewed effort to enlist slaves. The transition was aided by the conditional endorsement of Maryland's governor, Augustus W. Bradford, himself a slaveowner but also a committed Unionist. Furthermore, the recruitment of slaves was upheld in a ruling by Judge Advocate General Joseph Holt, as well as in an opinion issued by one of Maryland's most respected jurists, Hugh Bond.

At first, slaves were enlisted only with the consent of their masters; later, recruitment was authorized despite slaveholders' protests when it was deemed vital to the success of the war effort. In such instances, masters considered loyal to the government received fair compensation—no more than $300 per slave. Disloyal owners were paid nothing.[31]

Slaveholders greeted the new policy with vehement, and sometimes violent, protests. In October, one of Birney's recruiters, Lt. Eben White, attempted to liberate slaves from a plantation in St. Anne's County, only to be confronted by the shotgun-toting owner and his son, both avowed secessionists. An angry confrontation ended with White shot dead and his recruiting party dispersed. Before they could be apprehended, the assailants fled to Virginia, where the father remained throughout the war and the son entered the Confederate army. Federal officials retaliated by confiscating their estate, on which they settled homeless blacks; they refused to return the property to the family after war's end.[32]

＋・ ≡◆≡ ・＋

Those who joined the enlisted ranks of the 4th USCI did so for a variety of reasons, including a desire to aid the Union effort, to escape servitude or a menial job, to provide themselves and their families with a living wage, and to prove their manhood in a manner long denied them by a society mired in prejudice and discrimination. Two of the most potent motivations were voiced by soldiers of contrasting social and educational backgrounds. First

Sgt. Edward J. Wheeler of Company A, who had escaped from a Maryland plantation in 1859 via the Underground Railroad and had received a good education in Canada, avowed that he had not enlisted "for money alone," but "to fight for the flag of our country" as a means of helping liberate less fortunate members of his race from slavery, poverty, and racism. With this goal firmly in mind, Wheeler promised, "I will fight as long as a star can be seen and if [it] be my lot to be cut down in battle, I do believe . . . that my soul will be forever at rest." While few, if any, of his new comrades would have phrased it so lyrically, many undoubtedly would have echoed his sentiment.[33]

A much different, but no less potent, inducement to enter the ranks was cited by twenty-four-year-old Jarrett Morgan, a semiliterate private in Company F, the son of a free mother and a slaveborn father. When responding to the recruiting pitch of an agent who beat the drum in Harford County, northeast of Baltimore, Morgan viewed enlistment as a desirable alternative to being drafted. Conscription had begun in some of the large cities of the North in June; under the terms of a Federal law that had been enacted four months earlier, free blacks would soon be added to the draft pool. Although Maryland would not resort to the practice until the summer of 1864, Morgan had no way of knowing it would be so long delayed in his state.

In basing his decision to enlist on such a practical consideration, Morgan typified thousands of other enlistees, white and black—save perhaps in the degree of his naïveté. Having been "bound out" since youth to a plantation on Deer Creek, near Dublin, Maryland, he had acquired a reputation as a master gardener. When committing himself to join the 4th USCI, he said, "I thought that the war would be something like gardening." Years later, he reflected, "I found it out to be something very different from that."[34]

The white officers who sought commissions in the 4th did so for some of the same reasons cited by the enlisted soldiers, as well as for other motivations entirely. As was the case with officers of every USCT regiment, some were professional soldiers seeking promotion. Others had served as enlisted men in the prewar Regulars or in early-war volunteer outfits; they saw appointment to a USCT outfit—where competition for commissions was thought to be not as stiff as in many white regiments—as a stepping-stone to a more exalted position.

In fact, however, standards for obtaining shoulder straps in USCT outfits were fairly high. The vast majority of those applying for commissions in African-American regiments were compelled to appear before the officers' examining boards that had gone into session in Washington as well as in six other cities in the North and the occupied South. When quizzed by panel members on general intelligence, tactical knowledge, and other subjects, so many applicants had been rejected that preparatory schools for would-be officers had been set up, the most celebrated being the Free Military School of Philadelphia. As an inducement to attend classes, the War Department granted thirty-day furloughs to all who enrolled in these institutions. The course of instruction offered in Philadelphia and elsewhere ensured that by early 1864, only 5 of 150 applicants who went before the review boards failed the examination.[35]

Even tactically astute officers could be lax in their duties as well as insensitive or indifferent to the special needs of black troops, and a certain number of these found their way into the ranks of the 4th, as they did into every USCT outfit. A few other officers in the regiment were unfit to lead due to incompetence, intemperance, or some other defect. Nevertheless, the majority appear to have been good soldiers, equal to their responsibilities and worthy of the trust reposed in them by the government.

The 4th was especially blessed in the quality of its field officers and the members of the regimental staff. Early in August, Lt. Col. George Rogers, an Ohio-born abolitionist and a veteran of service in white outfits, assumed command of the regiment, permitting Colonel Birney to concentrate on his recruiting duties. From the outset, Rogers ruled with a firm but fair

U.S. Colored Troops taking the oath of allegiance to the Union. AUTHOR'S COLLECTION

hand. He carefully managed the early training of the outfit, winning the confidence and respect of the rank and file. In his labors, the Ohioan was ably assisted by the diminutive but energetic Maj. Augustus Boernstein, a native of Austria and a veteran of European service who showed himself to be not only an efficient drillmaster, but also a generous benefactor. Boernstein bankrolled the regimental band, funding the purchase of drums and horns. The remaining instruments were financed by a Soldiers' Aid Society composed of white and African-American ladies from Baltimore.[36]

Other beneficial additions to the officer corps included the regiment's skillful and caring medical team, consisting of Surgeon John W. Mitchell and Assistant Surgeons George G. Odiorne and Kenneth Wharry. Equally proficient, and deserving of the regiment's confidence and trust, were Adj. Marcellus Bailey, Regimental Quartermaster Alfred P. Barnes, and Chaplain William H. Hunter. The 4th's only African-American officer, Hunter was a happy exception to the discriminatory practices of the War Department. Born into slavery in North Carolina, the thirty-two-year-old clergyman had gained, as a young man, both freedom and religion. After a brief residence in Washington, D.C., he had moved to Baltimore, where he ministered to an African Methodist Episcopal congregation. Through his devotion to the soldiers of the 4th, many of whom he taught to read and write as well as counseled on spiritual matters, Hunter never failed to prove himself, in the words of one superior, "able and agreeable and hard working."[37]

From mid-July through early September, officers and men came together on the dusty parade ground of Camp Belger to demonstrate their determination to make the 4th United States Colored Infantry a fighting force in deed as well as in name. At first progress was slow and painful, and results were discouraging, for few enlisted men had even a modicum of military experience. Yet the regiment's growing pains were no more pronounced or lengthy than those that beset any white regiment that had gone to war in 1861–62.

In fact, from the first, the regiment was capable of dramatic displays. On August 10, Christian Fleetwood, along with dozens of other civilians, black and white, rode an excursion train from downtown Baltimore to witness a flag presentation and dress parade on the 4th's campground. The proceedings would have lacked polish and poise, for the newly minted soldiers had taken to the drill plain only a few days earlier. Even so, the proceedings—which included a ceremony in which the recruits pledged their fealty to the Union cause—were so inspiring that Fleetwood soon determined to cast his lot with the 4th.[38]

The master clerk spent two weeks putting his accounts in order at Hall & Company and concluding his editorial duties on the *Observer.* On August 17—five days in advance of his friend Handy—he returned to Camp Belger, where he passed a perfunctory physical examination, jotted his name on the enlistment rolls, and reported to Quartermaster Barnes, who issued him the same items of attire and equipment that the earlier recruits had received: a forage cap, or kepi, bearing a brass bugle and, above it, the numeral 4; one uniform coat of dark blue wool; one overcoat; one pair of light blue woolen trousers; one pair of bootees, or brogans; two pairs of drawers; two pairs of stockings; two shirts; one knapsack; one canteen; one haversack, a case for carrying rations; one cartridge box; one cap pouch; and two blankets, one of wool, the other rubber.

Only two days after receiving these items, Fleetwood sewed on the sleeves of his uniform coat the double chevrons that designated him as the highest-ranking enlisted man in the 4th United States Colored Infantry.[39]

CHAPTER 2

Off to the Wars

THE CITY HAD NEVER SEEN ANYTHING LIKE IT. ON THE AFTERNOON OF Thursday, September 17, the 4th United States Colored Infantry, more than 1,000 strong, marched from Camp Belger through the streets of Baltimore before a civilian crowd, alternately bewildered and excited by the unexpected display. The neophyte soldiers may have marched in something less than perfect alignment, but they did so in full military dress, their spanking-new uniforms of blue on bright display, brass buttons, belt plates, and the bayonets of their recently acquired Enfield rifles gleaming in the late-summer sunlight. In advance of the columns, the drums, flutes, and horns of the regimental band paved the regiment's way with music.

Never before had a regiment of African-Americans paraded through the heart of Baltimore. The novelty of the sight held the attention of most of the spectators, while the symbolism behind it prompted black citizens to beam with pride and shower the troops with cheers. Other onlookers— secessionists, rebel sympathizers, and those Unionists who objected to black men in arms—treated the marching men to hoots, catcalls, and an occasional brickbat. For the most part, however, order prevailed, thanks to the presence along the route of dozens of city policemen. As the march continued to the sounds of fife and drum, the cheers grew noticeably louder, while the boos slackened and virtually ceased. Marching proudly in the front ranks, Christian Fleetwood believed that he and his comrades were gradually "winning the praise of even our enemies."[1]

His opinion was seconded by the man who rode immediately in front of him. Col. Samuel Augustus Duncan, a pair of silver eagles newly perched on his soldiers, noted with satisfaction that although "it was the first time that the city had ever seen a regt. of negroes in her streets, and some enemies of the movement had thrown out hints that the regt. could not be marched through Baltimore," the day passed off without a disturbance

21

Col. Samuel A. Duncan
U.S. ARMY MILITARY HISTORY INSTITUTE

worthy of the name. Later, he wrote his mother, "It was on the whole a very satisfactory exhibition, and did much, as I have good reason to think from the many remarks reported, to soften the prejudices against col[ore]d troops—nowhere stronger, perhaps, than here."[2]

Duncan had a major stake in the way the 4th was perceived, and received, by the local populace, for the regiment was his—he had assumed command of it the previous day. Largely as a reward for the success of his recruiting efforts, William Birney had been appointed a brigadier general of volunteers and was awaiting a transfer to Charleston. There he would assume command of a brigade composed of several African-American outfits assigned to the Department of the South. The search for a successor to head the 4th had been going on for weeks before the September 17 parade, the process slowed by red tape and a dearth of qualified applicants. In the end, however, a worthy candidate had been selected.

The twenty-seven-year-old Duncan, a native of Meriden, New Hampshire, was a man of intellect, breeding, and military acumen, with an active social conscience and a desire to make African-Americans an effective tool in the struggle to restore the Union. Five years earlier, he had graduated

from Dartmouth College summa cum laude. After two years as principal of
a secondary school in Quincy, Massachusetts, he had returned to his alma
mater to obtain a master of arts degree and to join the faculty as an instructor of languages and mathematics. Duncan had remained in the classroom
through the first year of the war, but in September 1862, following the
failure of Maj. Gen. George B. McClellan's campaign on the Virginia
Peninsula and Lincoln's subsequent call for additional recruits, the professor
had accepted a company-grade commission in the 14th New Hampshire
Volunteers.[3]

He had expected to see active duty at an early date, but although his
abilities quickly brought him promotion to field rank, he found his outfit
relegated indefinitely to the defenses of Washington, D.C. By the summer
of 1863, months of inactivity, coupled with dissension among the rank and
file and rivalries among the officers, had left Major Duncan restless and
frustrated. Late in July, he complained dramatically to his family that while
other regiments had been turning back Lee's invasion of the North, "here
are we—thrown by an unkind wave upon the beach, while the giant tide of
war, its glorious exploits & achievements, goes rushing past. Idlers! Idlers
we deem ourselves—in a great city, yet exiles, exiles from participation in
the more stirring events of this eventful period."[4]

Duncan's fellow officers were aware of his discontent, but they
were not anxious to see him leave the outfit for more active service. As the
regimental historian observed, the major was "an ornament to the 14th,
and . . . representative of the best material it contained." The high regard of
his peers and superior, however, did not ease Duncan's state of mind. Noting his dissatisfaction, a civilian friend suggested that a "commission [in] a
black regiment will be likely to put you where powder & lead were thrown
about with perfect looseness." The same thought had already occurred to
the major, who also realized that the USCT offered an opportunity for
professional advancement.[5]

Unlike many officers in white outfits, Duncan had no misgivings about
leading African-Americans. In September, he informed a recent addition to
his long list of correspondents, Julia Jones of East Washington, New Hampshire, that it was "much to a man's credit and honor to lead a black regt."
His New England abolitionism, his liberal education, and his activist spirit
combined to make him a champion of minority rights. Yet, although he
was sincerely concerned with the welfare of black Americans, some of
Duncan's attitudes marked him as a product of his time, his environment,
and his class. He believed in racial equality as an abstract principle, but he
also believed in the cultural and intellectual superiority of white society. As
he wrote Miss Jones, his interest in a USC regiment notwithstanding, "as

you suggest, I would choose whites for my associates." He also ventured the opinion that commanding African-Americans was a worthy endeavor for any officer, but only as long as "he does it successfully, as a white man."[6]

Sometime in August, Duncan had appeared before the principal board for examining candidates for commissions in the Colored Troops, the one that sat in Washington under the supervision of Brig. Gen. Silas Casey. Although he had never attended any of the schools that claimed to prepare candidates for the examination, Duncan scored the highest among the nearly 200 officers and would-be officers who appeared before Casey's board that summer. At first he was told he would receive a colonelcy in Birney's original regiment, the 2nd USCI. Not until September 10 did he learn he would command the 4th instead.[7]

Duncan's initial impressions of the manpower at his disposal reveal that his attitudes on racial matters remained mixed and sometimes contradictory. When he wrote his mother about the parade through Baltimore, he remarked that the 4th was "as fine a looking body of men, so far as physique and muscle are concerned, as [he had] ever seen." He said nothing of the deportment or discipline of the men beyond the fact that they appeared "in a much better condition than [he] expected—more nearly organized and better drilled." For this happy condition, he credited the officers, not the men themselves. Even so, he believed the rank and file had great potential: "The blacks learn as rapidly as the white soldiers, if not more rapidly."

Despite his generally high opinion of the enlisted men, and although he was impressed with the attainments of Fleetwood and the other educated members of the 4th, Duncan put more faith in their physical capabilities than in their intellectual capacity. Like many USC officers, even when praising his troops, he sometimes attributed to them stereotypical characteristics, claiming, for example, that their stamina for marching, their ability to go long periods without adequate food and shelter, and their willingness to endure the numberless privations common to soldier life were inherently superior to those of white troops. Reflective of another cultural assumption, he never ceased to be struck by what he saw as the blacks' endless capacity for merriment. As he told his mother, "It is fun to see these fellows go thro' their drollery and cut up their shines. The way they shout and sing would surprise the denizens of quiet Meriden."[8]

Although Duncan viewed his men as paragons of strength and endurance, in many ways the 4th USCI was typical of every volunteer regiment, white or black, that answered the nation's call in 1861–63. At 1,007 officers and men, it was slightly larger than most of the earlier infantry outfits. The number stood as a testament to the recruiting talents of Colonel Birney and his agents, even though it had taken seven weeks, not the two

Birney had envisioned, to complete the 4th's organization. In its demographics, however, the 4th closely matched nationwide norms. The average age of its members was approximately twenty-two, although the outfit contained several men below the minimum official enlistment age of eighteen. The distinction of youngest member was shared by two fourteen-year-old privates in Company A, Moses Newman and William H. Hutchins. The eldest recruit was John R. Ross of Company C, a forty-nine-year-old machinist from Avondale, Maryland. The median height of the regiment—about five feet, seven inches—was also close to the national average. Individual heights ran the gamut from the four-foot, four-inch Andrew Ward of Company I to Company K's Grafton Cosley, a farmer from New Market, Maryland, who at six feet, six and a half inches towered above every comrade.

Only in the variety of civilian occupations did the 4th appear to stand out among USCT regiments. As was true of virtually every volunteer regiment in Union service, the 4th boasted a preponderance of farmers and laborers. While the term *farmer* appears to have been an accurate indicator of prewar profession, in many instances *laborer* served as a none-too-subtle euphemism for ex-slave. The 4th had its share of other menial occupations, including carpenter, butcher, barber, porter, waiter, bricklayer, and blacksmith. Yet skilled and professional positions also abounded, suggesting that the freeborn members of the 4th enjoyed better job opportunities than many of their brothers-in-arms. More than a few identified themselves as stonecutters, teachers, druggists, lawyers, writers, and hotel proprietors. One recruit grandly described his civilian occupation as "planter."[9]

Colonel Duncan's early observations of the officers of the 4th were as marked as his views of the enlisted force. He was impressed by the academic credentials and professional achievements of some, as he was by the combat experience of others—experience he lacked. One month after assuming command, he informed his mother:

> Some of the officers are very fine, accomplished gentlemen, and intelligent & efficient men. I refer especially to my Lt. Col. Geo. Rogers,—an old campaigner under Grant, and to the Major, A. S. Boernstein, a native German [*sic*] but highly educated, showing a practical acquaintance with military matters from an experience with the army in Missouri, as well as previously in the last Italian War. . . . I think we three make a team that works pretty well together.

Others who had his high regard included Chaplain Hunter, the spiritual anchor of the regiment; the efficient quartermaster, Albert Barnes;

Lt. Col. George Rogers
U.S. ARMY MILITARY HISTORY INSTITUTE

Company G's Capt. James H. Wickes of Boston, who had interrupted his engineering studies at Harvard to enlist; and such able and conscientious subalterns as William H. Appleton of Company E and Alfred M. Brigham of Company I.

Favorable impressions aside, Duncan viewed none of his subordinates as someone he cared to socialize with ("to my officers . . . I am under no obligations"), and he preferred it that way. By keeping his regimental relationships strictly professional, he could maintain decorum, objectivity, and evenhandedness. The distance he placed between himself and the other officers enabled him to assess and, when warranted, to criticize their attributes and performances.

At times his assessment of subordinates could be severe and even cutting. Upon assuming command, for example, he felt obliged to alter the 4th's camp arrangements so radically as to suggest that his predecessor, Rogers, was lax or incompetent, or both. The Austrian-born Boernstein he sometimes characterized, rather condescendingly, as "a little . . . Dutchman, [who] talk[ed] vehemently, gesticulate[d] all the time," and became

Maj. Augustus S. Boernstein
LIBRARY OF CONGRESS

excitable in a crisis. While he considered Chaplain Hunter a true asset to the regiment, he could not refrain from calling him "as black as the ace of spades." Then, too, within days of joining the regiment, he set up thrice-weekly meetings in which those officers he considered insufficiently versed in their adopted profession—and they were several—could be tutored in tactical instruction by a certified expert, their colonel.[10]

Although Duncan intended to whip officers and men into fighting trim as early as possible, while at Camp Belger they received only a smattering of training. At the end of that period, some officers had not yet reported to the regiment, and many men lacked a complete set of arms and equipment. Ideally, the men would have remained in camp for several weeks more, until Duncan's training regimen had taken hold. But on September 23, General Foster telegraphed Commanding Gen. Henry W. Halleck from Fort Monroe, inquiring whether the 4th was available for duty in his bailiwick, and adding: "I need their services." Two days later, Foster repeated his inquiry to Secretary Stanton. According to the departmental commander, the regiment was required at nearby Yorktown, where the local garrison was "very much enfeebled by sickness." Stanton granted the petition, and before sundown on the twenty-fifth, Colonel Duncan and his men were notified to stand ready to march.[11]

Yorktown, twenty miles northwest of Fort Monroe, site of the climactic campaign of the American Revolution, might have seemed an odd place for the 4th USCI to take the field. McClellan's attempt to capture Richmond via the Peninsula had fizzled out more than a year earlier, and except for a brief, abortive move against the city during the Gettysburg Campaign, the War Department had given no further thought to an offensive in that quarter. But when he evacuated the Peninsula, McClellan had left behind several thousand troops to guard the southeastern approaches to the enemy capital. Outposts remained in operation not only at Yorktown, but also at Williamsburg, Hampton, and Newport News, while larger Union positions dotted the south side of Hampton Roads. In these locations, Foster's troops guarded supply depots, raided guerrilla enclaves, and supported operations

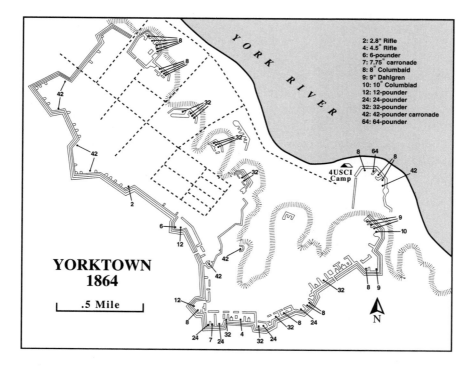

YORK RIVER

2: 2.8" Rifle
4: 4.5" Rifle
6: 6-pounder
7: 7.75" carronade
8: 8" Columbiad
9: 9" Dahlgren
10: 10" Columbiad
12: 12-pounder
24: 24-pounder
32: 32-pounder
42: 42-pounder carronade
64: 64-pounder

4USCI Camp

YORKTOWN 1864

.5 Mile

N

by the Army of the Potomac, which was now grouped around Culpeper and Brandy Station, sixty miles above Richmond.[12]

By the twenty-eighth, marching orders having been confirmed, the 4th began to strike tents west of Baltimore. At 8:00 the next morning, Colonel Duncan led the outfit down to the city's wharves, where the men crowded aboard the transport *Millie Penty.* Shortly before 2:30, amid the cheers and well wishes of friends and family members, including Sergeant Major Fleetwood's mother and sister, the boat put out into the Patapsco, bound for the Chesapeake Bay.[13]

The voyage down the Bay proceeded at a leisurely pace, aided by what Fleetwood described as "fine weather." Through that "beautiful night," he and his comrades slept on deck as they moved, almost imperceptibly, toward the seat of war. While some men easily fell asleep, others lay awake, staring wordlessly at a sky vaster than the sea that churned beneath them, their imaginations roaming freely. Some thought of the winding, uncertain road that lay ahead and hoped they would meet the demands of their new profession in a way that reflected credit on themselves, their outfit, and their families. Other men, already feeling the tug of loneliness, dwelled on the homes and loved ones they were leaving behind. A few recalled wives and children who had been "sold south" by heartless masters, wondering if they would meet again this side of heaven. Still others contented themselves by rehearsing what they would do when they met in battle representatives of the society that had kept them in bondage for so many years.

The voyage ended on the afternoon of the thirtieth, with the regiment safely arrived in Hampton Roads. Because of the lateness of the hour, the men did not embark at Fort Monroe—one of only two Southern garrisons that remained in Union hands—until the following morning. Bright and early on October 1, following a second night's sleep aboard the *Millie Penty,* the men were ushered onto the docks, arranged in marching formation, and pointed north. Before morning was over, they were well into their first forced march.[14]

In midafternoon, at the end of a dusty hike under an Indian summer sun, Colonel Duncan led the regiment through the gate of "Fort Yorktown," a rectangular perimeter of redoubts, redans, bastions, and other defenses that sprawled south and east of the Colonial-area village on the York River. The fort was defended not only by infantry and land-based artillery, but also by the guns of U.S. Navy warships in the York. Sections of the works had been erected on the foundations of the defenses that American, British, and French troops had thrown up in the fall of 1781. For the most part, however, the fort reflected the labor of the Confederate forces, initially under Brig. Gen. John Bankhead Magruder, who had occupied Yorktown eighty years after Lord Cornwallis surrendered to the forces of Washington and Rochambeau.

The most formidable sectors of the works protected the heavy batteries that McClellan had erected in April 1862 after deciding to besiege Magruder's men. "Little Mac" had expected to batter the enemy garrison (later commanded by Robert E. Lee's immediate predecessor, Gen. Joseph E. Johnston) into surrender with his long-range cannons, but he never got the chance. On May 3–4, twenty-four hours before the Federals were to open fire, Johnston evacuated the place and headed for Richmond, slipping the trap McClellan had so meticulously prepared. Town and fortifications had remained in Union hands ever since, although later garrisons never approached the size of McClellan's army.[15]

As the 4th USCI marched inside Fort Yorktown, it attracted the quizzical looks of the several regiments and batteries of white troops that had long occupied the area. It also drew openmouthed expressions of surprise from local African-American civilians. Most of the blacks, denizens of "Slabtown," a cluster of fifty or more cabins and huts that squatted outside the southern boundary of the fort, were fugitive slaves who had attached themselves to the local forces. In many respects, Slabtown was representative of the other slave communities on the Peninsula. A larger, better-arranged example was Camp Hamilton, the freedmen's village outside Fort Monroe, whose existence owed to Ben Butler's decision to protect human contraband.[16]

Few of the white troops and even fewer of the African-Americans had seen a USC outfit in full array. For days thereafter, curious glances followed the men of the 4th wherever they went. Most of the whites—members of Brig. Gen. Isaac J. Wistar's brigade of Foster's command—were wary of the 4th's fighting abilities and doubtful the regiment would prove an effective addition to the garrison. Wistar himself, a politician-general like Ben Butler but without Butler's open mind and liberal instincts, reflected the sentiment of many, perhaps most, of his troops when he described the USCT as "a Government pet and plaything . . . not good to tie to in battle."[17]

For their part, the inhabitants of Slabtown—once they recovered from the shock of seeing black men in uniforms and under arms—were delighted by the 4th's coming. Throughout its tenure at Yorktown, the regiment greeted visitors from the shantytown, with many of whom they shared their rations and even their pay. Whenever possible, the civilians returned the hospitality, treating off-duty soldiers to the endearing comforts of hearth and table.

Regardless of their attitude toward black troops in general, Wistar and his men welcomed the 4th USCI out of sheer necessity. As General Foster had so feelingly observed, climate and geography had combined to make this section of the Virginia tidewater an unhealthy venue. "The whole region," Colonel Duncan discovered, "is more or less malarial. The troops here . . . during the summer were fearfully prostrated by fever & ague & typhoid . . . the wretched water and terrible filth of the place rendering it exceedingly unhealthy beyond the possibility of prevention."[18]

Duncan was not alone in condemning the local conditions. At this same time, a member of another regiment, also new to the region, declared that the first sight to meet his eye was the abundance of fresh graves that surrounded the "accursed sand hole" of a garrison. The man found the leading military hospital in the area filled almost to bursting and the others only slightly less crowded. More patients could be expected, for within days of the 4th's arrival, smallpox appeared in Slabtown. Until the outbreak subsided, no member of the garrison was permitted to visit either the contraband camp or Yorktown itself, which Duncan described as consisting of "about 30 houses, small[,] old & decayed."[19]

The colonel originally intended to pitch camp inside Fort Yorktown, but an inspection of the works prompted second thoughts. The fastidious officer was appalled by what he found: "The interior is full of ravines, which are filled with the impurities accumulated there during the rebel occupation. An age cannot purify it, save by fire." Had he wished to be fair, he would have added that most of the filth was the product of the Union occupation, which had lasted far longer than the enemy's.

Turning his back on the noisome ravines, the 4th's commander selected a stretch of open ground on a river bluff just beyond the eastern face of the fort. The spot, near the site of British Redoubts 9 and 10, whose capture had sealed the fate of Cornwallis's army, Duncan called "the best location of the whole neighborhood. The air is pure, and the water abundant and excellent." He chose wisely indeed, for although the diseases endemic to the area sickened many of the white troops over the next several months, Sergeant Major Fleetwood reported that throughout the period, the 4th USCI enjoyed, on the whole, excellent health.[20]

The robust condition of the regiment also owed to the care given it by its trio of surgeons, as well as by the commander of the main hospital at Yorktown, Dr. J. G. Porteus, and his matron of nurses, Miss Melissa Vail. Other factors included the abundant and generally nutritious rations the regiment enjoyed throughout its stay, and perhaps also the daily issuance, beginning in early November, of beverages spiked with quinine—a cup of coffee at breakfast and a gill of whiskey before lights-out. Yet even with these advantages, the descriptive rolls of the regiment indicate that twenty-six of its men died from various causes during the 4th's time at Yorktown;

Lt. Marcellus Bailey
U.S. ARMY MILITARY HISTORY INSTITUTE

sixteen had succumbed to disease. Two of the dead—Privates Nathan Owens and William Banks—are buried in the yard of the national cemetery that was erected in 1866 within the perimeter of the fort.[21]

Once Duncan had designated the campsite, the 4th's quartermasters laid out its confines, which encompassed company streets and an adjacent parade ground. The men then began to erect their "dog houses," or shelter tents. Fatigue and police duty occupied the rest of the day; toward its close, everyone was drawn up in column on the embryonic drill field, where Adj. Marcellus Bailey read aloud general orders that fixed the regiment's daily routine. Until further notice, the day would begin at daybreak, when the buglers assigned to Wistar's headquarters blew reveille. Drill—the most basic and also the most important skill the regiment had to acquire—would commence just after breakfast and would last until 8:00 A.M. At that hour, guard mounting would take place, during which men would be detailed as sentinels and pickets. Policing of campground and quarters would begin at 9:00, followed by battalion drill, in which two or more companies would maneuver as a unit. At noon, the outfit would be called to dinner. The better part of the afternoon would be devoted to drill, in both battalion and regimental strength. Supper call would be sounded at 5:00 P.M., after which the men would attend to various chores, and the officers would recite tactics in the colonel's tent. At sunset, there would be a retreat ceremony and often a dress parade. Promptly at 9:00 P.M., the men would be ordered to extinguish lights and bed down.[22]

Their day would end with a flourish. Until mid-1862, Union troops on the Peninsula had marked lights-out with a rather nondescript bugle call known as tattoo. The previous summer, in the aftermath of the failed offensive against Richmond, one of McClellan's brigadiers, Daniel Butterfield of New York, had composed a new call, first played in his brigade's camp on the James River. Within days of its introduction, Taps, also known as "Butterfield's Lullaby," had found acceptance not only throughout the Army of the Potomac, but in virtually every Union encampment in the Eastern Theater. Thus, each night they spent in Yorktown, the men of the 4th USCI retired to a haunting refrain that seemed to beckon all soldiers, the dead as well as the living, to their rest.[23]

If drilling occupied the greater part of each recruit's day, he also spent much time at target practice. There he familiarized himself with the care and handling of his shoulder arm, the .577 Enfield rifle musket. This English-made arm, which had first seen service in 1854, was capable of delivering an accurate fire at a target more than 1,000 yards away. It used a .568 variant of the conical minié ball, whose hollow base expanded upon discharge, enabling the round to grip the grooves cut inside the rifle barrel.[24]

The Enfield, and the other rifles on which Federal and Confederate troops relied, had revolutionized infantry warfare. Its muzzle velocity, the accuracy of its fire, and the speed with which it could be reloaded (a veteran could squeeze off three well-aimed shots per minute) had made that venerable maneuver, the bayonet charge, an exercise in futility. The trouble was that the instructional manuals of the day, based on which every volunteer regiment learned how to behave in battle, had not caught up with the technological innovations. As if armies continued to be armed with smoothbore weapons accurate at less than half the distance of the Enfield, the textbooks promoted frontal assaults and other high-risk tactics. The upshot would be a continuing round of assaults in the manner of Pickett's Charge at Gettysburg, which had ended in defeat, chaos, and unacceptable loss.[25]

Casualties inflicted by firearms were not limited to the battlefield; more than a few occurred on the 4th's rifle range. Although no accident ended in a fatality, some caused serious injury. One day during target practice, Pvt. Joshua DeCoursey of Company E suffered severe powder burns because of a comrade's carelessness. As Corp. William Henry recalled, "A man standing behind him shot over DeCoursey's shoulder and nearly blinded him, and he could scarcely see after that." On another occasion, an errant round struck the leg of Lieutenant Brigham, putting him in the hospital for some weeks. Both men recovered sufficiently to resume active duty.[26]

At some point, the men of the 4th were instructed in artillery practice as well as infantry tactics. Heavy cannons continued to occupy the redoubts with which McClellan had surrounded Yorktown. Apparently General Wistar considered it prudent to teach foot soldiers how to augment the gun crews in the frightening if unlikely event that Rebels attacked the garrison in force. Jarrett Morgan, for one, never forgot his introduction to the artilleryman's craft. He remembered his instructor as "a veteran of the Mexican War . . . a gray-haired man, very tall, very thin, exceedingly sharp-eyed, a dandy gunner." Once a cannon had been loaded with a practice round, the instructor would position himself behind the breach, shout "Ready! Fire," and yank the lanyard. "Such a noise!" Morgan recalled years later. "If you stood on your tip toes when the guns were discharged it did not hurt you, but if you stood flat on your feet! Oh-oh-oh! It was awful!"

On one occasion, artillery instruction was interrupted by the discovery that a handful of enemy sharpshooters had sneaked to within rifle range of the garrison and had perched in some strategically located trees. It was a foolish idea, for as soon as the snipers opened fire, the instructor trained his cannon on them and discharged a round. Seconds later, as Morgan recalled, the Rebels "came rollin' down outer there," screaming their willingness to surrender.[27]

Occasionally, a plethora of work details would prevent the 4th from spending its allotted time at drill. Within three weeks of the outfit's arrival on the Peninsula, three of its companies had been shipped across the mile-wide river to Gloucester Point, where they temporarily manned Fort Keyes and other, smaller defenses that guarded the eastern approach to Yorktown. As Colonel Duncan informed his mother on October 18, "Two of the other companies are employed daily upon the fortifications enclosing York-town—mainly in repairing the works thrown up by the rebels last year. This, you see, keeps five companies employed constantly. In addition, our camp guard, a garrison guard, and wood parties, make our details so heavy that we get little time for drill." He added, however, that General Wistar "promises us time soon. Another Colored regt. is expected soon, who will relieve us every other day."[28]

In fact, on the very day Duncan wrote, the 6th United States Colored Infantry, which had been organized in Philadelphia early in the summer, reported for duty at Fort Yorktown. Its arrival was a blessing for the 4th, not only because it lightened the workload, but also because it shared the unwanted attention of the white portion of the garrison, which sometimes went out of its way to make the 4th feel unwelcome. The Pennsylvanians also provided the 4th with a ready source of comradeship, of shared experiences, hopes, and fears. Although the commander of the 6th, Col. John W. Ames, pitched his camp more than a mile from Fort Yorktown, the regiments fraternized on a daily basis, swapping rations, notions purchased from the sutler, and tall tales. In this manner, Christian Fleetwood made a close friend of his counterpart in the 6th, Sgt. Maj. Thomas R. Hawkins, whose education and interests matched his own.[29]

Even before Hawkins's arrival, Fleetwood had attracted a large circle of army friends, with whom he sometimes shared a tent and often a meal. These included Corp. G. Michael Arnold and Sgt. John H. Hance. An articulate freeman from Kentucky, Arnold had been assigned as regimental hospital steward, a demanding position that he filled efficiently enough to win the praise of Dr. Mitchell. Hance, the first sergeant of Company B, was well educated and politically aware; he and Fleetwood spent many an hour debating the issues of the day.[30]

The comrade with whom Fleetwood would forge the most cordial relationship arrived in Yorktown after the 4th had settled in. Reporting to regimental headquarters on October 10, Chaplain Hunter met Fleetwood, who spent a part of each day at Colonel Duncan's side, filing general and special orders and poring over muster rolls, morning reports, and company and regimental returns. Minister and Sunday school teacher hit it off immediately; thereafter, the two appeared inseparable. They discussed the Bible, explored theological issues, and worked together to meet the needs, spiritual and physical, of the regiment. Fleetwood assisted Hunter in securing accommodations for chapel services, the first of which was held the day after the clergyman's arrival. Thereafter, only the press of official duties prevented the sergeant major from attending church and assisting Hunter's ministry in any way possible.[31]

Before year's end, Fleetwood and other enlisted men had helped Hunter erect a cabin to provide a more permanent venue for services. In a letter to the *Christian Recorder,* the organ of the African Methodist Episcopal Church, Sergeant Wheeler observed that "in the evening we had prayer-meeting; and we intend holding class-meeting and prayer-meeting every Thursday and Monday evening." The chapel doubled as a schoolhouse in which Hunter, with the assistance of Fleetwood and other well-educated comrades, taught illiterate members of the 4th, as well as the men, women, and children of Slabtown, to read, write, and cipher. Colonel Duncan remarked that the good chaplain "handle[d] the rod and the Pointer to [such] great advantage that the intellectual capacity and military efficiency of this outfit increased noticeably."[32]

The school thrived into the spring of 1864, when it was apparently absorbed into a larger educational system for freedmen established on the Peninsula by civilian relief workers. These included Quakers and abolitionists from Pennsylvania, New York, and New England, whose coming had been encouraged by Benjamin F. Butler. The political general, who had recently returned to Fort Monroe as General Foster's replacement, had taken a strong interest in the welfare of the black soldiers and civilians in his department. By May 1864, one of these teachers, a young Quakeress from Philadelphia, could boast that her colleagues had "enrolled nearly three hundred pupils in their day school, and they have a large night school of adults." She credited Butler for this result, but in truth it was due to the zeal and energy of Chaplain Hunter, aided by Fleetwood and other enlisted members of the 4th USCI.[33]

Less than a week after reaching Yorktown, the greater part of the 4th made its first foray into the enemy's country. On October 5, in the early morning darkness, 744 officers and enlisted men were roused from sleep, fed breakfast, and ordered to assemble on the parade ground. Promptly at 5:00, Colonel Duncan and the other field officers led the outfit down to the wharf, where it boarded transports in company with detachments of four other units. The ships ferried across the York the troops and horses of the 11th Pennsylvania Cavalry and the 1st New York Mounted Rifles, as well as the guns and gunners of three artillery sections, two from the 8th New York Battery, the other from Battery E, 1st Pennsylvania Light Artillery.

General Wistar, commanding the expeditionary force, was close-mouthed about its mission and destination, but in time the men learned that the intent was to surprise, attack, and capture or disperse the Confederate Volunteer Coast Guard, a loose-knit organization of land and naval units known to be operating on the eastern side of Virginia's Middle Peninsula.

The journey across the river to Gloucester Point took about a half hour. Once on the far shore, the transports unloaded their human and equine cargo, which, after a slight delay, began moving inland. Their ultimate destination was Mathews County, on the southeastern side of the Peninsula. Their subsequent operations would be covered by three naval gunboats, as well as by eight tugs manned by army personnel and armed with cannons from the Yorktown defenses. The navy and army vessels had been positioned off the tip of the Peninsula to prevent any Rebels from evading Wistar by fleeing across the Rappahannock River to the Northern Neck.[34]

The movement inland began smoothly enough. It might have been otherwise, however, had not Colonel Duncan agreed to subordinate himself to Col. Samuel P. Spear of the 11th Pennsylvania, whom Wistar had designated as second-in-command of the expedition. Since his regiment constituted the largest element of the expeditionary force, Duncan believed he should rank next to Wistar. Yet Spear had been operating on both sides of the York, with much success, for several months; thus Duncan had dropped his mild protest, in the process acknowledging his colleague's "great excellence and wide experience." If nothing else, the incident indicated that although a citizen-soldier, Duncan had the sensitive pride of an old Regular when it came to the prerogatives of rank and seniority.[35]

The first day out, the combined-arms force covered a lot of ground but encountered few uniformed Rebels. While the mounted units under Spear, who had been assigned the most critical part of the mission, pushed north toward Gloucester Court House, Wistar, with the infantry and the artillery, moved northeastward. By evening, Wistar's men had reached that portion of Mathews County that lay between the North and Piankatank Rivers. Covered by the movement of the army and navy vessels that ran up the North, the 4th USCI reconnoitered that narrow neck of land but located no enemy troops. That night, Duncan and his regiment, worn out from their first long march, slept soundly in their wooded bivouac, as did the artillerists who slumbered beside them.

The next morning, as Wistar's detachment held its position, Spear's horsemen moved slowly toward it from the west, beginning a three-day sweep of the country between. As Wistar noted, during that period the Pennsylvanians and New Yorkers visited "every work, corner, creek, and landing place" in the county. They succeeded in bagging about 100 prisoners—members of the Regular Confederate army and navy, as well as guerrillas and civilians accused of helping commissary officers forage for Lee's army. The troopers also wrecked about 150 boats and confiscated horses, mules, and beef cattle that the foragers had corralled. These achievements had come at the cost of one trooper killed; his assailant, a notorious local guerrilla, had been caught and hanged.[36]

The role of the 4th USCI in this operation was largely limited to picket and reconnaissance duty along the Rappahannock. The regiment also relieved a few local farmers of the foodstuffs they had intended to sell to the government in Richmond. Christian Fleetwood later admitted that he and some comrades partook of the "stolen goods" (only later would he come to regard confiscation as an act of military necessity), including the contents of chicken coops, springhouses, and vegetable gardens.[37]

Early on the eighth, Wistar reunited with Spear and declared Mathews County sufficiently free of guerrillas, foragers, and coast guardsmen. Then he started everyone on the thirty-mile return trip to Yorktown. Heretofore, the 4th had been denied an opportunity to show its mettle; now, however, it proved something to Wistar and his white troops. While more than a few cavalrymen and artillerists dropped out of the column this day, the 4th covered the entire thirty miles without breathing hard. By 10:00 P.M., when the regiment returned to its camp at Yorktown, its marching performance was the talk of the garrison.

The feat did not escape the notice of the expeditionary commander, who, in his report of the operation, paid the rookie outfit an extraordinary compliment: "The negro infantry marched better than any old troops I ever saw. On two days they marched . . . without a straggler or a complaint, and were ready for picket, patrol, or detachment duty at night." Choosing to overlook evidence to the contrary, Wistar added that "not a fence rail was burned or a chicken stolen by them." All in all, "they seemed to be well controlled and their discipline, obedience, and cheerfulness, for new troops, is surprising, and has dispelled many of my prejudices."[38]

Officers and enlisted men alike reacted strongly to this tribute, which long remained a source of unit pride. It told them that their contribution to the war effort was appreciated and that their claim to the title of soldiers was being taken seriously at the highest levels. They would have been happy to know that the tribute was seconded by their own commander, who wrote his family that "the endurance and the patience of the men, uttering no complaints, was remarkable." Despite the grueling pace, "the men were shouting and singing most of the way, and when reaching camp they fell to dancing jigs."[39]

Duncan later added to his tribute by doubting that the soldierly qualities of his men were confined to marching: "I think they will be equally brave in battle." On that score, however, the future would have the final say.[40]

CHAPTER 3

Willing Hearts and Strong Hands

SOON AFTER RETURNING FROM MATHEWS COUNTY, COLONEL DUNCAN wrote, "We are merely <u>stopping</u> at Yorktown" and would probably be elsewhere, perhaps "upon a campaign," in a matter of weeks, if not days. He was no seer: The 4th was fated to remain there well into the spring of 1864. The lengthy stay would prove a boon to the regiment, for despite its commander's confidence that it would acquit itself proudly in battle, it could use all the training it could get before thrown into the fire of active campaigning.[1]

The 4th could afford to remain behind the fighting front because the war in Virginia had reached a stalemate, or something close to it. The Army of the Potomac spent October and November trying to outmaneuver the Army of Northern Virginia between the Rapidan and Rappahannock Rivers. Meade was looking for an opening in hopes of bringing on a decisive battle before winter curtailed operations. An opportunity to trap and smash the Confederates did not materialize, and when a final, desperate attempt at an offensive fizzled out along a Rapidan tributary called Mine Run early in December, the war seemed no closer to a conclusion than it had before Lee's invasion of Pennsylvania.[2]

In the Western Theater, Ulysses S. Grant's troops began the autumn resting and reorganizing after capturing Vicksburg and opening the length of the Mississippi River for Union shipping. Elsewhere in the West, other Federal forces were active, if not uniformly successful. In July, the Army of the Cumberland, under an erstwhile subordinate of Grant's, Maj. Gen. William S. Rosecrans, had maneuvered Braxton Bragg's Army of Tennessee out of its home state and into northern Georgia. An overconfident Rosecrans pursued in loose formation; as a result, he was surprised and defeated on September 20 along Chickamauga Creek. His army fell back to Chattanooga, where Bragg besieged it; soon Grant was hurrying there at the head of a relief force that included two infantry corps detached from Meade.[3]

The 4th USCI followed events in middle Virginia and the West as best it could from its camp on the Peninsula, a frustrating process at best, given the slow and irregular delivery of newspapers. Still, even out-of-date papers were in demand at Yorktown. Officers and those enlisted men who could read would recite their contents aloud for the benefit of less educated soldiers. The number of illiterates, however, continued to decline as more and more soldiers attended Chaplain Hunter's school. Although no man could be compelled to do so, it was observed that a majority of the regiment passed through the schoolhouse, if only once or twice. A considerable number thereby received the only classroom instruction they were ever exposed to. At least a few used it as a springboard for a more complete education after returning to civilian life.

A basic schooling was not the only advantage of which the regiment could boast while at Yorktown. Being assigned to a fixed location meant that the men usually ate well. Rations were abundant, and they were not limited to the basics of the soldier's diet—salt beef, salt pork, and the crackerlike hardtack. There were regular issues of desiccated, or dehydrated, vegetables and canned goods including condensed milk. The men often dined on fresh vegetables, and they rarely lacked for condiments or sweeteners.

Not surprisingly, officers and the higher-ranking enlisted men enjoyed better fare than their comrades. At various times, Christian Fleetwood ate steak, ham, oysters, onions, salad greens, and pies of various kinds, while consuming all the coffee he wanted. At night, having tended to the regimental books and his voluminous personal correspondence, the sergeant major enjoyed chocolate and other sweets, and he smoked at least one cigar before turning in. His diet was so rich, however, that at times his digestive system rebelled. He was plagued by bouts of diarrhea, which eventually brought on a case of hemorrhoids serious enough to incapacitate him from time to time.[4]

If the regular rations did not sate the appetite of the regiment, it could purchase additional and more exotic foods—everything from lager beer to canned lobster salad—from the sutler, a civilian merchant licensed to travel with and sell to the army. Virtually every Union regiment had its own sutler, selected from a wide array of prospective vendors by vote of the outfit's officers. The officers did not always choose wisely: While at Yorktown, the 4th was served by Reverdy J. Bowdin, a shrewd businessman who charged dearly for his wares. Bowdin inveigled so many who owed him money to sign over their pay to him that half the regiment was constantly broke.[5]

As dissatisfaction mounted, early in November the officers voted to suspend Bowdin's license until he reformed his business practices. Apparently he failed to comply, for early in 1864 he was discharged for violating price guidelines set by the War Department, as well as for "general inefficiency." His successor, W. C. Cooper, kept his position longer than Bowdin, but in the end he, too, developed a reputation for price gouging and was sent packing. A third sutler, G. W. Skiff, appears to have attached himself to the 4th at some point, but neither his conduct nor the length of his tenure is a matter of record.[6]

At Yorktown, the men lived as well as they ate. Until winter weather paid a call, shelter tents served the 4th more or less comfortably, although several comrades had to share the accommodations, "spooning" together to make maximum use of sleeping space and body warmth. By mid-November, however, canvas or muslin was insufficient to prevent hypothermia. At Duncan's order, the men scoured the surrounding forest for building materials. Rough-hewn lumber eventually produced a village of huts and cabins that dwarfed Slabtown. The men chinked the walls with mud, carted inside the portable cookstoves the garrison's quartermasters had furnished them, and fashioned chimneys from hollowed-out barrels. Then the residents—ten or twelve men to a cabin—fired up the stoves to produce the heat essential to life in winter quarters.

Again, the living conditions of the officers and the senior enlisted personnel were superior to those of the private soldiers. The colonel resided in a complex of A-shaped tents that had been winterized and propped on wooden planks. Fleetwood, along with Handy, Arnold, and four other noncommissioned officers with whom he occasionally messed, fashioned a spacious cabin, which they christened the Hotel de St. Main. No less grandly, the inhabitants dubbed themselves the Knights of St. Main. Fleetwood was elected to lead this new order of chivalry, with Arnold as his "Lt Col & Surgeon in chief" and Handy as "Lt. col & Chief of Staff"; the others assumed the titles of the lesser nobility.[7]

Another advantage of remaining for a sustained period at a single duty station was the ready availability of pay. Whereas regiments campaigning in the field often complained that the army's paymasters could not find them or, having found them, feared to join them at the front, units stationed at Fort Yorktown had no such problems. And yet, on the subject of pay, the enlisted men of the 4th had grounds for complaint. The seven dollars they received monthly was a continuing source of discontent to all USCT, who shared the same hardships and hazards as the better-paid white soldiers.

The issue was one of basic fairness, and thus a legitimate topic of debate. If the men agitated for higher pay, however, they risked looking like mercenaries. As First Sergeant Wheeler explained to the readers of the *Christian Recorder,* "You must not think . . . that we are fighting for money alone, but that, as soldiers, we ought to have our equal rights." Not only the soldier was harmed by this officially sanctioned injustice: "Our families are suffering for the want of sustenance. . . . We have been praised for our marches and our endurance of fatigue, but praises do not supply our families' wants at home."[8]

A few members of the regiment protested the inequity by refusing to accept their pay, but not everyone could or would make such a sacrifice. An anonymous sergeant of Company H, writing in the columns of a New York–based freedmen's newspaper, the *Anglo-African,* decried the "miserable pay of seven dollars per month," but he accepted the situation. He, too, had considered refusing the money, saying, "If the government was so poor that it could not pay, I would make it a present of what is justly my due." Then, however, he recalled the parable about the workers in the vineyard: "When they were called to be paid off, some murmured, but others were satisfied; so I will be satisfied until a further day."[9]

That day did not arrive until several months after the 4th left Yorktown for the field of active duty. In the annual report of his office, issued at the end of 1863, Secretary of War Stanton called on Congress to legislate the equalization of pay between Caucasian and African-American soldiers. Many congressmen endorsed such a bill, but their more conservative colleagues delayed its introduction until June 1864. By then black troops had proven their value in battle so forcefully that not even the most discriminatory legislators could ignore it. However, like the bounty law passed by the Maryland Assembly, it took several months before the pay bill, once passed, was strictly enforced. By war's end, surviving USCT were finally being remunerated on a par with their white comrades. Yet by failing to make the pay differential retroactive, the government never fully rectified the wrong it had done to the African-American soldiers.[10]

Although the compensation issue was a potent source of dissatisfaction, events that occurred before and after winter quarters went up served to bolster regimental morale. In addition to the Knights of St. Main, other enlisted men formed social groups that promoted good fellowship and furnished off-duty diversions. According to Fleetwood, at least one or two nights a week the men held songfests around the campfire, harmonizing on everything from spirituals to popular ballads. Sometimes banjoists and guitar players, including some of the officers, provided accompaniment. Members of the 6th USCI and, once in a while, some of the white troops at York-town joined in the sing-alongs. In turn, the men of the 4th took part in social events hosted by their garrison mates.[11]

On occasion, the regiment sponsored elaborate socials. These galas, which featured music as well as good food, much of it provided, at the usual exorbitant prices, by the sutler, were open to the residents of Slabtown and other local civilians. When weather and duty schedules per-mitted—most often, on Saturdays and Sundays—the regimental band held concerts, either inside the 4th's camp or in the streets of the town. The band was such a popular source of entertainment that when the 4th left Yorktown for the front and the musicians remained behind, unit morale suffered. Rather than accompany the outfit into the field, the band was attached to a succession of corps and division headquarters for the duration of the war. Some months after the Confederacy's demise, it was returned, without explanation, to the 4th.[12]

Holidays spawned social events that involved the entire outfit. The band played throughout the day, and high-ranking officers including Wistar and Duncan treated the troops to patriotic speeches. The first such occasion in the 4th's experience was Thanksgiving Day, November 26, 1863, a date made memorable by the receipt of good news from Tennessee. In a series of recent engagements south of Chattanooga, the relief troops under Gen. Ulysses S. Grant had lifted Bragg's siege, thrashed the Rebels, and sent them staggering back into Georgia. If his earlier triumphs at Fort Donel-son, Shiloh, and Vicksburg had not already done so, these latest victories made Grant the Union's preeminent warrior as well as a household name in both North and South.[13]

In the camp of the 4th, the day began soon after sunrise with a sermon by Chaplain Hunter, attended by the entire regiment. Ward Handy noted that the clergyman "preached a stirring discourse from this text: 'Thou crownest the year with thy goodness, and thy paths drop fatness' (Ps[alm] lxv., 11)." The sermon was "listened to with profound attention by both officers and soldiers."

At the conclusion of the service, the men were dismissed to participate in what Handy called "sports and plays incident to camp life." The merri-ment lasted only about an hour; at 8:00, drums beat throughout the camp, and the 4th reassembled on the parade ground. The men exchanged quizzical glances; no one knew the reason for the recall. The suspense was dispelled when Duncan strode to the head of the regiment and read aloud a dispatch from Grant's headquarters.

When finished reciting details of the recent victories, the colonel informed the men that General Wistar "desired them to cheer in such a manner, if their feelings so led them, that the sound of their rejoicing might be heard at Fortress Monroe." Duncan surveyed the well-aligned ranks before him and called out: "Men, are you ready to give those cheers now?" Handy recorded that every member of the regiment shouted, "Yes!" An instant later, "led by the Colonel himself," they let loose with three cheers for "Unconditional-Surrender Grant." When the commotion ceased, Duncan cried out: *"Three more for the completed emancipation of the African race!"* At his words, the regiment went wild, cheering, said Handy, "with an enthusiasm that beggars description. . . . I would have pitied a brigade of 'rebs' just then if our boys had been let loose upon them; they would have scattered them as chaff before the wind."

Duncan's remarks so touched his men that after everyone had been dismissed, a delegation of noncommissioned officers headed by Fleetwood and Arnold met to frame an appropriate response. At their urging, Chaplain Hunter agreed to put their sentiments into words. Early in the afternoon, the companies were called back into formation and marched as a body to regimental headquarters. There they called on Duncan, who received them outside his tent.

After a moment's pause, Hunter delivered a brief oration in which he thanked the colonel for the sentiments he had expressed to them all. The chaplain explained why they had come:

> Not to present you with a sword or any other weapon, but to assure you that you have our fullest confidence, and that with willing hearts and strong hands we would ever battle for and defend the flag of this our glorious country from all enemies . . . and whenever you shall be called upon to lead us in battle, our deeds of daring and valor shall be such as shall *never* bring confusion to your face or sorrow to your heart.

Sergeant Handy observed:

> The reply of Col. D. was brief, but to the purpose . . . [and] the men were more than ever confirmed in their opinion that the right man is in the right place. As the Colonel concluded his speech, cheer after cheer arose upon the air, and more than one heart whispered, "God bless him!" The men retired highly elated to their quarters. Roll-call was sounded, and so ended our Thanksgiving day—a glorious one indeed. God grant we may have more of them.[14]

Capt. John W. Dillenback
U.S. ARMY MILITARY HISTORY INSTITUTE

By the time the men went into winter quarters, many had begun to wonder when—if ever—they would see active campaigning. For weeks after
the strike at Mathews County, most of the regiment was confined to camp.
There the 4th continued to improve the local works, while the white
troops in the area tramped about the countryside on scouting patrols and
foraging expeditions. It began to appear as if the high command considered
the 4th fit only for menial labor.

Early in November, the picture seemed to change. Late the previous
month, Companies F and I of the 4th had been sent, under German-born
Capt. John W. Dillenback, to Williamsburg, where they augmented that
outpost, commanded by Col. Robert M. West of the 5th Pennsylvania Cavalry. A little over a week later, the remainder of the regiment, under Colonel
Duncan, joined Dillenback's detachment in Virginia's Colonial capital. On
November 9, the entire outfit accompanied West and a detachment of his
regiment to a point about fifteen miles above the town in a fruitless search

for Confederate guerrillas. By the time everyone returned to Yorktown on the eleventh, the 4th had fired no more than a couple of long-range shots at suspicious figures—about the same level of activity it had experienced in Mathews County. Christian Fleetwood recorded the results of the brief expedition as one member of the 4th and one cavalryman wounded by sniper fire, and one pig liberated from a Williamsburg farm.[15]

If the regiment was growing restless for service of consequence, it saw a glimmer of hope when, just after Thanksgiving, it made the acquaintance of the new departmental commander. Although field operations were essentially over for the year, the War Department projected an active role, come spring, for the 27,000 troops on and below the Peninsula. Lincoln and Stanton had hoped that John Foster would prove himself combative enough to lead this force in close support of the Army of the Potomac. By late October, however, the authorities had concluded that Foster was not the man they needed in that sector.

Ben Butler came quickly to mind. Though aware that the canny and ambitious New Englander might prove a political rival to him during next year's presidential campaign, Lincoln believed he needed the War Democrat's support for his own reelection bid. Moreover, Lincoln considered Butler an aggressive field commander who would use every available resource, including black soldiers, to defeat the Confederacy. Although the general had been on inactive service since his December 1862 relief from New Orleans, he had been making well-received speeches in behalf of the war effort. Throughout that period, his many supporters had been pressuring the administration to reinstate the general to field command. Thus on October 28, Lincoln took a calculated gamble by returning Butler to Fort Monroe as Foster's replacement.[16]

Immediately after retaking the field, Butler made an inspection tour of his domain, beginning with the 12,000 troops who manned the District of North Carolina. Turning north on Thanksgiving Day, he reached Yorktown, where he conferred with Wistar and took a brief tour of the garrison. From there he headed for Fort Monroe, but he returned to Wistar's headquarters on December 9 for a more thorough inspection, including a review of the entire command.

The initial impression the 4th USCI formed of the new commander was of a pudgy, balding man pushing fifty, with unusually short arms and legs and a "lop eye" that made him look devious or dissipated, or both. But if Butler was not physically imposing, he promised to satisfy the 4th's craving for more important duties in the field. Butler's reputation as an avid supporter of African-American soldiers was not limited to raising regiments of them. He did not hesitate to assign them important duties or commit them to front-line service.[17]

Maj. Gen. Benjamin F. Butler (seated, fifth from the left) and staff, 1864. U.S. ARMY
MILITARY HISTORY INSTITUTE

Only four days before he reviewed Wistar's troops, Butler had solidified his image as a champion of black soldiery. On December 5, he had issued General Order No. 46, Headquarters Department of Virginia and North Carolina, which had been read aloud to units throughout his new command. The document addressed more than a dozen issues, all related in some way to the recruitment of African-American troops, which Butler described as "the settled purpose of the Government." It began by saying that "every able-bodied colored man who shall enlist and be mustered into the service of the United States for three years or during the war, shall be paid a bounty, to support his immediate wants, the sum of ten (10) dollars." Here was a policy sure to draw the warm approval of regiments such as the 4th. No less important to the USCT, as to the inhabitants of Slabtown and Camp Hamilton, was the second provision of Butler's edict, which promised that "suitable subsistence" would be furnished to every soldier's dependents through a Department of Negro Affairs, to be administered by one of Butler's most trusted subordinates.

Other provisions of the order addressed some of the inequities that characterized the army's treatment of black soldiers. One mandated that African-Americans receive the same clothing, arms, and equipment as provided to white soldiers. Another provision concerned the thorny issue of pay. While Butler had no authority to erase the pay differential between black and white troops, he decreed that black noncommissioned officers would receive the same additional pay as whites of the same rank.

Demonstrating his aversion to government-mandated discrimination, Butler called on Congress to close the pay gap at the earliest opportunity. The language in which he framed this plea would have resonated with every member of the USCT: "The colored man fills an equal place in [the] ranks while he lives, and an equal grave when he falls." Still other provisions of his decree governed the employment of civilian laborers within the department, prohibited the impressment of black people by officers seeking servants, and proscribed penalties for white troops who obstructed the recruiting or employment of African-Americans. The order went far toward gaining the new commander the loyalty and trust of every black person in his department.[18]

As 1863 drew to a close, members of the 4th renewed their hope for purposeful activity, or at least for some event that would inject color and excitement into their life. That event—a truly memorable one—occurred on December 16–17. Afterward, the men were inclined to be more careful about what they wished for.

The evening of the sixteenth began quietly enough. By 7:00, many of the troops in and near Fort Yorktown had already turned in. Pacing sentinels guarded their comrades' sleep, although the nearest armed Confederates were miles away. Suddenly, unexpectedly, the stillness of night was broken by the crackle of flames, then by shouts of alarm. The source of the commotion was a frame building on one of the streets of Yorktown, northwest of the fort. In an instant, the garrison was a blur of activity. As an eyewitness reported in the columns of the *Cavalier,* a soldiers' newspaper printed on the confiscated presses of the venerable *Virginia Gazette,* "The usual quietude and sense of security from danger that had so long pervaded Yorktown was disturbed by the startling alarm of 'Fire!' and soldiers and citizens rushed from their quarters to behold one of the most alarming sights that the imagination could picture."

The conflagration had begun in the kitchen of a building that one of Wistar's white regiments, the 148th New York, had been using as a hospital. Although patients and attendants were safely evacuated, the raging fire quickly threatened adjacent houses that had been converted into arsenals. Those dwellings held "a quantity of almost every variety of explosive missiles."[19]

General Wistar having gone to Fort Monroe on official business, Colonel Duncan, by virtue of seniority, was in temporary command of the post. Through the use of pumper apparatus that drew water from the river by hose, Duncan managed to contain the fire for an hour or more. Eventually, however, the flames spread to the point that they began to sear the walls of the powder houses. Within minutes, "the bursting of heated shells gave terrible warning of an explosion . . . [although] none knew at what moment the expected crash would come."

Survival instincts propelled the 4th USCI to seek shelter. Half-dressed soldiers rushed from their huts and tents to take cover behind sturdier-looking sections of the fort. Some hunkered down in rear of the batteries; others fled into the woods near Slabtown. Once they felt reasonably safe from flying shells, they peered through the trees and over the parapets of the fort to follow the progress of the inferno and wait for the inevitable explosion.

At about 8:00, the flames reached one of the arsenals, detonating the shells stored inside. Two resounding blasts occurred in quick succession:

> The earth tremble[d] for miles around as though shaken by some awful revulsion of nature. Burning timbers were scattered in every direction, and showers of whistling shot and howling shell were hurled through the air, which was darkened by clouds of smoke and sand. . . . From among the scattered and burning fragments of buildings that strewed the ground thus was poured forth a continual shower of shell and brick that . . . fell thick and fast on every hand.

The fire raged on into the morning, creeping slowly but steadily toward a powder magazine inside the north face of the fort. At about 4:00 A.M. on the seventeenth, a shell that had been detonated and sent flying by the fire pierced the magazine. An explosion more thunderous than the preceding ones ripped two 20-pounder cannons from their nearby bases and hurled them seventy feet in the air. The guns landed in the just-abandoned camp of the artillery unit that attended to them. Doors, windows, and walls along the north face of the fort, which had resisted the earlier explosions, were blown out and their fragments scattered promiscuously about.[20]

Even greater damage might have occurred had not a steady rain begun to fall shortly before dawn, dousing some of the burning structures and protectively soaking other powder caches inside the fort. Duncan surveyed the garrison by daylight and was astonished to count so few casualties. As he wrote his father, "Why men were not killed I can never understand— But there were none killed, and not more than 5 or 6 very serious accidents." He added, wryly, "I think I have now a pretty good idea of what a bombardment is—altho' I have never been in battle."

In later days, the colonel headed a board of inquiry that met amid the debris to determine the extent of the damage and fix blame for the accident. In the end, however, the inquiry produced only what Duncan called "a good deal of paper & ink and red tape." No definitive conclusions were reached as to the cause of the fire, and no heads rolled as a result. In the end, the main significance of the catastrophe was the realization that troops in garrison, as well as those in the field, risked serious injury and death twenty-four hours a day.[21]

In the aftermath of the conflagration, the 4th USCI began to look more patiently toward year's end. The regiment marked Christmas with a dress parade, after which the men repaired to their quarters to share good food and good fellowship. In the Hotel de St. Main, Fleetwood and his fellow Knights had a "big time . . . eating & drinking" until midnight. At regimental headquarters, Duncan and his subordinates dined even more sumptuously; the colonel regretted that his family in New Hampshire could not be on hand, "as we had enough to spare."[22]

Holiday cheer continued into New Year's Day, when the enlisted men of the 4th dined by invitation in the camp of the 6th USCI. While the rank and file intermingled, their officers, as Duncan reported, "got up a good appetite by a fox hunt." Despite the raw, windy weather, and although "the race did not last long—The dogs took the varmint in about 15 minutes," the aristocratic trappings of the event appealed to the 4th's commander: "This used to be a grand sport among the natives here when old Virginia was in her glory."[23]

It remained grand sport, even with Virginia bleeding and broken from the ravages of a war whose end was not in sight. That fact troubled some observers; others hoped the fighting would go on until certain goals had been attained. One who felt this way was Sergeant Major Fleetwood, who noted in his diary: "The close of the year finds me a soldier for the cause of my race. May God bless this cause, and enable me in the coming year to forward it on."[24]

—→ ⊨✦⊨ ←—

When 1864 came in, the temperature plummeted and snow fell. The weather lengthened the sick list of the regiment, which heretofore had not been a source of concern to the surgeons. Despite the elements, the 4th soon experienced a spate of active duty. At 2:00 P.M. on January 11, the men were hauled out of their snug cabins and stockaded tents and led across the frozen earth toward the fortified garrison. "Passing in at one gate of Fort Yorktown," Fleetwood reported, "we traversed it to the music of our own drum corps, the men marching with the precision of veterans." Numerous white troops were on hand to see them off: "The most violent opponents of our troops," the sergeant major wrote, "could not withold [*sic*] expressions of praise for their soldier-like bearing."

The march took the men to river's edge. At the docks, in company with a squadron of the Mounted Rifles, they boarded transports that conveyed them to Gloucester Point, where they went into a frigid bivouac. Fleetwood fared better than his lower-ranking comrades. Searching for a more sheltered place to sleep, he happened upon a picket post where packing boxes formed a square that offered resistance to the frosty wind; even better, a roaring fire had been built in the center of the square. "Wending my way thither," he wrote, "I toasted my toes at the fire, curled up in a tent-box, and in a few moments slept like a—I was going to say king, but I will say soldier, which is better."[25]

The next morning, the men reassembled, and Duncan guided them to Fort Keyes, where they were met by baggage wagons carrying brand new shelter tents—the men would not have to spend a second night exposed to the cold. They could not avoid working in it, however. As the colonel explained, the local defenses had "fallen into much decay, the guns having all been removed." It was the 4th's job to rebuild the walls of Fort Keyes and clear ground for the mounting of new cannons.[26]

The men tended to this work throughout the twelfth. For a part of that day, they were assisted by men of the 11th Connecticut, a regiment that had long been stationed in the area. The outfit had recently reenlisted as a body for three more years of service; as a reward, it was about to go home on a thirty-day furlough. Apparently it decided to make a parting gesture, for that morning, several of its men began arguing with the fatigue parties of the 4th. Racial and other epithets were exchanged, followed by punches and kicks. The row was broken up before it could involve the main bodies of either outfit. Still, hard feelings persisted, and both outfits were pleased when, the next day, the whites departed for home and the African-Americans replaced them inside the works they had helped rebuild.

The 4th kept working. Within a couple of days, the fort had been fixed up to the point that, as Fleetwood said, the men "felt quite at home." They got so comfortable, in fact, that when ordered back to Yorktown on the morning of the nineteenth ("just long enough," the sergeant major complained, "to have the old camp entirely dismantled and get settled in our new one"), many hated to go. But they had no choice, for a New York heavy artillery regiment had been assigned to man the refurbished position on a permanent basis. By 8:00 that evening, following a wind-whipped recrossing of the York, the 4th was back in its winter habitation outside Fort Yorktown.[27]

When Colonel Duncan led the regiment into camp, the journey marked the last time he would command the 4th for nearly two years. Back in Yorktown, the outfit made the acquaintance of a recent addition to the garrison, the 5th United States Colored Infantry, a regiment raised in Ohio and composed almost entirely of free blacks. Its arrival meant that three USCT regiments had been assigned to Yorktown, enough to support a brigade organization. That same day, Wistar named Duncan to lead all three outfits in the capacity of acting brigadier general. The assignment had come about logically enough, for Duncan was senior by date of commission to Colonel Ames of the 6th and Col. James W. Conine, who commanded the Ohioans. Even so, it was a career milestone for Duncan, who had won the confidence and trust of his superior.[28]

The 4th USCI was proud of its colonel's accomplishments and thus pleased by his promotion. Yet it was sorry to lose contact with him, especially because the regiment lacked a full complement of commissioned officers. Lieutenant Colonel Rogers had taken leave to attend to personal business in Ohio, and thus Major Boernstein, the single field-grade officer remaining with the 4th, exercised command for some weeks after Duncan was promoted. There were, or were about to be, vacancies in the ranks of line officers as well. These would come about through circumstances less pleasant than those that took Duncan away.[29]

Already Company B was missing its leader, Capt. Joseph D. Wolfe having been cashiered in late December after being found drunk on duty. Other vacancies appeared the following month. One week after the 4th's return from Fort Keyes, Major Boernstein arrested Capt. Seth W. Maltby of Company E for unspecified conduct unbecoming an officer. A few weeks later, Boernstein also placed 1st Lt. William P. Worrall of Company B under arrest.[30]

While silent on the nature of Maltby's and Worrall's transgressions, the record suggests that one or both officers were guilty of the same charge as that leveled against Wolfe. This was one offense that both General Butler and Colonel Duncan were determined to eradicate through punitive action. In General Order No. 3 for 1864, issued on January 17, Butler announced that to be guilty of drunkenness, an officer did not have to be officially on duty at the time he was charged, as had been the case previously. In justifying his decree, the Massachusetts lawyer argued that because his department was surrounded by enemy territory, the officers should be considered *always* on duty, whether in their tent, on the drill field, or anywhere else.

In one of his last official acts before relinquishing regimental command, Duncan endorsed Butler's action, calling drunkenness "the greatest evil existing in the army." In disseminating Butler's decree, the colonel appended both a hope and a warning: "that neither the good name of the Regiment be disgraced nor its efficiency be impaired by any act of drunkenness on the part either of officers or men." At first Maltby and Worrall attempted to fight the charges against them. On February 25, however, Maltby resigned his commission rather than submit to a court-martial, and on March 28, Worrall was notified that he had been dismissed from the service—an action tantamount to a bad-conduct discharge.[31]

A fourth officer lost to the regiment was 2nd Lt. Charles P. Brown of Company D. His offense was of an entirely different nature than Maltby's or Worrall's. On February 6, in the midst of active operations, Dr. Mitchell was prevailed upon to declare Brown too sick to accompany his unit on a march. The lieutenant was ordered back to camp, although not to the hospital. Five days later, he was summoned to regimental headquarters by Lieutenant Colonel Rogers, recently returned from furlough. As Brown recalled the interview, Rogers said, without preamble, "that I had better tender my resignation and that it would be accepted" at once. Before the stunned lieutenant could reply, Rogers accused him "of being sick a good deal, and for long periods at a time." This charge was serious enough, but as Brown stated, Rogers added that "he believed me incompetent for any position, stating (by way of insult) that the First Sergt of my company was a better officer than I."

Brown protested that on the sixth, the surgeon had declared him unfit for field service, that he had been sick "only fourteen days" since the regiment took the field, and that when well he had "never failed to do [his] duty." For these and other reasons, he refused to submit his resignation. Rogers countered with what his subordinate considered an attempt "to get me out . . . that I should be closely watched, that he would have me before a board of examination which would cancel my commission &c &c."

Brown stood his ground, repeating his intention to remain in service with the 4th. For some weeks, he stuck to his purpose, although, he said, Rogers's "conduct toward me has been to make my position disagreeable, and not of the dignity that belongs to it." According to Brown, throughout this period, Rogers used "very insulting and profane language to me, sometimes in the presence of the men under my command." His superior insulted him in other ways, too, such as by confining him to camp when every other officer was out on a detail or a march.[32]

Eventually, Brown claimed, Rogers's conduct had become too "painful to my feelings and degrading to my dignity and efficiency as an officer."

The lieutenant petitioned departmental headquarters to grant him an honorable discharge. At first, at Rogers's doing, he was dismissed from the service. Early in April, however, and apparently through Ben Butler's intervention, Brown was given the release he sought. So, too, was Lieutenant Worrall, who had also argued his case before the commanding general. Yet if Butler found mitigating circumstances in either man's case, he never publicized them.[33]

Although it proved to be a false start, a movement that occurred in the first week in February involved the 4th in what appeared to be an early opening to the spring campaign. The operation originated with Colonel West, who had formed a plan "to strike for the relief of our suffering soldiers in the Richmond prisons." The recent escape of numerous inmates of Libby Prison had dramatized the squalid conditions of that jail for Union officers, as well as those at the enlisted men's prison on Belle Isle, in the James River. According to intelligence gathered by West's scouts, no more than a few dozen Confederates guarded the southern approach to Richmond via the Chickahominy River. The colonel had concluded that if it moved speedily under the cover of darkness, an expeditionary force could gain entrance to Richmond via Bottom's Bridge. Once in the city, it could not only liberate POWs, but also destroy offices, factories, and warehouses operated by, or for benefit of, the Confederate government.

Butler took an immediate liking to West's plan, which, if implemented successfully, would greatly enhance the general's political aspirations as well as his military career. As Lincoln had feared, Butler had his eye on the 1864 presidential nomination, either as a Republican or as a third-party candidate. Any man who occupied Richmond, even if unable to hold it for more than a few hours, would become a hero in the North. Although the project had originated with West, and although Wistar, as the colonel's immediate superior, would carry it out, Butler, the local commander, would reap much of the credit for such a coup.[34]

In late January and the first days of February, logistical preparations were hastily concluded, and troops from Williamsburg and Yorktown were put on marching notice. At 2:00 P.M. on the fifth, the call to move out reached the 4th's camp, where the men strapped on their field gear and Fleetwood laid aside the copy of *Les Misérables* he had been reading. Before 3:00, Wistar was cantering up the Peninsula at the head of a force of almost 4,000—the 4th USCI and the other regiments in Duncan's brigade, plus three regiments of white infantry and two batteries of artillery. The column reached Williamsburg after nightfall, "very tired & footsore," as Fleetwood put it. There West joined the expedition as Wistar's second-in-command; with him came 2,500 cavalrymen under Colonel Spear.[35]

The departure of so large a force from Yorktown in broad daylight undoubtedly alerted enemy scouts to the operation. Even if Wistar had moved with great stealth, since mid-January Robert E. Lee had been conveying to the officials in Richmond rumors that Butler was forming an expedition to liberate Libby and Belle Isle. The crowning blow to mission secrecy was the recent escape of a Union prisoner from Fort Monroe, where he had been jailed for shooting a superior during a drunken spree. The murderer became a deserter and traitor when he made his way inside Confederate lines and brought fresh reports of Wistar's expedition to the city's military commander, Brig. Gen. Arnold Elzey.[36]

The result was that the 4th, under the command of Major Boernstein, and its comrades under West, Duncan, and Spear made a long, grueling march in frigid weather for naught. The cavalry, the vanguard of the column, reached Bottom's Bridge at about 10:00 A.M. on the seventh, only to find the span unplanked and the far shore lined with defenders. When Wistar discovered that the only other crossing points in the neighborhood had been blocked with fallen trees and other obstructions, he realized that the mission had no hope of succeeding.

Reluctant to return to base without making an effort to cross, Wistar ordered Spear to make a mounted assault on the main Rebel position. Covered in rear by the Enfields of the 4th and the rifles of the other foot units, Spear reluctantly carried out the order. After suffering a decisive repulse and the loss of nine men and ten horses, his survivors galloped for the rear in panic. Thereafter, the expeditionary force contented itself with long-range skirmishing before turning back to Yorktown.[37]

That night, the 4th bivouacked in the cold near New Kent Court House. En route to Bottom's Bridge, the men had slept without fires, a vain effort to preserve the element of surprise. The bone-chilling memory was firmly in their minds even now, when permitted to light fires to ward off the chill. As Fleetwood observed, everyone involved was "intensely disgusted" with the failure of the raid. On the morning of the sixth, Wistar's subordinates had explained to the troops the nature and importance of their mission. The news, and the enthusiasm with which it had been conveyed, had convinced the 4th that a great victory was at hand. Having risen so high, their hopes had fallen a long way since then.[38]

The men of the 4th were still grumbling when they reached winter quarters late in the afternoon of the ninth. Their only consolation was that only one injury, and no fatalities, had accrued from the failed mission. On the return march from Williamsburg, a detachment of Spear's troopers had spurred without warning through a portion of the 4th, causing the regiment to clear the road in great haste. Isaiah Murdock of Company F tripped and fell into a ditch, where he was trampled by a cavalry mount. The result was a broken leg that laid him up for about six weeks. Somehow, Private Murdock's injury seemed an appropriate way to mark the close of the 4th USCI's involvement in one of the most promising, and most disappointing, operations ever conducted in southeastern Virginia.[39]

CHAPTER 4

Errands of Destruction

ALTHOUGH IT TOOK NEARLY A MONTH TO GET UNDER WAY, WISTAR'S expedition inaugurated a period of field service busy and colorful enough to satisfy even the most jaded campaigner. For three weeks after its return to Fort Yorktown, the men had little to take their minds off the recent unpleasantness beyond the usual drill and fatigue duty. Although occasionally enlivened by a dress parade or a review by Wistar or Duncan, the daily routine was an ordeal. In enduring it, however, the 4th had an increasing amount of company. In mid-February, yet another USCI regiment, the 22nd of Col. Joseph B. Kiddoo, a Pennsylvania outfit, augmented the local garrison. Although Kiddoo and Duncan would become close friends, the 22nd did not become a part of the latter's brigade. At first independent of any larger organization, the 22nd eventually joined Holman's 1st USCI and the 10th U.S. Colored Infantry of Lt. Col. Edward H. Powell in a brigade commanded by Brig. Gen. Edward A. Wild.[1]

A radical abolitionist from Massachusetts, Wild was a veteran of the Peninsula Campaign, where he had been wounded in both arms, one of which was later amputated. An even greater controversialist than Butler, the fiery-eyed brigadier had a reputation for using black troops to lay a heavy hand on enemy citizens and their property. In December, he had led 1,700 USCT on a raid through northeastern North Carolina, during which he hanged captured guerrillas, burned the homes of Rebel sympathizers, liberated 2,500 slaves, and allowed his troops to plunder so wantonly that, as one resident claimed, an observer could "trace the track of the raid for ten miles by the turkey buzzards, feeding on the carrion made by the destruction of animal life." Like Butler's reinstatement to Fort Monroe, Wild's coming indicated that a gloves-off policy would prevail in the Department of Virginia and North Carolina, and that African-Americans would play a leading role in the proceedings.[2]

Brig. Gen. Edward A. Wild
U.S. ARMY MILITARY HISTORY INSTITUTE

The 4th USCI was relieved of the daily grind on the first day of March, when, along with the rest of Duncan's command, it was ordered back to Williamsburg. This time, the brigade's mission was strictly defensive. It would provide cover for an approaching cavalry force under Brig. Gen. H. Judson Kilpatrick, one of Meade's most ambitious and enterprising subordinates. Having studied Wistar's abortive raid, Kilpatrick had persuaded his superior that a well-led mounted force could succeed where an infantry-heavy expedition had failed. Late in February, Kilpatrick had moved against Richmond from the north in command of two columns of horsemen totaling 3,500 officers and men. The expedition had begun promisingly, but in the end both columns were defeated by faulty planning, miscommunication, harsh weather, and unexpected resistance from the defense forces of the capital, mostly militia and government clerks temporarily under arms. Stymied on the outskirts of the city, having lost the element of surprise along with his nerve, Kilpatrick had aborted the mission and headed for the safety of Yorktown.[3]

If Wistar's raid had been a difficult experience for the 4th and its comrades, the march to locate Kilpatrick and secure his escape was a nightmare. Midafternoon of the first found the USCT "slipping, stumbling, falling" up the Peninsula in terrible weather. "It rained, snowed & blew," wrote Lieutenant Brigham, "beside being very cold, [with] mud and slush in abundance." Despite the elements, the brigade made forty-file miles in two days. This feat, so reminiscent of the 4th's performance during its first outing to Mathews County, prompted Duncan to brag that "the white Brigade doesn't exist that could have done it."[4]

The weather did take a toll. Having been unwell for some days, upon reaching Williamsburg, Christian Fleetwood collapsed from exposure and exhaustion. When Kilpatrick and his dispirited raiders passed through the town on the fourth, the sergeant major was still weak and woozy. The next day, he accompanied the regiment to Yorktown in an ambulance.[5]

Once back in camp, Fleetwood recovered sufficiently to take part in another excursion that began later that same day, the fifth. At 10:00 P.M., the entire regiment, now under Lieutenant Colonel Rogers, left the Yorktown wharf on a steamer bound for the south side of Hampton Roads. The next morning, the men debarked at Portsmouth, one of the largest garrisons in Butler's department. They were then put on a troop train heading west and alighted at a depot named for the local commander, Brig. Gen. George W. Getty. Near Getty's Station, the 4th again bivouacked in the field. The reason for the excursion escaped everyone. As Lieutenant Brigham put it, "It is possible we are going to Richmond but can't tell."[6]

In the short term, at least, they were going nowhere. For the next three days the 4th remained near Getty's, guarding sections of the railroad that ran to Suffolk. Presumably they were there to protect Union communications against local Regulars and guerrillas. On the ninth, the job—whatever it was—ended, and the regiment departed the area as abruptly as it had arrived. Lieutenant Colonel Rogers led the men back to Portsmouth, where they boarded a transport for what they supposed was a return to Yorktown.

Instead, the steamer carried the regiment up the York to its confluence with the Mattaponi River, northeast of Richmond. The 4th went ashore in King and Queen County, on the Middle Peninsula. There it met Duncan and the remainder of the brigade, which had been augmented by Kiddoo's infantry and Kilpatrick's and Spear's cavalry. Just offshore, three gunboats covered the movements of the entire force, which was about to embark on a punitive mission near King and Queen Court House. Near that village, on March 2, the smaller of Kilpatrick's raiding columns, led by Col. Ulric Dahlgren, had been ambushed and decimated, and its leader killed, by

Confederate Regulars, home guards, and civilians. Kilpatrick was out to avenge his subordinate at the expense of the local populace, and he had persuaded Ben Butler to assist him.[7]

For the officers and men of the 4th USCI, the ensuing operation, which lasted until the twelfth, was a reprise of the foray through Mathews County, although more heavy-handed. For three days, Kilpatrick and his supports burned homes and barns, seized animals, carted off foodstuffs, and took into custody several dozen prisoners, some of whom may have played a role in Dahlgren's demise. By the time the Federals started on the homeward journey, the locals had been, in Kilpatrick's words, "well punished for the murder of Colonel Dahlgren."[8]

Chastisement had required physical exertion. Almost every hour during those three days, the Federals had been discomfited not only by soldiers and bushwhackers, but also by arcticlike winds, snow, frozen mud, all-but-impassable swamps, and what Fleetwood called "interminable woods." The return to Yorktown, by foot down the Middle Peninsula, was itself a grueling experience. The men reached Yorktown, after being ferried across from Gloucester Point, on the evening of the twelfth, but only after one of the most severe marches ever conducted in that region.[9]

The 4th enjoyed five days in camp before being ordered out on yet another mission to Mathews County, this time under Colonel Ames of the 6th USCI. At about noon on March 17, the men boarded the transport *Convoy* for the run down the river and the bay. Other steamers at the dock took on Ames's regiment and the men and animals of Spear's 11th Pennsylvania Cavalry.

For some reason never explained to the men, the fully loaded vessels remained at the dock until sunset. When they finally weighed anchor, the men of the 4th were restless and out of sorts. Believing they were off on another scorched-earth operation, some determined to take out their discontent on any civilians who crossed their path.

Just after midnight, *Convoy* hove to at a landing on the Piankatank River about eight miles southwest of Mathews Court House. Most of the soldiers had slept on deck throughout the long, dreary voyage. Christian Fleetwood, one of the few to secure good quarters below, had just gotten to sleep when the gangplank was lowered and the regiment was ordered off.[10]

After disembarking, Lieutenant Colonel Rogers kept the men well in hand, awaiting orders to proceed. These were not received until 3:30 on the morning of the eighteenth, whereupon Ames directed the grumpy 4th to "march with all possible dispatch to Mathews' Court House, occupy the place, detail a captain and his company for provost duty, seize all suspicious characters, and take such private property as might be useful to contrabands, and to prevent any plundering by the men." Under the circumstances, that last prohibition might prove difficult to enforce.

"All possible dispatch" went by the boards when the march began: The head of the column did not reach the courthouse until well after sunup. Getting this far had been a tedious, frustrating business, the result of a general lack of familiarity with the neighborhood, the difficulty of securing local guides, and the resistance offered by members of the 5th Virginia Cavalry, who had been spending the winter far from the main camp of J. E. B. Stuart's division near Orange Court House. The Virginians had slowed their opponents, but they had drawn little blood. For their troubles, they had lost one man, captured by Spear's troopers.[11]

While the more mobile Pennsylvanians scouted in various directions, the 4th and 6th remained at and near Mathews Court House, picketing the length of the three-mile strip between the Piankatank and North Rivers. The next morning, everyone under Ames returned to the landing and reboarded the transports. Thus far the operation had accomplished nothing save the liberation of about 300 slaves, some of whom would be recruited into the ranks of the USCT. Thus few soldiers were surprised to find that they were not going home just yet. The transports took them up the Piankatank to Jones's Landing, on the edge of Middlesex County. As soon as they got ashore, the men of the 4th marched northward toward the village of New Market, which they reached at about 6:00 P.M.[12]

Even more so than Mathews, Middlesex County abounded in farmlands that had yet to feel the fist of war. The countryside had long supported Lee's army, which it was now helping to sustain in winter quarters. As such, Middlesex was a legitimate military target, one that Colonel Ames intended to strike. The 4th joined in this effort early on the twenty-first, following a night of listless picket duty. Lieutenant Colonel Rogers divided the regiment into several detachments, each led by a captain or lieutenant, and sent them through the countryside with orders to confiscate all manner of provisions.

The 4th's attitude toward the impressing of enemy resources had changed since the regiment's last visit to the Middle Peninsula. No longer did the men seize property only with severe misgivings. In fact, as Rogers observed, the men had come "to consider the expedition a kind of plundering foray." When sent out from New Market on the twentieth, many engaged in unlicensed thievery, raiding homes, farms, and stores, appropriating for personal use whatever struck their fancy. Suspecting as much, after the last detachment had returned to bivouac, Rogers conducted an inspection of the premises. He uncovered "a motley collection of all kinds of fowl (dead and alive), fresh and cured meats, and a promiscuous heap of the smaller appliances of the culinary art, together with cloths, linens, ornaments of dress, and little objects of vertu [knickknacks]."

Appalled by his discovery, the lieutenant colonel ordered his officers to "shoot on the spot any enlisted man who disobeyed an order to refrain from or cease plundering." First Lt. Charles R. Holcombe of Company E promptly complied, wounding a member of his unit who refused to desist from raiding a chicken coop. Rogers pronounced it "a most fortunate occurrence . . . [that] went a great way toward restoring the discipline of the regiment."

In defense of the 4th, a relatively inexperienced outfit would have been hard-pressed to make a clear distinction between authorized confiscation and unlawful seizure of private property. Even so, long after the regiment accompanied its comrades back to Yorktown, Rogers continued to worry that the expedition had produced "a very demoralizing effect on this command." General Wistar agreed with this conclusion. The 4th's behavior in Middlesex County had reactivated the prejudice of the garrison commander. Rogers's condemnation of pillaging, Wistar wrote, was "peculiarly applicable to colored troops, who, according to my observation, especially require to be held with [a] firm hand in order to get from them the full duty of soldiers."[13]

Early in April, Fleetwood, having finished the Victor Hugo novel he had been reading for the past several weeks, began perusing a biography of Ulysses S. Grant. The sergeant major, who prided himself on keeping abreast of current events, wished to know as much as possible about the officer under whom he expected to go into battle come spring. Grant had been a major topic of conversation at Yorktown for the past month, when Lincoln had appointed him general-in-chief of all the Union armies at the revived grade of lieutenant general, a rank previously held only by George Washington and Winfield Scott, the hero of the Mexican-American War.[14]

In mid-March, the 4th USCI and its garrison mates had been intrigued to learn that Grant, who realized that the war would be won or lost in the Eastern Theater, intended to make his field headquarters with the Army of the Potomac. Meade would continue in direct, tactical command of that fighting force, but Grant would define its objectives. In his absence, his trusted subordinate William T. Sherman would command the three armies

Grant left behind in Tennessee. While Meade's troops operated against Lee's army, the forces that constituted Sherman's Military Division of the Mississippi would advance on Atlanta, the transportation hub and manufacturing center of the Deep South. The operations of the two armies, as well as those of smaller Union commands in western Virginia, the Shenandoah Valley, and elsewhere, would be coordinated as closely as long-distance communications would permit.[15]

One of those smaller armies began to take shape while Fleetwood read up on the new general-in-chief. On April 1–2, Grant had visited Fort Monroe, where he outlined the part Butler's troops would play in the coming campaign. Months earlier, the soldiers stationed on the Peninsula as well as on the south side of Hampton Roads had become part of the XVIII Army Corps. Heretofore a loose conglomeration of outpost units, the corps would now become a more cohesive command under the leadership of Maj. Gen. William Farrar "Baldy" Smith, a West Point graduate and a brilliant engineer officer whom Grant considered a top-notch field commander as well.[16]

Grant projected an active role for the 23,000 troops under Smith, the nucleus of what would become the Army of the James. To this force, he planned to add 10,000 officers and men currently operating in South Carolina, members of Maj. Gen. Quincy Adams Gillmore's X Corps. The result would be an army about one-third the size of Meade's, yet large enough to support the Army of the Potomac. That support would be critical to the success of the entire campaign. As Grant envisioned it, Meade's soldiers would confront Robert E. Lee's people north of the Confederate capital. Meanwhile, the Army of the James would sail up its namesake river to attack Richmond from below. If the city, which was protected by heavy works but not an overabundance of troops, proved to be beyond quick capture, Meade would try to thrust Lee's army inside it and then join the Army of the James in besieging it. Eventually, the Confederates would have to come out and attack or remain inside and starve. Either outcome would end the war in the East fairly quickly, ensuring Lincoln's reelection.

If Lincoln had gambled in reinstating Butler to a field command, Grant was taking the same risk. Although the general-in-chief disliked having to entrust a critical mission to a nonprofessional soldier, he realized that Butler was too important to remove: The president continued to require his goodwill and backing. Grant felt somewhat relieved by the knowledge that Butler's ranking subordinates, especially Smith, were educated and experienced enough to prevent their boss from stumbling. Given the lack of a substantial force to oppose it, and if it enjoyed the requisite amount of good luck, the Army of the James should occupy Richmond within a week of the resumption of operations.[17]

Maj. Gen. William F. Smith
U.S. ARMY MILITARY HISTORY INSTITUTE

Had the 4th USCI understood its role in the campaign about to open, it would have rejoiced as a body. The regiment dearly wished to capture the city that symbolized the South's oppression of African-Americans. That desire was reinforced by the continual entry into the lines at Yorktown of slaves and captured USCT who had escaped from the capital or its environs. On April 10, Michael Arnold informed the readers of the *Anglo-African* that one such fugitive, formerly the servant of a Confederate officer, reported having seen "four colored soldiers chained hands and feet in a [Richmond] cellar, and fed on bread and water." The man also reported that Richmond's free black men were being drafted to finish building the fortifications surrounding the city: "Those from 16 years to 70 are subject to the draft. The rules of work are four days in each week, the balance of the time is given that you may make enough to protect yourself from starvation. The women, too, are drafted, to mend, dye and patch the clothes which they rob our soldiers of when prisoners of war." All the while, the black people were subject to "the infamous and insulting language which characterizes the Southerner." Alive to rumors that the troops at Yorktown might be heading for the enemy capital, Arnold closed his dispatch with hopes that his next letter would be sent from Richmond.[18]

If the regiment suspected that it was bound for Jeff Davis's city, it must have been concerned by a communiqué received on April 9, ordering the 4th to Point Lookout, Maryland. That picturesque strip of beach at the tip of the state's Western Shore housed one of the largest POW camps in the North. The assignment raised fear that while comrades under Butler and Wistar struck for the seat of the Confederate government, the 4th would be reduced to keeping watch over already-vanquished Rebels far from the front.

The men worried for nothing; the new mission would be too short-lived to keep them out of the spring campaign. It would, however, compel them to abandon the dwellings they had built at Yorktown. On the morning of the tenth, the regiment turned its quarters over to the newest member of the garrison, the 2nd New Hampshire Volunteers. Then Lieutenant Colonel Rogers herded the outfit together and led it, one last time, to the local wharf. Before noon, a steamer was conveying the 4th up the York and out into the Chesapeake Bay.

By 8:00 P.M., the vessel had steamed into the mouth of the Potomac River opposite Point Lookout, headquarters of the District of St. Mary's, the most far-flung corner of Ben Butler's fiefdom. The men were kept aboard ship through a night made miserable by a steady rain. Not until 6:30 on the eleventh did the regiment straggle ashore and march to its new quarters outside the prison compound. There it shared a muddy campground with two other regiments of white New Hampshiremen. It got down to work late the same day.[19]

The duty the men performed during the fortnight on the Western Shore was varied and onerous. They guarded prisoners, helped repair sections of the stockade, and picketed the Bay and Potomac shores of the Peninsula. The officers' workload was much lighter, making Lieutenant Brigham fear that it was "too nice a job to last long." Yet even the enlisted men found their tour of duty psychologically rewarding. For one thing, it gave them a close-up view of enemy soldiers stripped of worldly goods and aristocratic pretensions. In fact, the inmates of Point Lookout were some of the most bedraggled specimens of humanity the 4th had ever laid eyes on.[20]

Every day, the regiment got a close view of this forlorn-looking rabble. Jarrett Morgan recalled: "I had to walk back and forth on a high scaffolding from which I could look down over them. They did look terrible. Filthy, dirty, ragged, starved, miserable. They were making rings out of beef bones to sell in order to make a little money." Despite the enmity he felt for these people and for the institution they had perpetuated at the expense of his race, Morgan also found himself pitying them.

One day, a prisoner detached himself from the others and approached the scaffold. Morgan thought he looked familiar but could not recall where he had seen him. The man stared up at the platform and asked, "Isn't this Jarrett Morgan?" The voice ignited a spark of recognition, and the private replied, "Are you Mr. Joe Parker?" The ragged fellow nodded. When bound out as a "house boy" to Isaac Wilson of Deer Creek, Harford County, Maryland, Morgan had played freely with the other children of the neighborhood, black and white, including his employer's nephews, Joe and Will Parker. Years later, by then in their late teens, the brothers had entered Confederate service, Joe as a member of the 43rd Virginia Battalion, the war's most famous unit of partisan rangers. On the eve of enlisting, Joe had come by to bid farewell to his old playmate, clasping Morgan's hand and rejecting the servant's admonition that he would be killed or captured: "The darned yankees'll never get me." The memory of that last remark made their meeting on the present occasion all the more poignant.

Touched by the unexpected reunion, Morgan vowed to do what he could to ease Parker's miserable condition, but he never got the chance: "We were not allowed to talk to the prisoners, but I managed to get a word in to him now and then as . . . I walked to and fro on the scaffolding. But I was taken down from there next day, and I never saw him again 'till long after the war. But he got home before I did." The young Rebel survived his imprisonment and was released at war's end, whereas Morgan remained in military service for another year. When he finally got back to Maryland, the two renewed their friendship and kept in close touch until Parker's death many years later.[21]

——+—≡✦≡—+——

Those who guarded prisoners were not alone in shouldering a heavy work-load. From the moment he set foot on the sandy peninsula of Point Look-out, Christian Fleetwood was kept busy trying to reduce a mountain of paperwork, much of it relative to the transfer from Yorktown, and finding enough men to handle the incessant demands of the compound commander. Only one day after arriving, he threw up his hands in frustration: "Oh Lord! The details!" He, for one, was not sorry when the 4th's assignment ended abruptly on the twenty-fifth and the men were shuttled down the Bay aboard the transport *George Leary*.[22]

The return trip was made memorable by the onboard issuance of beer, apparently a reward for the commendable restraint the 4th had displayed at Point Lookout. It had not shot a single POW for offenses real or alleged, a rare occurrence at a camp whose guards were known for their quick trigger fingers. The beer proved to be a bad idea: Fleetwood had to break up at least one fistfight between inebriated passengers.

The *George Leary* returned the men of the 4th to the Peninsula, which was now bathed in the warmth of spring, but not to Yorktown. Early on the twenty-sixth, the steamer navigated a path through a forest of transports and warships in Hampton Roads. Before noon, the men had gone ashore at Old Point Comfort, the site of Fort Monroe. The destination surprised the regiment; it also hinted that something big was in the offing.[23]

Instead of being assigned quarters in or just outside the garrison, the 4th was marched to Camp Hamilton, the fortified outwork that had originated as a haven for contrabands. The regiment was reunited there with Colonel Duncan and the rest of the brigade, augmented by more recently arrived USCT. Over the past few weeks, Wild's brigade, four regiments strong, had assembled in and around Fort Monroe. Now it joined with the three outfits under Duncan to form an all-USCT division under Brig. Gen. Edward Ward Hinks of Massachusetts, an officer with an exemplary combat record and who was known to be sensitive to the needs and talents of minority soldiers.[24]

Brig. Gen. Edward W. Hinks
PHOTOGRAPHIC HISTORY
OF THE CIVIL WAR

Hinks's was not the only division on hand in Hampton Roads. On the run from Point Lookout, the 4th's transport had rounded the Middle Peninsula, which it found overflowing with white units. The 4th learned that Yorktown, as well as Gloucester Point, had become a staging area for elements of Smith's command and for the advance contingent of the X Corps.

The presence of so many troops and ships in this backwater of the war told the 4th it would soon be off on a field mission to dwarf all that had gone before. Another clue to an imminent movement was the hectic pace of activity at Camp Hamilton; Lieutenant Brigham reported soon after arriving, "We are busy from morning till night getting [defective] property condemned, issuing clothing, making pay vouchers &c." Yet another piece of evidence was a rumor, later confirmed, that Lieutenant Colonel Rogers had recently petitioned department headquarters for the immediate return from detached duty of Captains Wickes, John W. Parrington (Company A), and William V. King (Company C), and First Lieutenants Holcombe and Wareham C. Hill (Company D). Only Wickes, whom General Hinks was about to appoint provost marshal and adjutant general of his division, and Holcombe, who had been charged with going AWOL to Baltimore, failed to rejoin the regiment posthaste. That so many officers would be recalled to the regiment at the same time hinted strongly that the 4th was on the verge of taking the field.[25]

But if the regiment was about to strike a blow for freedom and Union, where would it land? "Where we are to go from here no one seems to know," wrote Brigham. The lieutenant could not even be sure whether the "large fleet of transports & gunboats in the Roads" was meant for them. Yet he spoke for the entire regiment—in fact, for every officer and man encamped between Fortress Monroe and Gloucester Point—when he added, "All I hope is that when we do strike we shall be successful."[26]

⚊•⚊

Originally, H-Hour was set for May 4. That morning, Meade's army broke camp on the Rapidan and moved south toward the Virginia Wilderness, while the forces under Sherman took to roads leading to northern Georgia. Eager to play his role in Grant's multifaceted plan, Ben Butler loaded men, cannons, wagons, ammunition, and provisions aboard the transports anchored off Fort Monroe and points north. But due to the tardy arrival in Hampton Roads of Gillmore and the main body of his corps, men and materiel spent almost twenty-four inactive hours aboard ship. Not until 4:00 A.M. on May 5 did the vessels get under way. With those carrying Hinks's men in the lead, the ships steamed through the Roads, then churned up the winding, brackish James, their passage covered by warships from Adm. S. Phillips Lee's North Atlantic Blockading Squadron.[27]

The journey upriver in the ever-brightening sunlight was an experience no member of the 4th USCI could ever forget. Lieutenant Brigham called it "the grandest sight [he] ever saw, some thirty steamboats, besides gunboats, monitors, &c, all in one line steaming up the river." Colonel Duncan, while more expansive in his description of the flotilla, also felt that "it was a truly magnificent sight." He depicted it for the benefit of his friend Julia Jones:

> Monitors, Gunboats, Ironclads, transports of every conceivable pattern and capacity—black with the soldiers of the Union— came pressing on. I shall never forget how, early in the forenoon, the Greyhound [Butler's headquarters sloop] steamed past us. . . . Gen. Butler stood upon her deck, his hat in his hand, & the fresh wind streaming his thin hair behind him. Approaching our boat, his right arm was moving energetically like a piston; and amid the din of voices and the whirring of the boat, we could not fail to hear his shout, "Push on! push on! push on! More steam! More steam! Hurry up!" It was a most lovely May morning. The air was warm and balmy. The shores were lined with the fresh full foliage of Spring. Every body & every thing seemed to smile & catch the inspiration of the scene. It was hard to realize that we were bound on an errand of destruction & desolation.[28]

Although the fleet was observed by Rebel scouts on the riverbank, it proceeded unimpeded until, late in the afternoon, it reached the head of the westward-leading Appomattox River, about fourteen miles below Richmond. Since the upper reaches of the James were known to be obstructed by pilings placed there by the Confederate navy, this was as close to the enemy capital as Butler would get by water.

Grant's plans for Butler's army included the holding of strategic points on the James. The task had been entrusted to Wild's brigade, detachments of which had landed at Wilson's Wharf, on the north bank of the river about fifteen miles from the mouth of the Appomattox, and at Fort Powhatan, an ancient earthwork on the opposite bank about five miles farther upstream. With his line of communications now secure, Butler was to occupy the peninsula formed by the two rivers, known as Bermuda Hundred, while also taking City Point, a landing and railroad terminus on the south side of the Appomattox eight miles northeast of the strategic city of

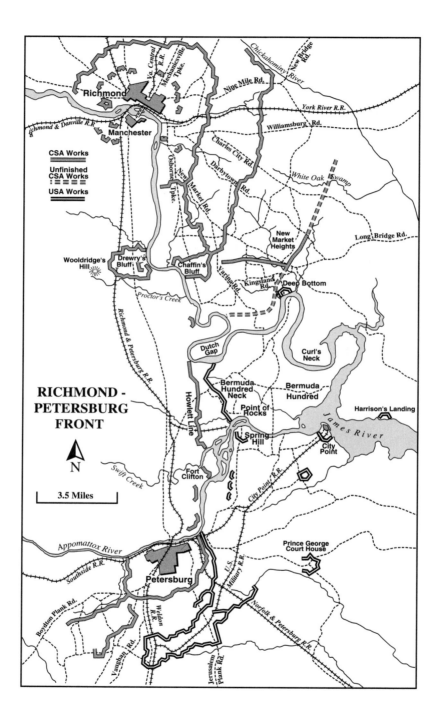

CSA Works
Unfinished CSA Works
USA Works

Richmond
Manchester

Va. Central R.R.
Mechanicsville Tpke.
Chickahominy River
New Bridge Rd.
Nine Mile Rd.
York River R.R.
Williamsburg Rd.
Richmond & Danville R.R.
Charles City Rd.
Darbytown Rd.
White Oak Swamp
Osborne Tpke.
New Market Rd.
Long Bridge Rd.
New Market Heights
Wooldridge's Hill
Drewry's Bluff
Chaffin's Bluff
Varina Rd.
Kingsland Rd.
Deep Bottom
Proctor's Creek
Richmond & Petersburg R.R.
Dutch Gap
Curl's Neck
Bermuda Hundred Neck
Bermuda Hundred
Harrison's Landing
Point of Rocks
James River
Howlett Line
Spring Hill
City Point
City Point R.R.
Swift Creek
Fort Clifton
N

RICHMOND - PETERSBURG FRONT

3.5 Miles

Appomattox River
Prince George Court House
Southside R.R.
Petersburg
U.S. Military R.R.
Boydton Plank Rd.
Weldon R.R.
Norfolk & Petersburg R.R.
Vaughan Rd.
Jerusalem Plank Rd.

Petersburg. The white troops of the XVIII Corps were to land at Bermuda Hundred; the remainder of Hinks's division would seize City Point.[29]

While the upper objective was not known to be held in force, it was feared that the landing to the south was well defended. Thus, as the fleet neared the confluence of the rivers, the 4th USCI and its comrades scanned the shoreline for entrenchments and fortifications. Colonel Duncan wrote: "We expected a fight for its [City Point's] possession, and we prepared accordingly. I might say that we hoped for a fight, for the [rest of] the army lay out in the James, and we would gladly have given them a chance to see us 'go in,' in order that we might convince the skeptics" of the fighting ability of the African-American soldier. Though they lacked battle experience, his men appeared confident of success; Michael Arnold noted that throughout the trip, his comrades sang "John Brown's Body" and other patriotic songs, while offering up cheers for Lincoln, Grant, and Butler. The men's enthusiasm grew with each passing mile: "The farther up the river we go the more they seem to rejoice."[30]

But City Point failed to provide the 4th with the test it craved. When, at about 5:30 P.M., the transports made fast at the local wharf—until recently the berth of flag-of-truce and prisoner-exchange vessels—no hint of an enemy presence could be discerned, beyond a signal platform and a large Rebel flag flying from it. Playing it safe, the men clambered up the shoreline bluffs with their rifles at the ready. Moving quickly inland under cover of the gunboats—one of whose shells exploded just above the signal perch, reducing it to splinters—the 4th and its sister regiments secured the landing. Against minimal resistance, Duncan's 2nd Brigade, 3rd Division, XVIII Corps, captured thirty-five signal personnel and confiscated their banner.[31]

If few soldiers came forth to greet Duncan's men, a demonstrative reception was provided by the African-American residents of the neighborhood, whom Arnold saw "running to and fro, so glad were they at the sight of black Yankees." One older gentleman tugged at the coat sleeve of a corporal and asked if he was indeed a Union soldier. Once assured of that fact, the civilian exclaimed: "'Fore God, I'se bin looking for de Yanks dis two years!"[32]

The signal detachment had been corralled too quickly to warn Richmond of Butler's coming. Especially when his white units occupied Bermuda Hundred without a fight, the army leader grew confident that the defenders of Richmond knew nothing of the danger they were in. In this supposition he was essentially correct, for the capital remained as lightly defended as it had been when Wistar and, later, Kilpatrick and Dahlgren advanced on it.

Butler, however, should have realized that surprise was a fleeting thing and that his objective would not remain unprotected forever. Already, in fact, Jefferson Davis was seeking assistance from Maj. Gen. George E. Pickett, leader of the 13,000 Confederates in and around Petersburg. Of greater danger to Butler's plans, several thousand potential defenders were en route from the Carolinas under Pierre G. T. Beauregard, one of the Confederacy's earliest heroes, commander of the batteries in Charleston Harbor that had inaugurated the war, and second-in-command of the victors at First Manassas (First Bull Run). Since achieving those triumphs, the Louisiana Creole had fallen out with President Davis, whose military policies he had scorned. As punishment, he had been assigned to a rearward command, the Department of South Carolina, Georgia, and Florida. But despite a gargantuan ego and his penchant for alienating civilian superiors, Beauregard was an able strategist and a tenacious fighter. Although supplied with fewer troops than his opponent, he would prove more than a match for Benjamin F. Butler.[33]

With Bermuda Hundred and City Point in Union hands, Butler ought to have given quick thought to moving on Richmond. Instead, he had his men fortify both places beyond the possibility of recapture. Above the Appomattox, Smith's troops, eventually assisted by the new arrivals under Gillmore, dug trenches along the length of the peninsula and threw up a strong line of defenses across Bermuda Hundred Neck, where the peninsula narrowed to a width of three miles.

Then Butler sent elements of both corps westward to break the railroad between Richmond and Petersburg and obstruct the parallel-running turnpike. This effort, which consumed several days that would have been better spent on the road north, ended unsuccessfully due to the inability of Smith and Gillmore—both of whom were prickly and temperamental—to cooperate with and support each other. Much smaller enemy forces kept railroad and pike open to traffic, including Beauregard and his hard-marching Carolinians. By May 14, the Creole was in position to defend the capital with some 17,000 troops of all arms—a feat made possible not only by Butler's poor sense of priorities, but also by the unprofessional behavior of the West Pointers who had been expected to keep him from blundering.[34]

While the white troops toiled to secure Bermuda Hundred, the USCT at City Point were no less busy or productive. Small fortifications soon rose on all sides of the nondescript settlement that overlooked the landing. By midday of May 6, the 4th USCI occupied one of these earthworks and prepared to hold it against an assault by Beauregard or Pickett. Three days passed, however, without attracting even a half-hearted challenge. The 4th took the opportunity to get in some drill, visit the bivouacs of nearby regiments, and when the temperature climbed, to cool off with a swim in the Appomattox.[35]

Between the sixth and eighth, detachments of the regiment and some of the other components of Duncan's brigade ventured down the winding Appomattox in search of the enemy. They reconnoitered, but did not attempt to hold, several points on the south side of the river, including a tree-fringed plateau called Spring Hill. More gingerly, they probed toward Fort Clifton, a large Confederate earthwork on the north side of the river, barely two miles from Pickett's headquarters.

At midday on the ninth, the USCT moved in greater strength against Fort Clifton to support a sudden advance from the north by a white brigade and a run down the Appomattox by army and navy gunboats. The many-pronged attack faltered, however, when the fort's long-range guns held the white troops at bay and sank one of the vessels. For a few hours, the men of the 4th dosed the fort with rounds from their Enfields, but to no discernible effect. At length, the assault was called off, and the regiment returned nonchalantly to City Point, where Christian Fleetwood, for one, "turned in for a snooze."[36]

It seemed, in fact, that the entire army had gone to sleep. By sundown on the ninth, Butler's subordinates had spent four days lethargically attempting to interpose between Richmond and Petersburg and neutralize the outposts on the Appomattox. That night, their disgusted superior turned his full attention on Petersburg, which he had sized up as equal in strategic value to the Confederate capital. He proposed an all-out assault on the city, to take place early on the tenth—only to cancel it hours after he broached it to Smith and Gillmore.

In the interim, he had received word by telegraph that Grant and Meade had maneuvered Lee's army out of its position below the Rapidan River and were driving it steadily toward Richmond. The intelligence was not entirely accurate: Rather than advancing south with a full head of steam, the Army of the Potomac was moving slowly through the Virginia Wilderness against stubborn opposition. How soon Meade's troops could reach Richmond was anyone's guess. Still, the news reminded Butler of his orders to cooperate with Meade in attacking or besieging the capital. Thus, instead of striking Petersburg, he spent May 10 assembling his white troops at Bermuda Hundred. The following morning, he led most of them toward the southern defenses of Richmond, near Drewry's Bluff on the James River.[37]

While the X and XVIII Corps headed north, Hinks's USCT remained at and near City Point to guard the army's rear and communications. The assignment seemed to suggest that Butler lacked faith in the African-Americans, but it was a logical move: The black soldiers had none of the combat experience that most of their comrades under Gillmore and Smith enjoyed. At this stage in their development, the USCT were better suited to fight from behind prepared works than attack across open ground against intricate defenses.

Being left in the rear did not mean they would be denied an active role in the unfolding campaign. On the twelfth, at Butler's urging, Hinks led the 4th and 6th USCI of Duncan's brigade, plus a company of the 2nd United States Colored Cavalry and two artillery sections, including one from the only African-American battery in the Army of the James, down-river to Spring Hill. That position now anchored a pontoon bridge that Butler's engineers had laid across the Appomattox opposite a Bermuda Hundred landmark known as Point of Rocks. This time the plateau was occupied; the 4th and its comrades began building an earthen redoubt later christened Fort Converse. The work was vital to maintaining a foothold on the river, but the men were beginning to wonder when they would stop throwing dirt and start throwing lead. Mike Arnold reflected the prevailing mood when he wrote that he hoped "soon to be led to victory under the gallant Hinks and modest Duncan, without spades, picks, and mud-works."[38]

Within a couple of days, Duncan's men had completed and armed with artillery what their leader called a "very respectable" set of works "that will play the deuce with Johnny Reb when he attempts our capture." The first attempt was made at 11:00 A.M. on the eighteenth, when, according to Fleetwood, the enemy "woke us with a few shells," a prelude to a reconnaissance-in-force of the 4th's position. Under cover of a brief cannonade, a force that Duncan estimated at 600 cavalry, backed by 100 infantry, came charging along the river toward the 4th's position, keening the Rebel yell. It was later learned that the Confederates had vowed to "wipe out that nigger regt." that occupied Spring Hill.[39]

The attackers drove in the pickets of the 4th, but this was the extent of their success. Before they came into carbine or rifle range of the defenses, Duncan's cannons opened on them with brutal effect. Shell and shrapnel tore into the cavalry, which turned and galloped to the rear. Their infantry friends pressed forward, only to stagger under the fire of the 4th's Enfields. The ground at the base of the regiment's works was soon littered with a dozen bodies. The rest of the attack force, Duncan wrote, "retired, undoubtedly in disgust." Some held on to ground beyond rifle range, and for about a half hour, the opposing artillery carried on the fight. Then, suddenly, the enemy was gone, having withdrawn to Petersburg.[40]

For the 4th USCI, the price of victory had been two men slightly wounded. Thus the regiment had experienced an almost bloodless introduction to combat. It had stood the test well; not a man had left his post for the rear even when exposed to that fearsome cannon fire. As battles went, the affair at Spring Hill had been a small one, but it had enabled the outfit to show what Corporal Arnold called "the best of pluck and courage." That knowledge would engender unit pride, which in turn would sustain the outfit in the much heavier fighting that lay ahead. [41]

CHAPTER 5

Error and Redemption

IF THE 4TH HAD PASSED THE TEST OF BATTLE, THE SAME COULD NOT BE said of the army's white units. By the fourteenth, following two days of skirmishing with the advance elements of Beauregard's command, Butler, Smith, and Gillmore settled into attack positions just below the defenses of Drewry's Bluff, about eight miles south of the capital. That day the corps commanders captured a line of entrenchments in their front, but a nervous Butler postponed an assault on the interior line, then went over to the defensive.

He was still trying to decide whether to assault or to withdraw to Bermuda Hundred when, on the foggy morning of the sixteenth, Beauregard attacked instead. Although slightly outnumbered, the Creole used surprise to maximum advantage. His enemy's faulty dispositions enabled him to break through on the right, a blow both physically and psychologically destructive. Then, in methodical fashion, he rolled up the Union line from east to west. By midday, the stunned, confused Federals were falling back; by late afternoon, they were streaming southward in full retreat. They might have been routed utterly had not one of Beauregard's subordinates, who had gone into position to smite the Union rear, failed to attack. The officer's timidity permitted Butler's survivors, by early evening, to reach the safety of their peninsula defenses.[1]

Hinks's troops were not required to vacate their well-secured positions in order to safeguard Butler's withdrawal. Even so, the debacle of Drewry's Bluff, which cost the army nearly 5,000 casualties against fewer than half as many for the Confederates, affected the black troops. In addition to lowering morale throughout Hinks's division, Butler's retreat left the command vulnerable to attack by Beauregard, who pursued his enemy to Bermuda Hundred Neck. Beginning on the seventeenth, the Louisianan launched a series of assaults on the peninsula works. His reconnaissance-in-force the

76

following day, which provided the 4th USCI with its baptism of battle, was one aspect of this offensive.

By the twenty-second, Beauregard had been butting his head for five days against a line of defense he now admitted was too strong to take by direct assault. Belatedly, he realized that to secure Richmond's safety, he did not need to overthrow Butler's army, only neutralize it. By fortifying across the neck of his peninsula, Butler had effectively chained his troops to a parcel of land of no military value. To ensure that the trap was airtight, Beauregard built a parallel line of works, effectively containing the Army of the James like "the contents of a bottle, strongly corked," as Grant later put it.[2]

With Butler's white troops rendered stationary, the Confederates could concentrate their attention and resources on the James and the south side of the Appomattox. On the twenty-fourth, a large body of cavalry attacked Wild's troops at Wilson's Wharf and Fort Powhatan. Both assaults were repulsed handily, winning favorable publicity for the USCT throughout Butler's ranks. Other Rebels probed the works at Spring Hill, though they did not attempt a full-scale assault. Believing they would remain quiescent, on the twenty-sixth Hinks withdrew the 4th USCI from Fort Converse to City Point, where, along with the 5th and 22nd Infantry and the African-American battery, it constituted a reserve brigade under Duncan's command.[3]

Although not happy with its rear-guard posture, the 4th doubted it would maintain it for long. As soon as it had departed Spring Hill, pressure on Fort Converse intensified. Sometimes the enemy resorted to unconventional tactics. According to Mike Arnold, on one occasion Beauregard's troops attacked not only with infantry and artillery, but also with packs of bloodhounds. As a means of taking prisoners, the gesture was both desperate and futile. "This mode of warfare," said Fleetwood's friend and fellow noncom, "at one time proved successful on unarmed slaves, but not so with free men who are armed from teeth to toe."[4]

On May 28, the 4th was ordered to stand ready to return to Spring Hill, preparatory to joining a movement against Petersburg—a movement that never took place. Ever since the tenth, Butler had regretted his decision to abort his offensive against the "Cockade City"; he had been seeking an opportunity to try again with the troops of Smith and Hinks. By the twenty-sixth, he had learned that the city's defenses had recently been depleted, and he scheduled a new attack for two days later. The only trouble was that Grant, who was aware of Butler's entrapment at Bermuda Hundred, considered the Army of the James, in its present position, doomed to immobility. He thought he could make better use of Butler's troops elsewhere—specifically, in Meade's sector.

By the twenty-eighth, the Army of the Potomac was crossing the Pamunkey River after having battled Lee to a standstill in the Wilderness (May 5–6), near Spotsylvania Court House (May 8–21), and along the line of the North Anna (May 23–26). As they had done so often during those three weeks, Meade's people were again attempting to pass Lee's right (lower) flank on the road to Richmond. Their next destination was Cold Harbor, a misnamed hamlet about ten miles northeast of the capital.[5]

On the twenty-sixth, Grant had wired Butler to send about 20,000 troops under Smith—whom the general-in-chief continued to regard as an able leader—to link with Meade on the road to Cold Harbor. Butler cast about for a reason to delay obeying the order until after Smith's men struck Petersburg. At first he used the lack of adequate shipping in the James as a pretext to hang on to Smith. Under cover of that excuse, he ordered the XVIII Corps, including Hinks's division, to prepare, as Christian Fleetwood put it, "to move on Petersburg and take [it] with the bayonet." At the eleventh hour, however, enough transports reached Butler's headquarters to make him call off the assault. Until the thirty-first, he busied himself, instead, with readying Smith's detachment for the run up the James and the Pamunkey to Cold Harbor. Yet instead of tearing up his plan for Petersburg, Butler merely pocketed it once more.[6]

Smith's departure from Bermuda Hundred was so chaotic that he managed to bring off only 15,000 officers and men, including a division-size contingent of the X Corps. The loss of even that many troops meant that Butler would have to stretch the remainder of Gillmore's command to cover gaps left in the line. To help with this process, Butler ordered many of Hinks's men to relocate from City Point and Spring Hill. On the twenty-ninth, the 4th USCI crossed the pontoons to Point of Rocks, then trekked north into position on the far right of the line. As soon as they arrived, the men were put to work improving the defenses that surrounded them. They lengthened breastworks, deepened trenches, and threw fresh earth on redoubts and redans—in effect, making impregnable barriers even more so. That done, the men stepped up to the dirt walls, stuck the barrels of their Enfields through the embrasures, and began trading minié balls with Rebel sharpshooters.

The 4th did not spend every waking hour digging or shooting. At regular intervals, detachments were relieved on the firing lines and sent to the comparative safety of the rear. There they messed, talked, sang, played cards, and fraternized with other regiments. On occasion, they greeted visitors to the front, including a couple of celebrities. On the twenty-ninth, they made the acquaintance of the mulatto James Wormley, one of Washington's most celebrated restaurateurs, and shook hands with one of the soldier sons of Frederick Douglass, the most famous black abolitionist of the day.[7]

The regiment had been at Point of Rocks only two days when its presence was again required below the Appomattox. Sometime before 10:00 in the morning of the thirty-first, Colonel Ames's 6th USCI, the only unit remaining at Spring Hill, came under attack by Confederates of all arms. The assault, which at first was thought to involve more troops than had struck on the eighteenth, so alarmed Butler that he ordered 600 members of Duncan's brigade—the better part of the 4th, under Lieutenant Colonel Rogers and Major Boernstein, both on horseback, supported by a small detachment of the 5th USCI—to the threatened sector.[8]

When the call came, most of the 4th, recently relieved from the main line, were resting in the shade of the few trees still standing in the rear. An anonymous enlisted man recalled: "The sound of cannon brought us forth, and, at a double-quick under a broiling sun, we hastened to the rescue. . . . Having, after some delay, crossed the river, we entered the fort, much to the joy of the gallant 6th Regiment."[9]

Unknown to the men of the 4th, Colonel Ames had informed General Hinks by courier that he did not need reinforcing. For one thing, his pickets, instead of rushing to the cover of their works as they had on the eighteenth, retired stubbornly this day, halting to fire wherever they found cover. The newly arrived 4th was impressed with the way its comrades disputed the enemy advance: "Experienced officers say they never saw picket lines held better." As a result, the attackers—some 700 cavalry, supported by two rifled cannons and a small force of foot soldiers—refused to assault Fort Converse. They hunkered down behind trees, rocks, and foliage, from which they showered the garrison with shells and bullets. Dismounted skirmishers crept closer to the fort, picking off members of the 6th with sniper fire.[10]

Ames, tiring of the standoff, early in the afternoon ordered the 4th to clear out the skirmishers. The colonel believed this feat achievable because the regiment's manpower appeared to match that of the enemy and its rifles were superior to the carbines and shotguns most horsemen toted. Still, the Confederates had artillery, which promised to add drama to the assault. The enlisted man who chronicled the regiment's arrival at Spring Hill wrote that a large detachment of the 4th, under Boernstein, had barely begun to advance in line of battle when its "skirmishers were hotly engaged, and the whizzing and singing of balls, and the indescribable sound of shells passing and repassing, made it exciting."

Despite the ferocity of the opposition, he wrote, "steadily we drove them [the Rebel skirmishers] back on to their main body." When the fire in front slackened, Boernstein, believing his job done, turned to lead the men back to Fort Converse. He discovered, however, that many skirmishers, having remounted, were following his men at a trot. The perturbed officer faced about yet again and called for a charge. As cheering men broke into the double-quick, the major spurred his charger up the road. The flabbergasted enemy lingered long enough to get off a ragged volley. A carbine round missed Boernstein only because his horse's head got in the way. Then the Rebels galloped off as if the fires of perdition were blowing their way.

The 4th pursued until artillery began to lash it with case shot. An unhorsed Boernstein hollered a warning, and his men hit the dirt just as a volley passed over their heads. They remained facedown in the road for several minutes before the cannons trundled away and Ames recalled everyone to the earthwork. "This time," observed the unnamed enlisted man, "we were not followed and returned as if from battalion drill." The unhurried withdrawal capped a display of "coolness and bravery" that had impressed every onlooker.[11]

The 4th's heroics had cost the outfit no fatalities, but several men had gone down with wounds. On the surface, the regiment seemed to have escaped relatively unscathed. But even slightly wounded men could be lost to action for months at a time, creating worrisome gaps in the ranks. One such casualty was Jarrett Morgan, who, while discharging his rifle at the retreating horsemen, had his right thumb nearly severed by a piece of shell. Sent to a field hospital in the rear, where the thumb was amputated, the private was later evacuated to the division hospital at City Point.[12]

After three weeks of recuperation, Morgan was transferred across Hampton Roads to the military hospital at Portsmouth, Virginia. This was one of several large, well-appointed hospitals in Ben Butler's department, but it must have been overcrowded just then, for soon after he arrived, the charter member of Company F was shipped north aboard a medical steamboat. He ended up in a general hospital in Newark, New Jersey, where he spent almost five months. During that time, through some extralegal arrangement, the hospital commander hired him out to a wealthy New York family, who employed him as a servant in their home. When he returned to Newark several weeks later, Morgan was declared recovered from his wound and fit for duty, but he was not permitted to rejoin his regiment. Instead, he was ferried partway across the Hudson River and assigned quarters in the barracks on Governors Island. He did not rejoin his outfit in Virginia until late in November.[13]

Morgan's six-month absence from active duty was unusual, as were certain aspects of his time away from the 4th. In its basic elements, however, his was a case with which the 4th USCI was all too familiar.

The day after its most recent encounter with "Southern chivalry," the 4th did picket duty at Spring Hill. When the Rebels offered no further trouble beyond long-range sharpshooting, the outfit packed up on the afternoon of June 2 and marched to City Point. After a few hours at division headquarters—during which General Hinks may well have congratulated Rogers and Boernstein for the men's conduct on the thirty-first—the outfit recrossed the Appomattox.[14]

Arriving at its old campground at Bermuda Hundred, the regiment found it shelled out in the wake of two days of attacks against both flanks of Butler's defenses. During the assaults, several white regiments had been cut up and a few forced into retreat; one had been captured nearly whole. Disgusted and weary, the 4th salvaged what it could amid the wreckage caused by cannon fire, drew replacement tents at the quartermaster depot, and established a new camp on Cobb's Hill, in rear of the army's left. That sector was considered far enough removed from enemy batteries that Butler's signalmen had erected an observation tower, almost 200 feet high, on the hill. According to the regiment's new adjutant, Alfred Brigham, "The whole line of the enemy can be seen" from the top of the tower.[15]

Relief from the frenetic action on the Bermuda Hundred front came on June 3, a quiet, listless day along the lines. Beauregard's troops were so quiet that the only sounds of battle to reach the 4th's ears drifted up from Cold Harbor, more than twenty miles away. Some listeners thought those sounds had an ominous ring. In fact, the troops of Meade and Smith were attacking across open ground against well-constructed breastworks supported by banks of artillery. The assault of June 3—the product of Grant's frustration at finding his path to Richmond blocked yet again by hard-marching Confederates—would cost the combined Union forces approximately 7,000 men killed and wounded, about 1,000 of them in the ranks of the X and XVIII Corps. At a cost of only 1,500 casualties, Lee thereby ended his opponents' efforts to reach Richmond from above. The Federals, whose left flank now rested on the Chickahominy River, had been pushed so far to the east that they lacked the maneuvering room to reach their objective.[16]

Over the next week, Meade and Smith maneuvered in Lee's front but did not assault it. They repulsed a few Rebel sorties, tended to their wounded, and beginning on June 7, interred hundreds of corpses that had been left between the lines to rot under a merciless sun. Meanwhile, at Bermuda Hundred, Butler spent the week planning how best to use the troops remaining to him.

The army leader still envisioned a major strike on Petersburg. Days after being forced to detach half his troops to Cold Harbor, he had sounded out Edward Hinks and the army's cavalry commander, Brig. Gen. August V. Kautz, on the possibility of attacking the Cockade City via the pontoon bridge to Spring Hill. Beauregard's assaults on Bermuda Hundred Neck had postponed the discussion, but it resumed on June 6 after a deserter from Petersburg informed army headquarters that the city was defended by a single regiment of Regular infantry, some heavy artillery, and militia— mostly old men and boys.[17]

The news fell sweetly on Butler's ears, for it promised to raise his political prospects. The convention of the Republican Party (now styled the National Union Party to curry the support of War Democrats), scheduled to open in Baltimore later in the month, was certain to renominate Abraham Lincoln. But signs of disaffection were already appearing in the ranks. A Radical Republican convention, which would select a candidate in opposition to Lincoln, was about to convene in Cleveland. Butler doubted that either the regulars or the extremists—or the Peace Democrats, for that matter—would choose an electible candidate. A war hero, especially one who achieved a dramatic victory at the height of the presidential race, might outmaneuver the party leaders and snatch the coveted prize.[18]

On the seventh, a hopeful Butler put Hinks and Kautz on notice that large detachments of their forces were needed for expeditionary service. The news, which quickly filtered down to the rank and file, did not raise everyone's expectations. Christian Fleetwood jotted in his diary: "Ammunition issued and talk of on to Petersburg. Doubt it."[19]

His skepticism was well founded. On the morning of the ninth, some 3,200 infantry and 1,000 horsemen moved south to capture Petersburg. Last-minute substitutions had changed the leadership and composition of the expedition. Having gotten wind of the operation, General Gillmore had claimed the right to command it. Despite his questionable performances against the Richmond and Petersburg Railroad and at Drewry's Bluff, the corps leader had the seniority the position demanded, and so Butler, against his better judgment, gave it to him. At once Gillmore, who distrusted the ability of the USCT, demanded that Hinks's contribution to the operation be reduced and a corresponding number of white infantrymen be added. Again Butler acquiesced. On the afternoon of the eighth, Hinks had notified Duncan's brigade to stand ready to march. Before evening, he canceled its participation and limited his column to Wild's brigade, which had been detached from its James River outposts.[20]

Gillmore's changes allowed the 4th USCI to escape a humiliating disaster. Petersburg was so lightly held that it should have fallen at first contact, thereby severing Lee's communications with the interior of the Confederacy—a blow that would have denied much-needed provisions to the army at Cold Harbor. But Gillmore and Kautz took up attack positions so far apart as to prevent them from coordinating operations. Each hesitated to strike until assured the other had done so. The fainthearted Gillmore confined himself to sparring with the city's few defenders. Late in the day,

Kautz finally attacked, but by then Gillmore had withdrawn to Bermuda Hundred, permitting the garrison to concentrate against the cavalry. Kautz pierced the outer works south of the city, but he failed to gain the heart of Petersburg before a motley force of Regulars and citizen-soldiers threatened his rear, persuading him to retreat.[21]

Butler was infuriated by the outcome, which not only lessened his political prospects, but also alerted Beauregard, who reinforced Petersburg so heavily that a second assault appeared out of the question. The commander took out his anger on Gillmore, whom he relieved from duty and sent to Washington for reassignment. Eventually the corps leader was replaced by a veteran of the Army of the Potomac, Maj. Gen. David Bell Birney. The newcomer was the younger brother of William Birney, whose USCT brigade had recently come up from South Carolina to augment the white troops of the X Corps.[22]

Although the 4th had been denied a role in one effort against Petersburg, it was given a second chance less than a week later. In the midst of his preparations for the June 9 operation, Butler had received a telegram from Grant at Cold Harbor, announcing his intention to move Meade and Smith across the Chickahominy and then the James. Grant's target was no longer Richmond, but its support center to the south. The general-in-chief was aware that Petersburg had been reinforced in the aftermath of the Gillmore fiasco, but even with the additions, Beauregard could not stop an assault by the Army of the Potomac and the XVIII Corps. Butler could expect the first troops to reach Bermuda Hundred by transport and/or overland march on or about the fourteenth; he was to support the movement with troops from City Point, including Hinks's division.[23]

When the 4th got the word that it would soon recross the Appomattox, some men expressed mixed feelings. They wanted in on any effort to wrest Petersburg or Richmond from the Rebels, but they had finally settled into a routine at Cobb's Hill, which lay far enough behind the firing lines that drill had been reinstituted. Recently, in fact, the regiment had held its first dress parade since leaving Fort Monroe and Camp Hamilton. The place also had its drawbacks, as Adjutant Brigham observed: "The water is not good here, there are no springs and . . . it is too near the surface to be good. I usually dilute mine with a little whiskey and quinine." Even so, the regiment had come to consider the place something very close to home.[24]

But late on the fourteenth, Hinks ordered Duncan to march at 1:00 A.M. with the 2,200 officers and men of his brigade—the 4th, 5th, and 6th USCI, to which Kiddoo's 22nd Regiment had been added. The immediate destination was a newly laid pontoon bridge at Broadway Landing, three miles west of City Point. The brigade spent the balance of the night getting ready; again ammunition was distributed, defective arms were exchanged for serviceable ones, and the men filled their haversacks with enough rations to last at least three days.[25]

Those who were able to grab a few hours' sleep were awakened shortly before midnight and placed in a column. One hour later, when they reported to Hinks at Broadway Landing, they found the bridgehead a scene of intense activity. Despite the darkness, they could discern marching men off their flanks and to their rear, some heading downriver toward the bridge at Point of Rocks. These troops—most of them members of a provisional USCT brigade under Colonel Holman—were moving as noiselessly as possible, hopeful that the enemy could be kept in the dark, figuratively as well as literally, about their movement.

When the 4th crossed to the south side, it found itself amidst an even greater crush of bodies. At City Point, the river was clogged with transports from which hundreds of soldiers were debarking. These were the survivors of the ill-starred force Baldy Smith had led to Cold Harbor—men who had endured a great deal of misery over the past two weeks and who intended to avenge themselves on the defenders of Petersburg.

Thanks to elaborate precautions—the loud playing of bands on the front lines, the theatrical-like movement of Meade's troops in clear sight of the enemy—Smith's people had slipped away from Cold Harbor without alerting their opponents. So, too, had elements of the Army of the Potomac, spearheaded by the II Corps of Maj. Gen. Winfield S. Hancock. While the Army of the James rode the Pamunkey and the James to Butler's headquarters, Hancock's men had begun a long march overland toward City Point. Grant expected them to link with Smith's force after the latter made the initial attack on the Cockade City. They would add their weight to the decisive push that Kautz's cavalry had failed to complete on the ninth.[26]

Upon reaching Broadway Landing, Duncan's brigade linked with two artillery batteries and the 1,300 USCT under Holman—not only the colonel's own 1st USCI, but also one wing of the 5th Massachusetts Cavalry, one of the few African-American regiments to have retained its state designation. The majority of the troops under Hinks enjoyed high morale and regarded the upcoming movement—what they knew of it—with more than a little enthusiasm. The 5th Massachusetts was an exception. Its men had taken the field astride fine-looking animals, only to be dismounted and forced to serve as infantry, although armed with pistols, carbines, and sabers instead of long-range rifles. The transformation had destroyed the unit's morale, but few of the cavalrymen's infantry comrades felt sorry for them; rather, they rejoiced that the high-and-mighty had been brought low.

The horsemen had only themselves to blame. Some months before his wounding, Jarrett Morgan had watched the regiment ride past: "My they looked nice! Spick and span. Clean sky-blue uniforms, polished brass buttons. They began making fun of us foot-soldiers. We were tired, dirty and ragged." The infantrymen were not disposed to take the jesting in good humor. After being stripped of their mounts, the erstwhile troopers marched by with heads hung low. At every opportunity, Morgan and his comrades showered them with hoots and catcalls: "Eh! Eh! didn't we put it on to 'em though!"[27]

The 4th and the other regiments under Duncan expected to move out for Petersburg via the direct road from City Point, soon after reaching the south side of the river. Instead, they were kept waiting until after 3:00 A.M. for the arrival of three bodies of white troops assigned to the operation: the XVIII Corps divisions of Brigadier Generals William T. H. Brooks and John H. Martindale and a detachment of the X Corps under Col. Louis Bell. The delay was vexing enough—it suggested poor planning on the part of Butler or Smith, or both—but when the whites arrived and the troops under Hinks, Duncan, and Holman started forward, they were halted minutes later to permit Kautz's cavalry to take the road. Kautz's intervention not only held up the foot soldiers two more hours, but it also forced them to march over a path coated with the droppings of several hundred horses.

By 5:00, the entire expeditionary force, 9,000 strong, was finally under way. Kautz, followed by the USCT, then by the units of Brooks and Bell, trooped down the City Point Road. Martindale's division took a parallel road that hugged the bank of the Appomattox. If all went as planned, each of these forces would play a major role in the coming assault. While Martindale guarded the flank and rear of the expedition, Brooks and Bell would attack along the City Point Road against Lunettes 1, 2, and 3, the northwesternmost of fifty-five batteries that covered the approaches to Petersburg above, east of, and below the city. While the initial assault was in progress, the USCT would shift a mile or more to the east until they gained the Jordan's Point Road. Turning south, they would attack Lunettes 4 through 7. If successful there, the African-Americans, supported by uncommitted white units, would attempt to widen the breakthrough by moving still farther east and south, in the direction of Lunettes 8 through 11.[28]

It was a viable plan, but it broke down even before it could be fairly tested. At about 7:00, the horsemen in the vanguard of Hinks's column unexpectedly encountered a heavily manned earthwork flanked by well-occupied entrenchments at Baylor's Farm, two miles in advance of the batteries. The cavalry and the African-Americans in its rear halted and shook out skirmish lines. When the skirmishers went forward, they discovered that the enemy position could be reached only by passing through a swamp-infested woods about a quarter of a mile wide, crossing a 400-yard-long plain cleared for artillery fire, and clambering up the steep hill on which the earthwork rested. Though the Federals could not make an accurate estimate, the defenses were manned by two infantry regiments and several companies of horsemen, backed by four 12-pounder cannons.

When Baldy Smith came up, he made a hasty decision. Because the white troops in whom he placed the majority of his confidence were well to the rear, he planned to attack with soldiers—white cavalry and black infantry—whose ability he doubted. Rather than assign the task to Hinks's men, he had Kautz dismount most of his command and lead it forward. It proved to be a bad idea. Unused to fighting afoot, the troopers penetrated the woods with difficulty; those that made it onto the plain beyond found their short-range carbines no match for the rifles of the Confederates. Halfway across the field, the troopers were hit with a scathing volley that sent most of them scrambling for safety behind a hill. There they were shielded from further harm but could not assist the offensive.[29]

A disgusted Smith turned to Hinks and ordered him to go in with his brigade and a half. Hinks passed the word, and minutes later—at or about 8:00—Duncan's men launched their first attack of the war in brigade strength. As the advance began, the 5th USCI held the right flank of the battle line, the 22nd the right center, the 4th the left center, and the 6th the far left. Behind Duncan's men, the 5th Massachusetts and the 1st USCI of Holman's brigade moved slowly forward. From the rear, the batteries attached to Hinks's command began to lay down a covering barrage.

Despite the obstacles in their path, Duncan's people went forward briskly and enthusiastically. Because they lacked experience, however, they failed to maintain alignment. All four of the brigade's regiments were roughly side by side as they entered the woods, but the movement attracted what Duncan called "a furious shelling." The cannonade so disarranged the formation that the 4th reached the far edge of the trees in advance of everyone else.[30]

Lieutenant Colonel Rogers and Major Boernstein, both on foot this day, attempted to keep the men well in hand until the rest of the brigade came up, to permit a cohesive crossing of the field. But the shelling, which had already inflicted the 4th's first combat casualties, so unnerved the men in the center of the regimental line—Captain Parrington's Company A, Capt. William V. King's Company C, and Capt. Sidney J. Mendall's Company I—that they refused to wait at the tree line. Impulsively and without orders, all three companies burst out of the woods and bounded across the naked ground toward the enemy.

This was a fatal error, and Lieutenant Colonel Rogers knew it immediately. He risked life and limb to chase after the men, screaming for them to return to the woods. His warning was drowned out by the din of Rebel rifle and artillery fire. The running men kept moving until the first volley of musketry ripped into them. Initially they fell by twos and threes, but once they attracted the full attention of the enemy, a converging fire was poured in on them and they went down by the dozens. Rogers could only stare in horror at the carnage before his eyes.[31]

The Confederate barrage was destructive enough, but when the converted foot soldiers of the 5th Massachusetts reached the edge of the woods, they unaccountably unleashed a fusillade against the left wing of the 4th. Already stunned by the fire in front, the survivors of the charge were staggered by the unexpected blow from the rear. The three companies did not get even as far as Kautz's troopers before turning and racing to the rear. With frantic gestures, Rogers and Boernstein guided them back to the shelter they had so recklessly abandoned.[32]

By then it was too late to avert major damage. In less than fifteen minutes, more than 120 members of the 4th had been killed or wounded. The fatalities included not only Captain King, but also Adjutant Brigham, who had joined in the charge for reasons of his own. Parrington and Mendall had been wounded, the former slightly, the latter severely. To the list of officer casualties one could add 2nd Lt. George H. Walrath of Company A, who this day succumbed to disease in a City Point hospital.[33]

The slaughter in the ranks of the 4th, while it reflected a want of discipline, had come about through understandable circumstances: Even veteran regiments had been known to break and flee when they became the target of a sudden, fearsome barrage. At least the 4th had run forward, not to the rear, as any raw regiment might have done under similar conditions. Then, too, the sacrifice the three companies had made contributed to ultimate success. By concentrating their attention on the left of Duncan's brigade—including a portion of the 6th USCI, which had advanced in rear of the 4th and had been cut up almost as severely—the Confederates had failed to oppose until well under way the subsequent advance of the rest of the brigade. As Duncan wrote in his after-action report: "Through the brisk fire now turned upon the right wing[,] the Fifth and Twenty-second Regiments swept gallantly up the intervening declivity and into the rebel works. The enemy fled precipitately, abandoning one 12-pounder, which fell into the hands of the Twenty-second, and was immediately turned upon the retreating foe."[34]

Lt. George H. Walrath
U.S. ARMY MILITARY HISTORY INSTITUTE

While Surgeon Mitchell and his assistants tended to the wounded and Chaplain Hunter prayed over the fallen, the rest of the brigade, including that part of the 4th not caught up in the deadly charge, occupied the captured works. It was observed that the men of the 22nd, exultant at having wrested a cannon from the enemy, hauled it thither and yon in a display of enthusiasm and pride. They were still capering about when General Smith rode up, astonished by the achievements of these troops whose abilities he had so long derided.

Smith conferred briefly with General Hinks, who had fallen from his fractious horse so hard as to reopen a wound received almost two years before. Hinks remained in nominal command for the rest of the day, although he was "physically unable to take so active a part in the operations" as he wished. After the conference broke up, the USCT were permitted to rest for about an hour while the soldiers of Brooks, Bell, and Martindale moved up to relieve them. When the advance resumed sometime after 9:00, the white units headed south toward Lunettes 1 through 5, while the African-Americans pushed across the fields toward the batteries north and northeast of Petersburg.[35]

U.S. Colored Troops and captured cannon, June 15, 1864. THE SOLDIER IN OUR CIVIL WAR

At approximately 10:00, the head of Hinks's column approached a line of heavy works astride the Jordan's Point Road, near where Wild's men had been stationed during the abortive assault of June 9. Like the defenses the white soldiers were confronting farther west, these were formidable-looking indeed: They consisted of cannon-stocked redoubts atop a tall ridge, protected in front by a slashing of trees; a 600-yard-long plain; a smaller, earthwork-crowned ridge; and, closer in, ditches six to eight feet deep and fifteen feet wide. Duncan approached the position slowly, tentatively, probing it with a heavy skirmish line and trying to soften it up with both of Hinks's artillery units. In the end, the colonel was forced to admit that the effort "accomplished little, save to distract the enemy's attention."[36]

By 1:00 P.M., his and Holman's brigades had been waiting, beyond effective cannon range, for almost three hours. At that point, Hinks ordered everyone to advance through the slashing and across the field to the first ridgeline, a move that would bring the USCT into line with Martindale's men on the right. Two battle lines were formed. The first consisted of the 4th USCI on the right, with the 22nd farther left, connecting with the 1st USCI of Lt. Col. Elias Wright. Duncan's remaining regiments formed the second line of attack. In the wake of its murderous error, the 5th Massachusetts had been placed well in rear of both lines as a covering force; it would take no part in the offensive.

When they swept forward, both lines made surprising progress. Thanks in part to the cover fire of their artillery, they surmounted the slashing and charged across 500 yards of open ground while taking relatively few casualties. The steadiness of their advance was intimidating: The Rebels abandoned the forward ridge even before the first line reached it. Upon arriving, the men of the 4th found the position occupied by a band of skirmishers from the 1st USCI.

This was as close to the main enemy line as Hinks's troops could expect to get for some hours. General Smith believed—and Colonel Duncan, for one, agreed—that further progress had to await the coming of darkness. The only trouble was that Grant had tried to impress upon Smith the importance of taking the city's outer works in daylight, so that its interior defenses might be carried before sundown.

The postponed offensive did not resume until 5:30, when Duncan advanced a strong skirmish line—three companies of the 4th under Boernstein, and four companies of the 22nd under a Major Cook—which would spearhead the assault. The skirmishers did their job well, thrusting their counterparts in gray from the edge of the field and into Lunettes 6 and 7. Then everyone waited for night to fall. Another hour crept by. Just short of 7:00 P.M., dusk having settled over the field, an outburst of rifle fire from the west told the USCT that the white troops were attacking the batteries facing them.

That was the signal to charge. The skirmish lines of each of Hinks's regiments save the 5th Massachusetts surged forward, following the lead of their color guards, who bore the national and regimental banners. While the 1st USCI charged westward against Lunette 6, the troops under Boernstein and Cook made for the three guns of Lunette 7. With volleys of shell and case shot slashing the sky above them, the skirmishers covered the remainder of the field at the double-quick, if not faster. On the far side, they jumped feetfirst into the ditches fronting the battery. Barely breaking stride, they clambered up the rear slope, each man vying with his comrades to reach the top.[37]

Once upon the parapet, they hurled themselves into the open space beyond, where infantrymen who supported the guns fired point-blank into them. Several attackers toppled, but others, as Christian Fleetwood recalled, "swept like a tornado over the works," bayonets agleam. As more and more men entered the fort, the defenders were steadily forced out. Those not felled by rifle blasts or cold steel were seized by panic; turning about, they ran for their lives. This uncovered the heavy ordnance that gave the position its staying power. Seeing the guns unprotected, the intermingled ranks of the 4th and 22nd swarmed over them and took full possession. Both outfits would claim primary credit for their capture.[38]

As soon as the works were carried, Duncan sent in the remainder of both regiments, plus the entire 5th and 6th USCI. Once their comrades came up, Boernstein's and Cook's skirmishers pounded toward the next batteries on the defense line. Against quickly diminishing resistance, Colonel Kiddoo's men carried Lunette 8 from the rear, capturing another gun. Lieutenant Colonel Rogers intended to support this effort, but when he found Lunette 8 already in Union hands, he led the entire body of the 4th through a ravine and across the 500-yard stretch of ground that separated Lunettes 8 and 9.

The weight of defeat already upon them, the defenders of Lunette 9 fled minutes before the 4th reached them. They sought refuge with the garrison of Lunette 10, but their stay was painfully brief. As soon as his men reached the ditch in front of the battery, Rogers led them up and over the palisade. Once inside Lunette 10, they put the Rebels to flight with the bayonet alone, in the process seizing another artillery piece and forcing the evacuation of Lunette 11. At this point, officers' orders finally halted them,

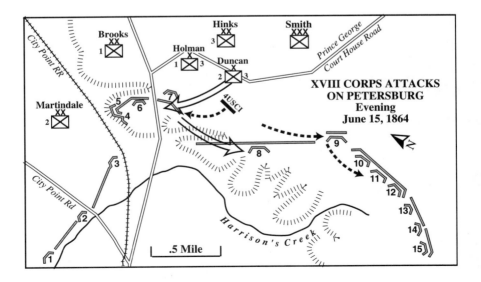

but already their success was complete. Added to those of their white comrades, the African-Americans' gains meant that a three-and-a-half-mile sector of the line that defended the most vital military position in Virginia was in Union hands.

Close to 9:00 P.M., Hinks joined Duncan and Holman and, although in obvious pain, helped them regroup around Lunettes 10 and 11. There the men involved in the day's captures were permitted to rest, while comrades who had been less heavily engaged were put to work building up the reverse slope of the occupied works as a shield against counterattack.[39]

But none came. Once the digging stopped, Hinks's regiments settled down for a well-deserved rest. For the 4th USCI, slumber perhaps came more quickly than it did for the other participants in the events of afternoon and evening. Early in the fight, the regiment had erred and had suffered for it, but it had redeemed itself in sublime fashion. Its men had emerged from their first true battle not only as veterans, but as victors. And they had been largely responsible for the praise with which their division commander showered his troops in his after-action report:

> In the gallant and soldierly deportment of the troops engaged on the 15th instant under varying circumstances; the celerity with which they moved to the charge; the steadiness and coolness exhibited by them under heavy and long-continued fire; the impetuosity with which they sprang to the assault; the patient endurance of wounds, we have a sufficient proof that colored men, when properly officered, instructed, and drilled, will make most excellent infantry of the line, and may be used as such soldiers to great advantage.[40]

CHAPTER 6

Heat! Dust! Flies!

IN A LETTER TO THE EDITOR OF THE NEW YORK *ANGLO-AFRICAN*, MIKE Arnold reviewed the results of the fighting on the fifteenth: "Our regiment has suffered severely. We mourn the loss of our fallen comrades; but with hope and confidence we still push on, hoping the day of the complete submission of the rebels, and the restoration of the laws of the Union, is not far distant."

It was true that the 4th, in common with so many other outfits, black and Caucasian, had paid a steep price in the pursuit of victory. Casualties had hit especially hard in the ranks of commissioned and noncommissioned officers. In addition to Mendall and Parrington, Captain Dillenback of Company A and 1st Lt. Daniel W. Spicer of Company K had been wounded. Noncoms killed or mortally wounded included 1st Sgt. Isaac E. Burgee of Company K and Sgt. John Shaw of Company A, plus two corporals of Company C, Rider Newman and John Warner, and one of Company E, James Gray. Among the wounded were Sergeants Elijah Ash (Company F) and Thomas Cooper (K), and Corporals John Adams (B), Joseph Baker (F), William Edwards (D), James Jones (B), Josiah F. Kane (G), John Thompson (K), and Calvin Timson (K).[1]

Despite its magnitude, the sacrifice the 4th had made on June 15 helped win only a temporary victory, one whose results were undone by the events of subsequent days. Because he had launched his primary attack so late in the day, Smith had been unable to consolidate his gains—which included sixteen cannons and 230 men captured—before darkness suspended operations. Years later, he gave his reason for not pushing on to the interior works: "My white troops were exhausted by marching day and night, and by fighting most of the day in the excessive heat." Smith added an excuse that both lauded and condemned the USCT: "My colored troops, who had fought bravely, were intoxicated by their success, and could hardly be kept in order." This was a blatant exaggeration; the sight of the 22nd USCI capering about its captured gun apparently convinced Smith that every African-American was too giddy to be relied upon thereafter.[2]

Given Grant's expectations for the day, Smith's performance was sadly lacking. He compounded it by going to the rear, apparently ill, thus leaving his command leaderless at a critical hour. When David Birney, at the head of the II Corps, reached the outskirts of Petersburg shortly before midnight, Smith's subordinates told him that nothing more could be accomplished north or northeast of Petersburg until daylight. Once Hancock arrived, Smith requested that his troops be withdrawn to a position closer to the Appomattox. Without comment, Hancock agreed to relieve the XVIII Corps with his own men. Thus nothing was done to exploit the success the white and USCT regiments had gained this day at such great expense.[3]

The reprieve gave Beauregard, who had assumed command of the local garrison, time to erect works closer to the center of Petersburg and to stock them with troops hustled down from opposite Bermuda Hundred. By dawn of June 16, the city was held by 10,000 defenders, four times as many as when Smith had arrived. Beauregard also put in a call to Cold Harbor for help. At first it did little good: Lee refused to believe that enough Federals had left his front to threaten Beauregard's city. Late in the morning of the sixteenth, the army leader finally dispatched a division under Pickett toward Petersburg, but the command was delayed when it encountered some of Butler's regiments. After his opponent depleted his line opposite Bermuda Hundred Neck, Butler had broken out of his "bottle" for the first time in six weeks. Large detachments of his army marched west to damage further the Richmond and Petersburg Railroad, only to run into Pickett.[4]

Butler accomplished little along the railroad; meanwhile, the Federals at Petersburg failed to exploit Lee's slowness to reinforce Beauregard. Early on the sixteenth, according to Christian Fleetwood, the 4th, along with several other regiments, "moved to the rear and rested." After hours of lying about in a quiet sector, Duncan's brigade was shifted closer to the line of works it had attacked the previous day. The men expected a general advance, but after an hour or so, they were returned to the rear and permitted to bed down for the night.[5]

The 4th was even less active the following day, although Meade's army, detachments of which continued to pour in from Cold Harbor, was heavily engaged. That afternoon Fleetwood's ears were assailed by what he called "the heaviest musketry I ever heard." And yet neither his outfit nor any under Hinks, Duncan, and Holman was committed to the fight. The 4th not only idled away the day, but also "lay . . . all night undisturbed." Fleetwood added: "Had fresh beef today. . . . Weather fair and warm."[6]

Finally, early on the eighteenth, the 4th was drawn up in column and led forward. Passing through the defenses it had so ferociously assaulted three days before, the outfit was halted short of those inner works that Beauregard's men continued to hold against all opposition. There the men were suddenly pelted by a hail of rifle fire. In seconds, the regiment lost one man killed and eight wounded. Then it broke for the cover of a hill, behind which it remained for the balance of the day. The position appeared so secure that Fleetwood spent hours reading letters from home and perusing a recent issue of the *Anglo-African*.[7]

The sergeant major was struck by the number of soldiers' letters the newspaper carried, many written to publicize a particular regiment's achievements, some to criticize the poor conduct of other units. Two weeks hence, and again a month later, Fleetwood would contribute letters of his own, to refute charges by a pseudonymous member of the 5th Massachusetts that the 4th had skedaddled from Baylor's Farm, forcing the dismounted cavalry to step forward and stem the rout. The sergeant major branded these aspersions on his outfit gross falsehoods, and he condemned anyone who made such statements while "sheltering his cowardly head under a *nom de plume.*"

With particular vehemence, he denounced the critic's contention that most of the 4th's casualties that morning had occurred in the woods to which the frightened men had retreated rather than in the field close to the enemy's works:

> I had charge of the party who went back over the ground hallowed by the blood of our fallen braves, and found them wounded, dying and dead, *both in the field and in the woods,* the majority of the wounded in the woods, where they had dragged themselves for shelter, though some fell from the effects of the shelling of the woods; but nearly all the dead in the open field. Let no dastard *dare* attempt to cast the mantle of dishonor over the corpse of the humblest hero who "Sleeps for the Flag."[8]

From early on June 16 to midday on the eighteenth, the several components of the Army of the Potomac—the II, V, VI, and IX Corps of infantry (the IX contained a small division of USCT)—attempted to enlarge the success gained on the fifteenth by the Army of the James. They failed miserably. Poor staff work, a breakdown in communication, and a general lack of initiative and aggressiveness on the part of Meade's subordinates, among other factors, combined to render this latest effort to seize the Cockade City an exercise in futility and frustration. The faulty tactics not only allowed Beauregard to withdraw from one hastily improvised defense line to another, but also permitted Lee to clear away the fog of war, march south in force, and line the inner works of the city with veterans in gray and butternut brown. By late on the eighteenth, Grant's once-vibrant opportunity to win the war in a single stroke had died along with thousands of young men, sacrificed on the altar of high-level blundering.[9]

Early on the nineteenth, the 4th USCI was permitted to quit the scene of squandered opportunities and dashed hopes. After being relieved by a portion of the VI Corps, Duncan's brigade marched toward City Point. That evening, after a brief stopover at Spring Hill, the command crossed the floating bridge to Point of Rocks.

Once back in its old camp on Cobb's Hill, the 4th tried to recapture the pace of life it had experienced prior to the descent on Petersburg. The sense of loss that the visibly depleted ranks generated made this difficult. Eventually, however, a conscious effort on the part of officers and men began to return the outfit to a semblance of normality. But they soon found that they would have to complete the process somewhere other than Cobb's Hill.[10]

One event that helped take the men's minds off the recent bloodletting was a wide-scale reorganization of their corps, which was announced within hours of their return from Petersburg. As part of this overhaul, Hinks's division was reduced from three brigades to two, under Holman and Duncan. At first the latter command consisted of the 4th, 5th, and 6th USCI, as well as the dismounted 2nd U.S. Colored Cavalry and, for a time, the 5th Massachusetts. The Bay Staters' conduct on June 15 and the slanderous charges its correspondent had leveled in the *Anglo-African* may well have produced a degree of discontent prejudicial to good order in the brigade. Before June ended, the regiment was removed from the field and sent to Point Lookout, where it not only guarded POWs, but also received remedial training as infantry. Taking its place was Kiddoo's 22nd USCI, whose return to Duncan's command was as roundly praised as the 5th Massachusetts' inclusion had been condemned.[11]

The reorganization portended a new change of base. Just after tattoo on June 20, the 4th received marching orders. The next morning, the men collapsed their tents, packed their gear, and broke camp. Once again they took the pontoons to Spring Hill, near which point they bivouacked in a woodlot. The morning after that, the outfit was awakened at an early hour to greet a pair of distinguished visitors. General Grant, short and stocky in the saddle, his teeth clamped around a cheroot, rode past the bivouac, accompanied by Abraham Lincoln. Astride a horse too small for his lanky frame, the long-legged president, in his dark suit and stovepipe hat, looked even taller than usual; some observers thought he also wore a look of concern. Made restless by the news out of Petersburg, he had come down from Washington to confer with his field leader, review the troops, and if possible, determine how the recent offensive had gone awry. "The men cheered loudly," noted Corporal Arnold, as the odd couple in whose hands rested the fate of the Union trotted past.[12]

One item on the pair's agenda was Grant's recent decision to lengthen his lines above and below Petersburg. The commanding general was not ready to concede that he must go over to the defensive and commence siege operations. On the twentieth, at his order, Butler had extended his lines toward the west side of Petersburg while also pushing a brigade across the James River to Deep Bottom, a creek mouth eleven miles south of Richmond. If and when the opportunity arose, the Army of the James could use this foothold to strike toward the enemy capital.

At the same time, Grant readied a cavalry raid, utilizing troopers from Butler's army as well as Meade's, to strike the railroads that ran south and west of Petersburg; the operation got under way on the twenty-second. Soon after the troopers started out, Meade sent a hefty force of infantry and artillery down the east side of one of the raiders' targets, the Petersburg and Weldon, which extended into North Carolina. Grant's goal was the area west of the rail line; a lodgment there would threaten a communications link even more critical to the survival of Petersburg and Lee's army, the Southside Railroad.[13]

Meade's expedition furnished the 4th USCI with its next assignment. On the twenty-third, after two days of lying about in the woods around Spring Hill, the regiment moved yet again to the scene of their triumph of the fifteenth. The next day, they reentered Lunette 10, freeing its occupants for work farther south and pulling picket duty on a rotational basis with the 6th and 22nd USCI. The captured earthwork would serve as the regiment's base of operations, off and on, over the next six weeks.[14]

While Duncan's brigade did guard duty, elements of the II and VI Corps fought to gain a footing along the Weldon line. The effort was a qualified failure: Meade extended his lower flank to a point west of the Jerusalem Plank Road but not far enough to control the railroad. By month's end, the cavalry expedition had also fallen short of success. Grant accepted the inevitable and settled down to besiege Petersburg.

That operation promised to be long and arduous. Given his manpower advantage, the commanding general did not doubt that eventually he would extend his lines so far as to stretch Lee's defenses to the breaking point. The question was whether a breakthrough would occur in time to ensure the reelection of the president, who was on the verge of accepting his party's nomination. If November found the armies at Petersburg stalemated, the electorate might be so disgruntled as to put a Peace Democrat in the White House. That might lead to a negotiated settlement of the conflict, one that recognized Confederate nationhood.

If the picture in Virginia was not particularly promising, it appeared no rosier in the Western Theater. On June 27, Sherman, frustrated at having been outmaneuvered on the road to Atlanta by Gen. Joseph E. Johnston, attacked head-on against a well-entrenched Army of Tennessee near Kennesaw Mountain, Georgia. The battle, so reminiscent of Grant's misguided assault at Cold Harbor, produced a casualty count almost as lopsided: The combined forces under Sherman lost more than 2,000 men as against fewer than 500 for Johnston. Like Lee, Johnston appeared able to keep his enemy off balance and at a disadvantage. Here, perhaps, was a recipe for Confederate triumph.[15]

It seemed an odd hour to begin a general movement, but at 3:00 A.M. on the twenty-eighth, the men of the 4th were turned out of their blankets and put on the road. Marching off under the moonlight, they left Lunette 10 behind. They trudged up the lower bank of the Appomattox until, just after daybreak, they arrived opposite Confederate-held Fort Clifton. According to Fleetwood, the regiment was ordered to dig and occupy rifle pits "in direct line [of] fire of both sides." As General Hinks and his subordinates ought to have foreseen, the 4th drew the fire of the garrison across the stream. Through the sheerest good fortune, no casualties resulted.

Only after darkness descended was the main body of the regiment relocated beyond range of Clifton's guns. Yet for some reason, regimental headquarters—which had been established in a "bombproof" hut protected on top by logs and braced in front with sandbags—remained in harm's way throughout the night. Fleetwood, for one, "slept ungreatly," feeling "too far from the boys to rest well." His unease was validated the next day when a Rebel shell came screaming overhead to lodge in a wall of the bombproof. Miraculously, it failed to explode.[16]

As the 4th USCI soon discovered, exposure to sudden shelling was one of the drawbacks of life on the siege lines of Petersburg. Through late June and well into July, every day or so a member of the 4th fell prey to artillery or sharpshooter fire. By mid-August, the regiment would lose twelve men killed and thirty-nine wounded in the trenches. Even those of high station, who did not always share the dangers of the rank and file, became targets. On July 9, Fleetwood was struck by a spent ball while occupying what he thought was a safe sector in the rear. Four days later, 2nd Lt. Stephen W. Reynolds of Company F took a nasty wound while ensconced in a well-dug rifle pit.[17]

It was a precarious existence, but in time the men became inured to it. As Corporal Arnold observed in mid-July, "The sharpshooters continue to bang away at each other from morning till night, and finally somebody gets hurt. . . . But our fellows have become used to this, and when it begins, should they be enjoying a cup of coffee and hard tack, ten chances to one they would not stir."[18]

Among all the hardships of siege life, second only to the incessant firing was the severe weather the men had to endure, whether inside Lunette 10 or in bivouac along the Appomattox. July and August produced a seemingly endless succession of intolerably hot days and nights too muggy to permit sound sleep. On June 28, a *New York Times* reporter attached to the Army of the James complained of the "suffocating heat! blinding dust! torturing flies!" There never seemed to be enough shade or shelter against the heat, even when the men occupied fixed fortifications.[19]

On those rare occasions when rain fell, it came down not in gentle drops, but in blinding sheets that flooded campsites and trenches. More than once it rained so hard, so fast, that sleeping men drowned before able to crawl out of their rifle pits. Nonmeteorological discomforts included the general scarcity of potable water, the vermin that infested Lunette 10 and the rifle pits along the Appomattox, and the men's inability to bathe or change clothing for weeks at a time.

This vicious combination of dangers and discomforts played hob with the physical and emotional health of the 4th. One result was that the regiment's sick list grew geometrically throughout the summer. Not only enlisted men left the trenches for the hospitals in the rear; so did company commanders, including James Wickes and Capt. Wareham C. Hill of Company B. Wickes, who had just left Hinks's staff to return to the field, remained apart from the regiment only briefly, but Hill was frequently absent due to a series of illnesses, including colds, chills, and dysentery. In postwar years, his friend and fellow captain Sidney Mendall enumerated the conditions responsible for Hill's frequent hospitalizations. His comments constitute a litany of the hardships every member of the 4th faced in the summer of 1864: "The regiment was . . . at frequent intervals under fire . . . digging in the pits, throwing up breast works [to] make fortifications—digging holes[,] making bomb proof covers for shelter and to sleep in when not on duty—these holes always damp often wet—the results were rheumatism[,] chills[,] malarial fever—diarrhea[,] lung troubles."[20]

Although often absent, Hill always rejoined his company as soon as the surgeons considered him physically able, even though his colleagues found him haggard and emaciated. His unflagging determination to serve helped him win promotion to major and, at war's end, the brevet, or honorary, rank of colonel. Other officers were not so conscientious; they exaggerated injuries or exploited phantom ills to escape the drudgery and danger of siege warfare for weeks or months at a time. Having suffered a minor wound to his left hand on June 15, Captain Parrington had been hospitalized at Fort Monroe ever since. Although his superiors, notably Major Boernstein, questioned the severity of his injury, Parrington managed to remain out of the field for four months. When he finally left the hospital, he somehow wangled an assignment to garrison duty at Harpers Ferry, West Virginia.[21]

Then there was Lieutenant Holcombe, who early in August left Company K for the hospital at Point of Rocks, claiming he had been injured by a shell "rolling over his back, which . . . injured him internally." Declared temporarily unfit for field duty, Holcombe remained on convalescent leave in Norfolk for nine months while his company dug trenches, dodged sniper fire, and sweltered under a torrid sun. During his time away, as the ever-skeptical Major Boernstein later discovered, the lieutenant "drank freely"; played tenpins, "in which game he succeeded in exhausting strong and healthy men"; and amused himself "in various other matters, not at all conducive to health."[22]

At least one officer found a way to escape the siege lines without damaging his standing in the regiment. Although it is not known if he solicited the assignment, late in July Lieutenant Colonel Rogers was named superintendent of the recruiting service for the Department of Virginia and North Carolina. His new duty station was the enrollment rendezvous in Union-occupied New Bern, North Carolina. Although Rogers's job was officially described as "the recruitment of men, by duly appointed agents from loyal States," it was generally believed he was going to raise a USCT regiment composed of slaves liberated by the invaders of the Tarheel State.[23]

Rather than stigmatizing him, Rogers's transfer met with the regretful approval of the rank and file of the 4th. The 4th hated to part with "one so noble, gallant, dashing and brave, and whose joy and delight was to hear or receive the order for his regiment to go to the front, or lead the advance," said John Hance. "May success attend him in his new undertaking." As for

Rogers's successor, Hance observed that with Augustus Boernstein in command of the regiment, "we are all right yet." He continued: "But I fear if he has two or three more horses shot from under him, and three or four more swords severed by shells, or a shoulder strap shot off [supposedly, all three had occurred during the siege], Edward [*sic*] Stanton will deprive us of him."[24]

The great majority of its officers remained with the 4th throughout this season of trial and tribulation. From time to time, however, some were adversely affected by the severity of life on the siege lines. A few sought escape in liquor, to the detriment of their careers. One who appears to have done so, 2nd Lt. Norman M. Rust of Company G, was barred from promotion and later, when he evidently failed to reform, was dismissed from the service.[25]

Some men, and even a few officers, allowed the oppressive conditions to get the best of their temper. Arguments among the rank and file, often over trivial matters, were common throughout the summer. On one occasion, Christian Fleetwood, who prided himself on his equanimity, engaged in a shouting match not only with the excitable Hance, but also with the soft-spoken Chaplain Hunter. Later all involved apologized and made a determined attempt at burying the hatchet. Even so, the aggravations of siege duty continued to affect Fleetwood to the point that he feared they would hamper his ability to function in his highly responsible position.[26]

Nevertheless, life in the forts and trenches of Petersburg was not unadulterated misery. Given the difficulties they faced on a daily basis, most of the men did a valiant job of keeping up their spirits. One way they did this was to organize amusements. In his diary of the siege, Christian Fleetwood made several references to social functions in the field. On July 21, he described an impromptu musicale by several members of the regiment (apparently none was a talented musician, for when a rain of shells sent everyone back to the firing lines, Fleetwood remarked that at least it "relieved the Dumb concert"). Two nights later, he made a more charitable reference to comrades "singing in the evening." Throughout August, he recorded instances of "fellows . . . singing, eating & drinking" and "talking, smoking, laughing and singing till sleep overhauled us." By mid-September, the regiment having moved from its exposed position to a more secure location along the James River, the sergeant major described a "moonlight ball and concert" attended by the regiment and guests from other USCT outfits.[27]

For a time, at least, the men had enough money to ensure that they ate well. Although a visit by the paymaster had not been a regular occurrence since early spring, he reached the 4th's camp at the close of August and distributed six months' pay to every member. Flush with cash, some soldiers gambled away their earnings at the first opportunity. Others spent their money at the sutler's tent in order to obtain rations that the government could not, or would not, furnish them. Throughout the siege, Sutler Cooper did a flourishing business in cigars, cakes, biscuits, fruits, vegetables, and other edibles imported from afar. Business truly boomed when the merchant acquired a bake oven and began to turn out dried-apple pies. Cooper's assistant, Charles Osgood, recalled:

> The oven would hold about 50 at a time, and at times there would be a crowd around the tent waiting for pies, eight or 10 deep, all clamoring for one when the baker brought them in. Every evening the team, four mules, came from Bermuda Hundred with a load [of pies], which would be disposed of before the next afternoon.[28]

Baked goods were not the only non-government-issue edibles that found their way to the regiment. At various times during the summer, Fleetwood wrote of enjoying not only "soft tack & fresh beef," but also "chop and ham," "Watermelon &c," "Melon & coconuts," "Milk punch," and "flapjacks [for] Break[fast], Dinner & Sup[per]." On several occasions he referred to "eating & drinking till late." At other times, not surprisingly, he mentioned "taking physic [medicine for an upset stomach] all day."[29]

Fleetwood and his comrades also partook of food for the soul and food for thought. Throughout the siege—if not always at regular intervals—the good chaplain held religious services in the field. Whenever he did, he attracted a large and enthusiastic congregation that often included worshipers from nearby regiments, white and black. Whenever possible, the clergyman also continued his program to tutor the illiterate and the undereducated. Not until late in the year, however, did the army furnish him with a permanent location for a schoolhouse.

Those who could already read whiled away off-duty hours by perusing books, magazines, and religious tracts (in one two-week span, the well-read Fleetwood indulged his taste for fiction by devouring *Tim Cringle, Lavinia,* and *The Soldier's Wife*). Whether or not facile with the pen, almost everyone kept in touch with loved ones at home through regular correspondence. As Mike Arnold informed the readers of the *Anglo-African,* even in the midst of siege operations, the "Post Office [and] Express Co. . . . are in full operation." Perhaps the most successful of Ben Butler's efforts to maintain the morale of his troops was an army-wide postal service that delivered an average of 50,000 letters per day. Butler also saw to it that the Adams Express Company maintained branches at Fort Monroe, Bermuda

Hundred, and other points on the army's line of operations. By the winter of 1864–65, the branch at Bermuda Hundred alone was distributing 2,000 parcels a day—mainly gift boxes from loved ones at home to the soldiers at the front.[30]

When the men tired of fraternizing with other members of their regiment, they visited the bivouacs of outfits within walking or riding distance. In mid-July, for example, Fleetwood and Hunter rode over to the Army of the Potomac's sector to visit the camps of the 30th and 39th USCI. Both regiments had been recruited in Maryland; the visitors found many familiar faces in their ranks. The following week, Fleetwood accompanied Sergeant Handy to the camp of the 29th USCI, another of General Meade's outfits. There the sergeant major "found more Baltimorians still. Some [came] to camp along with us." On these and other occasions, the men of the 4th enjoyed a "jolly time" in the company of their brothers in uniform.[31]

After November 1864, the 4th did not have to travel so far to visit its friends. This came about through a dramatic display of Butler's confidence in the USCT. Wishing to rid himself of some new, untried regiments of whites, the army leader traded an equal number of them for the entire complement of African-Americans in Meade's army. Thereafter the Army of the James comprised thirty-five regiments and batteries of black soldiers, more such units than served in any other army. The number of USCT subject to Butler's authority enabled him, in December 1864, to organize the XXV Corps, the first and only American army corps composed exclusively of Colored Troops. The unique organizational structure enabled Butler to give the troops the attention, care, and support they required. If his past actions had not done so, the corps' formation enabled Butler to demonstrate the validity of his boast that "colored troops thrive as well under me as anybody."[32]

While virtually every soldier under Butler and Meade cursed and complained about the siege, one regiment took action to end it. Late in June, former coal miners in a Pennsylvania infantry regiment, part of the IX Corps, Army of the Potomac, conceived the notion of tunneling under an enemy salient only 400 yards opposite their position southeast of Petersburg. The coal crackers believed that if enough blasting powder could be detonated inside the tunnel, a gaping hole might be blown in the Rebel line, opening a path to the heart of the city.

At first the idea stirred little enthusiasm at corps headquarters, but the miners, who craved an escape from boredom, began to dig anyway. They made so much progress in such a short time that their corps commander, Maj. Gen. Ambrose E. Burnside, not only approved the project, but also promoted it before a skeptical Meade and a doubtful Grant. In the end, the high command gave the mine their cautious endorsement and provided the Pennsylvanians with enough tools to complete it in record time.

The high-level support enabled the miners, working in shifts twenty-four hours a day, to finish the mine in less than a month. By mid-July, their tunnel extended more than 100 yards inside, and 40 feet below, Elliott's Salient. The Pennsylvanians then added galleries to each side of the main shaft. Over a several-day period, Meade's engineers stocked the galleries with 8,000 pounds of powder, enough to blow the salient—and the Rebels holding it—sky-high. A single, multispliced fuse connected the dozens of ammunition boxes and barrels, ensuring that the mass of powder would go up all at once.[33]

While still hesitant to put his faith in the project, Grant decided that in case it succeeded, some of Burnside's troops should be trained to attack in the wake of the blast. The Rebel works across from the IX Corps were intricate and deep; should a hole be blown in them, any effort to exploit it would have to be carefully planned. The composition of the attack force was left to Burnside, who chose his 4th Division, the all-USCT command of Brig. Gen. Edward Ferrero. While the mine neared completion, the African-Americans were moved to the rear, where they were drilled in anticipation of charging into downtown Petersburg.

Shortly before the mine was finished—the powder was scheduled to be touched off before dawn on July 30—Grant expressed concern over Burnside's selection. In the coming presidential race, Lincoln's party would need the support of every abolitionist. If the mine failed, enabling the Confederates to concentrate their fire against the attackers, the blacks would be slaughtered. Liberal Republicans, as also citizens of every political stripe, would accuse the army of sacrificing the minority troops. Meade agreed with Grant's reasoning; at the last minute, he prevailed upon Burnside to substitute an untrained white division for the well-tutored blacks.[34]

Originally, the assault was envisioned as strictly an Army of the Potomac undertaking. Also at the eleventh hour, Grant decided that Butler's command should support the rear and flanks of the attacking force. The politician-general agreed to provide a division from each of his corps. The combined force would be entrusted to the army's highest-ranking newcomer, Maj. Gen. Edward O. C. Ord, formerly a subordinate of Grant's in the West, whom the commanding general had assigned on July 21 to take over the XVIII Corps. The post had become vacant two days before, when Baldy Smith—whose relations with Butler had deteriorated steadily since the fiasco at Drewry's Bluff—made himself so obnoxious to his superior that the harmony-loving Grant relieved him of his command and sent him home to Vermont.[35]

After dark on the twenty-ninth, Ord notified both divisions to stand ready. A bit later, he carefully detached them from their positions above Petersburg and led them south. Sometime after midnight, they arrived in rear of the troops that Burnside had chosen to replace his African-Americans, the division of Brig. Gen. James H. Ledlie—an officer who, apparently unknown to Burnside, was both an incompetent and a coward. For hours, Ord's men waited inside a long, covered trench that led toward the mine and Elliott's Salient. Most had no inkling of what was supposed to occur this morning. The few who had heard rumors of a mine shaft crammed with ammunition gave little credence to the idea.[36]

Although the 4th USCI would take no direct part in the attack, the regiment, along with other elements of Duncan's brigade, vacated Lunette 10 on the twenty-ninth and moved south to occupy the trenches that Ledlie's men had emptied. The movement led the men to suspect that something out of the ordinary was in the offing. The impression was strengthened when the regiment was awakened before dawn on the thirtieth. Over the next hour, the men of the 4th peered into the darkness toward the rumored site of Burnside's attack.

Having helped rouse the men, Christian Fleetwood lay down on the ground in company with Mike Arnold and other noncommissioned officers and tried to catch a few extra minutes of sleep. At 4:45, the sergeant major was awakened in memorable fashion. The earth beneath him began to tremble—then, as it seemed, to shake violently. Some miles to the front, a giant geyser of dirt and debris suddenly shot up into the sky. A split second later, an almost palpable wave of sound rolled over the trenches, stunning the senses and instantly bringing everyone awake. "As we sprang to our feet," Fleetwood recalled, "Arnold clapped his hand to his right ear with an exclamation. From that time I found him deaf on the right side of his head."[37]

In the murky light, the men of the 4th stared south in openmouthed wonder. When the noise of the blast had dissipated and the dust-filled sky began to clear, they beheld, where a strong-looking sector of the enemy line had recently stood, a smoking crater 170 feet long, 50 feet wide, and 25 feet deep. At its bottom, buried in mounds of debris, were the bodies of dozens of Confederates and the shattered remains of cannons, caissons, limbers, and wagons—many of which had been blown 20 feet into the air before falling back to earth.

The rumors of a powder mine had been true, after all. Moreover, the weapon had performed brilliantly, opening Petersburg to capture and

Battle of the Crater, July 30, 1864. BATTLES AND LEADERS OF THE CIVIL WAR

occupation. All that remained was for Ledlie's men to charge through the jagged swath that had once been Elliott's Salient and claim their prize. But nothing of the sort occurred. Lacking both proper training and on-scene guidance—Ledlie was huddling in a bombproof well to the rear, guzzling whiskey commandeered from one of his surgeons—the white troops did not go forward for several minutes. When junior officers finally got them moving, a large number were quickly stymied by the crater; others unaccountably piled into the hole instead of skirting it. Meade's artillery attempted to cover them with a barrage, but it only attracted a counterbattery fire that destroyed what little cohesion remained in Ledlie's column. Finally, enough Confederates recovered from the shock of the blast and rushed to the threatened point to turn back the few Federals who had successfully passed the crater. By late morning, with hundreds of reinforcements on the scene, the advantage had swung decisively to the defenders.[38]

At this point, Grant and Meade should have called off the attack; instead, in a fit of desperation, they committed Ferrero's division, which, though out of position, was at least prepared for the offensive. By now, however, it was too late to avert disaster; the African-Americans were merely caught up in it. Although just as many white troops, if not more, turned and fled from the cannon fire and musketry being poured into them from many angles, the retreat of the black troops became one of the most vivid scenes in the tragedy. So many of Ferrero's men broke for the rear that they blocked the progress of Ord's troops, hundreds of whom, quite fortunately, never got into the fight. The African-Americans even knocked down and trampled General Ord, then dragged him several feet.[39]

Looking on from a distance, the 4th USCI felt shamed and disgusted by the rout of their brothers in Meade's army. Fleetwood's reaction was typical of the regiment: "Broke and run! Devil blame 'em!" Like many of his comrades, the sergeant major feared that the performance of Ferrero's division—as understandable as it was under the circumstances—would besmirch the reputation of the USCT of both armies. Another onlooker, Colonel Duncan, was more forgiving, declaring in a letter home, "To my certain knowledge they [Ferrero's men] behaved more handsomely than the white troops" involved in the debacle.[40]

But even such a charitable assessment could not hide the fact that another glittering opportunity to end the war in quick and dramatic fashion had gone by the boards. In the aftermath of the failure at the crater, it began to look as if the conflict was destined to go on indefinitely. The men of the Armies of the James and Potomac envisioned months of siege warfare stretching in unending succession into the future. That prospect prompted some men to wail and gnash their teeth; others cursed the fates that had conspired against them; still others shook their heads ruefully and tried to forget. In the ranks of the 4th USCI, most took the fiasco philosophically. They filed it away among the many might-have-beens of this war, picked up the rifles they had laid aside, and went on.

CHAPTER 7

"Boys, Save the Colors!"

PHYSICALLY, THE FAILURE OF BURNSIDE'S MINE HAD LITTLE EFFECT ON THE 4th USCI. When the Confederates opened on Ledlie's and Ferrero's men, they sent some rounds the 4th's way, but they inflicted few wounds. The most serious injury was to 2nd Lt. Peter Frazer of Company C, whose right leg was mangled by a shell, requiring its amputation near the knee.[1]

The 4th continued to occupy the IX Corps' trenches, where it supported a light battery, through the early evening of August 1. At dusk, the 4th moved out, trudged northward, and bivouacked in a ravine. The next day, it reoccupied the campground it had evacuated on the twenty-ninth, but it remained there only a few hours. At 4:00 A.M. on August 4, the men accompanied the rest of Duncan's brigade toward the Appomattox. They marched to Spring Hill, the sound of the guns at Petersburg growing fainter in the distance. Late in the morning, Major Boernstein led everyone across the pontoons to Point of Rocks, a campground the 4th had not occupied since June 14.[2]

The change of scenery did the outfit much good. Life in the trenches before Petersburg had taken a toll, more or less severe, of everyone. Here at Bermuda Hundred, although fighting raged every day along the front line, the tempo of combat could not compare with the Petersburg front either in intensity or in casualties inflicted. At Point of Rocks, the men did not attract the concentrated firepower they had been subjected to over the past six weeks. In the trenches, they had been able to estimate the strength and position of the enemy by a simple but effective method. As Michael Arnold explained, "To find out their whereabouts—place your hat on a stick; hoist it above the works, and let it remain for three minutes, and when taken down you discover that it is well ventilated." According to the hospital steward, it was "a matter of impossibility to enter the [rifle] pits in daylight unless on your hands and knees, [and even] then the chances were greatly against you."[3]

Brig. Gen. Charles J. Paine
PHOTOGRAPHIC HISTORY
OF THE CIVIL WAR

In their old, familiar surroundings, the men spent hours pitching tents and regrading company streets. Fleetwood reported himself "busy as you please getting up [regimental] Hd Qrs till afternoon" and also getting his "own Hd Qrs fixed." Then, however, he lay down for a short nap in the open air; presumably, others did the same. It had been a while since the men had done fatigue duty, and they were out of shape. Occupying trenches within range of dozens of cannons and hundreds of sharpshooters may have been hard on the nerves, but it demanded a minimum of physical exertion.

Over the next few days, the 4th got back to the basics of camp life. The officers resumed regimental inspections, guard mounting, dress parades, and battalion drill. Living so close to the Appomattox, the men were able to bathe and wash clothes for the first time in more than a month.[4]

Having spruced up, the regiment made a respectable showing on review when its new division commander visited camp. On August 3, Brig. Gen. Charles J. Paine had replaced Edward Hinks, whose disabilities had finally forced him to hobble home to Massachusetts. Hinks's injuries were severe enough that, like Lieutenant Frazer, he would never return to Virginia. He would be missed by the USCT, who had come to regard him as a competent field commander, as well as a friend of their cause.[5]

Hinks's successor engendered no such feelings, for the division was unfamiliar with his past service. Like Hinks an abolitionist from a wealthy New England family, Paine lacked his predecessor's prewar military experience. He was best known as a yachtsman, an avocation that may have taught him some managerial skills but hardly prepared him to lead soldiers in combat. Even Captain Wickes, who later accepted a position on Paine's staff, initially regarded him as an inexperienced interloper who had risen to high command mainly because of his long relationship with Butler.[6]

Paine's assumption of command roughly coincided with yet another shift of position by the 4th and the other components of Duncan's 3rd Brigade, 3rd Division, XVIII Corps. Beginning with the transfer of Company B on August 11, the outfit vacated its tranquil campsite along the Appomattox and moved to a scene of greater activity and danger, one it would occupy for the next six weeks. As they struck tents, the men muttered that their return to Point of Rocks had been too good to be true.[7]

The move took Duncan's people across the rear of the lines at Bermuda Hundred, as far as the James River. They were halted where the river flowed west to Trent's Reach before looping northeastward and doubling back upon itself in hairpin fashion. The narrow finger of land enclosed by the loop was known as Farrar's Island. The misnamed peninsula was also called Dutch Gap, in memory of a European immigrant who, some years before, had tried unsuccessfully to connect the two prongs of the hairpin by means of a canal.

The failed project had long intrigued the Yankee tinkerer who commanded the army named for this river. Ben Butler realized that to complete the canal, he need dig only 174 yards across the narrowest point on the peninsula. By doing so, he would cut almost five miles off the water route to Richmond. Ships moving in that direction would be able to bypass the heavy batteries Beauregard had emplaced along Trent's Reach. Provided with such a detour, even the fusty Admiral Lee might be enticed to run his fleet to the doorstep of the Rebel capital. In that event, troopships could place Butler's soldiers in positions from which to turn the defenses at Drewry's Bluff, on the west bank of the James, and Chaffin's Bluff, on the opposite side. Attacked from that direction, Richmond must surely fall. Butler might yet win the hero's mantle upon which his political aspirations seemed to depend.

Butler believed the project not only viable, but easy to accomplish. A hurried survey convinced him, as he informed Grant, that 55,000 cubic yards of peninsula had to be excavated to finish the canal, "or 10 days' labor for a thousand men." A later, more thorough inspection, however, revealed that the excavation site was, on average, 43 yards wide at the top, 27 yards at water level, 31 yards deep on its northwest side, and 12 yards wide on the southeast end. A tract of these dimensions would require the removal of almost 70,000 cubic yards of earth.[8]

In terms of manpower required, the difference between the two estimates was considerable. One thousand men would prove insufficient to meet Butler's timetable; several times as many laborers, soldiers and civilians, would have to work twenty-four hours a day to complete the job according to his projections. As it turned out, due to interruptions caused by military operations, and despite the aid of heavy equipment including a steam-powered dredge, the canal would take more than four months to complete. Grant gave Butler the go-ahead only because he accepted the initial calculations at face value.

For the 4th USCI, the new duty station combined the worst features of its two most recent venues: the heavy workload it had shouldered at Spring Hill and the stressful exposure to cannon fire it had experienced in the rifle pits at Petersburg. From day one, the regiment found itself engaged in arduous, sometimes backbreaking labor under a hot sun. In detachments working simultaneously from different points, the 4th dug at the hard earth with shovels and picks, and loaded the soil on horse-drawn wagons that carted it away. As the men worked, the greenish waters of the James were held in check by earthen bulkheads fifteen feet thick. The final job would be to remove those barriers with an explosive charge.

Having made his legal reputation as a champion of the working class, Butler saw to it that the laborers were remunerated above the normal pay rate. Each worker who put in a seven-and-a-half-hour day would receive 8 cents additional pay per hour, plus a gill of whiskey per diem or its equivalent in extra pay. Theoretically, at least, the workers volunteered for the duty; they worked alongside civilian employees of the army—mostly African-Americans, including many former slaves—who were paid the same wage as they. In actuality, details were made upon every regiment in Duncan's brigade, as well as on most of the other USCT units in Paine's division, as also upon white regiments whose presence was not required on the front lines.[9]

Despite the severity of the work, many members of the 4th labored enthusiastically for the extra pay. Others came to resent the menial labor demanded of them. As a sergeant in Company A declared, "We are . . . soldiers, not slaves!"[10]

Their officers, although not forced to wield a shovel alongside the men, expressed similar feelings. Captain Wickes, who had yet to leave the

4th for staff duty, was dismayed that most of the soldiers toiling on the canal were black. In a letter to Judge Hugh Bond in Baltimore, the commander of Company G wrote: "I am beginning to lose a great deal of my enthusiasm for the colored service from the manner in which the troops are treated by Butler and some of the Corps commanders. They are employed to do all the hard work, which White regiments will not do." His complaint had a personal angle, for officers whose units were committed to fatigue duty instead of field service were often passed over for promotion: "As officering them [USCT] is entrusted entirely to Butler, very little regard is shown to the custom of regular promotions. . . . This cannot but create dissatisfaction." Due to the perceived lack of professional mobility, "positions here are at a discount."[11]

The fatigue duty may have been productive of discontent among officers and men, but not of strategic results. By late August, Wickes was calling the canal "a great humbug." He complained: "Six hundred men have been working on it nearly twenty days, and not more than one third of the earth which is above the water level has been removed. About as much more is to be dug out below the water level, before it can be serviceable, and this last half will be attended with difficulties which will cause much slower progress." Other observers believed that even if completed, the waterway would avail the army nothing. As one of General Meade's staff officers put it, "When Butler gets his canal cleverly through, he will find fresh batteries ready to rake it, and plenty more above it, on the river."[12]

It was bad enough that the work was so grueling, but the enemy tried to make it intolerable. Almost from the hour the soldiers began digging, Beauregard established batteries whose long-range guns he trained on Dutch Gap. Although a large party of the X Corps manned breastworks across the west end of the peninsula, they afforded the diggers minimal protection. Admiral Lee stationed one of his gunboats in the James just below the gap, but she proved unable to quell the fire of a fleet of steam rams patrolling the Rebel end of Trent's Reach. On August 14, the rams churned upriver and began firing on the head of the gap. Meanwhile, two batteries on the north flank of Beauregard's line opposite Bermuda Hundred pounded away in unison at the laborers. Soldiers and civilians threw down their shovels and raced for cover, but thirty failed to reach safety before falling dead or wounded.

Union artillery at and below Farrar's Island replied to the barrage and finally silenced both river- and land-borne guns. In later weeks, Butler redoubled the canal's defenses, ensuring that an attack of the magnitude of August 14 would not recur. Even so, from that time forward, the workers shoveled with one eye peeled for enemy shells. Thus preoccupied, they may have failed to achieve as much as they had previously, causing Butler to devalue their contributions. Then, too, by mid-September, the army leader decided he needed a full complement of troops at the front. Thus he returned most of the military laborers to Petersburg, Bermuda Hundred, and Deep Bottom. Additional civilians were hired to replace them, but thereafter the work progressed more slowly. Not until year's end would Butler's canal be open for business—and by then the race for the White House would be long over.[13]

By mid-August, the war had taken a grievous toll of the 4th United States Colored Infantry. Both before and after the deadly fighting of June 15, the regiment had suffered continual losses to artillery and sniper fire, as well as to the kinds of illnesses caused or aggravated by life in the trenches and in the captured forts. By the time the outfit came under fire at Dutch Gap, its effective strength had been reduced to fewer than half the number that had left Baltimore for the seat of war eleven months earlier.

Attrition had hit the enlisted force hard, but it had also diminished the ranks of commissioned officers. On the twentieth, with Major Boernstein sick, Captain Wickes, as senior line officer on duty, assumed command of the regiment. He observed, "The position is by no means desirable at present, as so many officers have been absent through the last two months, that company & regimental papers have been greatly neglected . . . [and] in a state of interminable confusion." Something had to be done to recruit the 4th's strength, or it would become impotent as a fighting force.[14]

Aware of the problem and determined to fix it, Colonel Duncan gave permission for a recruiting party from his old regiment to return to Baltimore and search the city for new blood—it was calculated that at least 220 enlistees would be needed to bring the regiment up to fighting strength. Originally it was decided that Chaplain Hunter should head the team, also to consist of Sergeant Major Fleetwood and Sergeant Handy. The trio had been recommended for recruiting service weeks before, on the eve of Lieutenant Colonel Rogers's transfer to North Carolina. Rogers believed that the men's "acquaintance and influence with the more intelligent part of the colored people" of Baltimore ideally qualified them for the assignment.[15]

But not all three got to go. On the eve of heading home, Fleetwood found that his inclusion had been disallowed for unspecified reasons, a decision that left him "grievously disgruntled." The others, who had been granted sixty days' leave, left Dutch Gap on the eighteenth and were in Baltimore before month's end. Although the trip gave them an opportunity to visit their families and friends for the first time in a year, they might have stayed in Virginia for all they accomplished. As Hunter informed Duncan by letter on September 16, Col. S. M. Bowman, chief recruiter and mustering officer of Colored Troops for Maryland, had declared Baltimore off-limits to all recruiters except those who represented certain regiments: "There could be no recruiting for the regt. . . . Nothing can be done to benefit the service by my remaining here longer." Duncan agreed, and the recruiting party cut short its time in the city.[16]

In later weeks, the colonel tried to find ways of getting around Bowman's prohibition. He knew that a number of young men from Baltimore and the surrounding counties, then coming of military age, wished to join friends and family members in the ranks of the 4th. Therefore, he sought permission for recruits to specify a preference for a certain outfit and requested authority to grant their wishes. This expedient, however, was not approved, as Duncan probably foresaw.[17]

As a last resort, the regiment sought the help of recruitment brokers based in the Northwest, which remained a fertile source of free black manpower. Arrangements were worked out among officials of the Federal government, Maryland, and Ohio, and in September and October the middlemen sent a total of 196 recruits to the regiment from the Buckeye State, via Washington, D.C. All were carried on Ohio's enlistment rolls, thus relieving the state of an equal number to be secured through conscription, but preventing their addition to local African-American regiments such as the 5th USCI.

The quality of the recruits, and their value to the 4th, were matters of conjecture. Many reached Virginia as a new round of active operations was getting under way. Thus no time was available in which to train them in even the fundamentals of soldiering. Doubtful of their utility, Major Boernstein, who by late September had resumed command of the regiment, decided to leave them at Dutch Gap while the rest of the regiment repaired to the battlefield. Laborers were still needed to bring Butler's pet project to fruition, and even raw recruits knew how to wield shovels.[18]

⊶ ⚔ ⊷

By the middle of September, Grant had launched two major offensives north of the James, both operating out of Butler's fortified bridgehead at Deep Bottom. The first, which began in late July, had been primarily intended as a feint to draw defenders from the area of Burnside's mine. A subsidiary operation against the Rebel capital, mainly the work of Meade's and Butler's cavalry, fell short of success. The second offensive, launched in

mid-August, had been based on the supposition that the defenses the Confederates had constructed north of Deep Bottom had been depleted to reinforce a small army operating in Virginia's Shenandoah Valley. When the intelligence proved to be invalid and the Rebel lines were found to be strongly held, this offensive, too, was doomed to failure, although nearly a week of fighting was required to prove the point.[19]

By late September, Grant was ready to launch a third strike on the Northside, this time in conjunction with a movement on the lower end of Meade's line toward the Southside Railroad. Again rumors were rife that Lee had sent reinforcements to the Shenandoah, or was on the verge of doing so. Since early August, the former cavalry commander of the Army of the Potomac, Maj. Gen. Philip H. Sheridan, had been commanding a small army in the Valley in opposition to several thousand Confederates under Lt. Gen. Jubal A. Early. On the nineteenth of the month, Sheridan had attacked Early's forces near Winchester, Virginia, inflicting on them a decisive defeat. "Little Phil" had followed up his triumph with a successful assault three days later at Fisher's Hill.[20]

Combined with the news, recently received in Virginia, of Sherman's capture of Atlanta, Sheridan's operations, although small in scale compared to those in eastern Virginia and Georgia, revived Union fortunes and helped dissipate the war weariness that had infected the North. The string of victories appeared to ensure Lincoln's reelection, while ending Butler's increasingly unlikely presidential prospects. The army commander admitted as much when, before September ended, he publicized his unambiguous support of the Union Party ticket.[21]

To prove that his heart was fully in the war, not in the presidential race, Butler responded to Grant's latest initiative by drawing up a plan of operations north of the James that ran to more than twenty pages. The plan, copies of which went to Butler's new corps commanders, Birney and Ord, as well as to General Kautz, was aimed at getting "possession of the City of Richmond. Failing that, to make such serious and determined demonstrations to that end as shall draw reinforcements from the right of the enemy's line in sufficient numbers . . . to enable the Army of the Potomac to move upon the enemy's communications near Petersburg."

Butler's role in Grant's multipronged strategy called for him to commit more than 26,000 troops, almost three-quarters of the effective strength of his army. On the morning of the twenty-ninth, Butler was to cross the river in two columns: ten brigades under Birney at Deep Bottom, and seven XVIII Corps brigades via a new pontoon bridge near Aiken's Landing, two miles downriver. Ord's wing would strike toward the entrenched camp at Chaffin's Bluff, the outermost defense line south of Richmond.

The right-hand column under Birney, which included Kautz's horsemen, would attack the complex of fortifications on New Market Heights, a long, high plateau southeast of the capital. If Birney broke through on his front—he had failed to carry a line of works in the same area during Grant's second offensive—he was to move west, via the New Market and Darbytown Roads, to assist Ord in an all-out assault against Richmond's intermediate defense line.

The USCT would make a critical contribution to the operations on the Northside, but their organizational affiliation would be unusual. Instead of taking part in Ord's offensive, Paine's division was assigned a place in the X Corps column that would attack New Market Heights. In fact, the African-Americans would spearhead Birney's operations, leading the march to and across the bridge at Deep Bottom and making first contact with the Rebels farther north. Theirs was a responsible mission, to be sure, but also a risky one. Until reinforcements came up, they would be the focal point of Rebel fire on that sector of Richmond's lines.[22]

As befit its leader's managerial skills, the Army of the James moved out on schedule. Late on the twenty-eighth, most of the white regiments, as well as the X Corps' own USCT brigade under William Birney, moved on foot into position to cross the river. The African-Americans under Paine, however, boarded transports and gunboats at Dutch Gap for the run upriver. Perhaps an hour later, they debarked at Jones Landing, on the north side of the James, within easy marching distance of Deep Bottom. In sheltering darkness, they moved to the bridgehead and filed silently inside the works that secured Butler's foothold on Richmond's doorstep.[23]

Aware that an important, perhaps a momentous, undertaking would unfold in the morning, the men of the 4th slept fitfully, if at all, that night. Well before fog-shrouded daybreak, they were awakened and ordered to grab a quick breakfast. Coffee had barely begun to boil when the word was passed to stand ready to move out. Entrusting their knapsacks to the few comrades who would remain in bivouac, the men slung their Enfields over their shoulders, inspected their cartridge pouches, newly filled with forty rounds of ammunition, and made certain their cap and cartridge boxes and canteens were full. At the signal, they took up their positions in the marching column. Minutes later, the line began to move, and the 4th United States Colored Infantry—not quite 400 strong (with an additional 200 recruits at Dutch Gap)—passed through the Deep Bottom defenses, heading north.[24]

The route of march took the men up the Grover House Road, a country trail that crossed brier-infested bottomland dotted with ravines, marshes, and swamps. Beyond its intersection with the east-west-running Kingsland

Road, not quite three miles north of Deep Bottom, stretched a multilay-ered defensive line held by Confederate infantry, artillery, and dismounted cavalry under the overall command of Brig. Gen. John Gregg. A double line of abatis—the first an indiscriminate pile of felled trees, the second a sharpened-log *chevaux-de-frise*—protected an unfinished stand of breast-works.

The defenders of this elongated position—most of them members of Lt. Col. Frederick Bass's brigade of Texas and Arkansas infantry, Army of Northern Virginia—numbered only a few hundred. They were stretched so thinly along the line that gaps existed in many places, shielded only by the felled trees and, here and there, a shallow ditch. Bass's men, however, were closely supported on both flanks—on the east by the three regiments in Brig. Gen. Martin Gary's cavalry brigade plus the battery known as the Rockbridge Artillery, and on the west by two Virginia infantry battalions and the Richmond Howitzers.[25]

As the fog began to give way to the light of dawn, Duncan's abbrevi-ated brigade—the 4th USCI in front, its main body preceded by a line of skirmishers, and with the 6th USCI in echelon toward the left rear—headed toward the midpoint of the New Market line. Well to the rear came the remainder of Paine's command, the brigades of John Holman and Col. Alonzo G. Draper. Even farther back, and well to the west of the USCT, marched the all-white X Corps division of Brig. Gen. Robert S. Foster. Well beyond Duncan's right was the white division of Brig. Gen. Alfred Howe Terry and also William Birney's USCT brigade. Foster's column was advancing against that part of the line held by the Georgia brigade of Lt. Col. Dudley DuBose, on Bass's right, while Terry's men were veering toward the sector of the defenses where Bass's foot soldiers linked with Gary's troopers.

Before the 4th and its comrades to the left, right, and rear could close with the enemy, the rattle of musketry and the thump of cannons toward the west indicated that Ord's column had made contact with the defenders of Chaffin's Bluff. Ord's surprise assault would result in the capture of strategic Fort Harrison (later renamed Fort Burnham in honor of a fallen brigadier), but his men would run aground against forts on Richmond's intermediate line. Although Ord's men failed to gain entry to the enemy capital, their penetration of the outer line so troubled the Confederates that on the thirtieth, Robert E. Lee would personally direct a series of counter-attacks aimed at regaining Fort Harrison—each of which would fail.[26]

When it reached the Kingsland Road, the 4th halted, recalled its skir-mishers, and in response to orders from Duncan, spread out in line of bat-tle. Though beyond rifle range, the regiment was already under fire from the Rebel pickets, as well as from cannons whose shells screamed over their heads to burst in the open ground in rear. Even as the barrage continued, the men studied the terrain ahead. They found that they would have to cross a swampy branch of Four-Mile Creek, which meandered north and west across the Kingsland Road before skirting the western edge of New Market Heights. Although at that distance they could not discern any other obstacles, beyond the creek lay a deep, heavily wooded ravine. Only after passing these obstructions would the 4th confront the man-made barriers that protected Bass's position.

Butler's carefully developed plan, which had been shaped by past operations including Birney's August attack, called for New Market Heights to be assailed from the west, beyond Bass's right flank. The lay of the land, however, and the tactics of Birney and Paine shoved the advancing troops eastward until they found themselves approaching the opposite end of Bass's position, where Gary's carbineers also lay in wait.[27]

A head-on attack against two brigades would leave the 4th and 6th open to heavy casualties. The lack of support Duncan's outfits would receive from the rest of the division would only worsen their predicament.

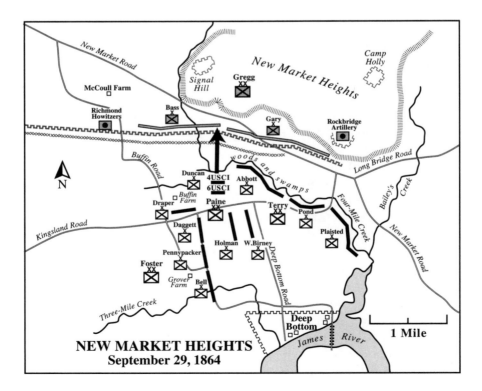

NEW MARKET HEIGHTS
September 29, 1864

Instead of keeping Holman's and Draper's brigades closed up on Duncan's flanks and rear, Paine held them so far back that they would prove of no use in the opening minutes of the assault. He covered Duncan's advance with a mere handful of dismounted skirmishers from the unbrigaded 2nd United States Colored Cavalry. Recalling its experience with the 5th Massachusetts on June 15, the 4th must have wondered if it would again have as much to fear from friendly fire as from Confederate opposition.

At about 5:30 A.M., the 4th got the word to attack. With a shout that ran along its length, the battle line surged forward, each man trying to follow the color guard that led the way over an open plain perhaps 500 yards in length. Minutes later, men were plunging into the swamp, rifles held high to prevent water contamination. This day, however, the almost-unconscious gesture seemed futile: The regiment's arms remained uncapped so that their owners would not be tempted to halt, aim, and fire. The Rebel position was to be taken in one sweeping movement, and by bayonet alone.[28]

Once mired in the swamp, the 4th became the target of Bass's infantry and Gary's troopers. Several attackers fell dead or wounded, a few sinking out of sight in the marshy ooze. The majority sloshed through the morass and, as soon as on dry ground, headed forward. Under an intensifying fire, some jumped, others tumbled, into the ravine they had not detected from the rear. Most struggled through the trees to the top; less fortunate comrades toppled backward into the ditch against the impact of minié balls and shell fragments. Regaining their footing on level ground, the survivors raced over the field toward the double line of abatis.

The first line did not stymie them; the attackers either leapt over the piled logs or tore them apart with their bare hands. With bullets flitting all around, they penetrated the barrier in groups large and small, then sped toward the *chevaux-de-frise*. This was a more formidable obstacle; it took much time to surmount. Time, however, was precious, for at this range the men were subject to an even thicker stream of missiles than before. Those who were hit fell heavily atop the works, some impaling themselves on the sharpened logs. Others tore at the abatis as they had the slashing, but with a growing sense of desperation. A few members of the regiment had been armed with axes and hatches in anticipation of reaching this barrier, but not enough tools were available to hew out a wide opening. Officers and men slipped through whatever gaps they could find, however narrow; some left pieces of their uniforms, and of their flesh, clinging to the stakes.

Despite the order given them, the few dozen men who made it through the *chevaux-de-frise* unwounded dropped to the earth to avoid a sudden stream of rifle balls. Men farther to the rear, noting the halt, stopped also; some ran back to the near side of the barrier. As if by mutual agreement, they remained there, catching their breath and steeling themselves for the push to the breastworks.

When the men failed to resume their forward movement, some of the officers—notably, Lieutenant Appleton of Company H—urged them back on their feet with shouts and gestures. Most of the men responded, although more than a few, including 1st Sgt. Thomas S. Kelly of Company C, held back, oblivious to repeated orders. Because Kelly was supposed to inspire his men by his example, he was later reduced to the ranks for cowardice. In levying the punishment, a regretful Major Boernstein noted that "in the ranks of 'the Fourth' there are few men to whom a charge like this could be applied."[29]

One reason some men hesitated to push on was that a leading member of the color guard, the bearer of the regimental standard, had been shot down. Hastening to his side, Sgt. Alfred B. Hilton, who carried the national colors, scooped up the fallen banner and, following Appleton's lead, started forward, one flag in each hand. With the exception of the few who, like Kelly, could not force themselves onward, the men of the regiment let out another shout, got to their feet, and bounded toward the enemy.

Hilton got only a short distance beyond the *chevaux-de-frise* before he, too, fell, his leg shattered by a ball. Again the attack column shuddered to a halt. Propping himself on his elbows, the color-bearer held both banners aloft while bullets tore into them, almost yanking the staffs from his hands. Unable to rise, he shouted to those nearest him, "Boys, save the colors!"

Two men rushed up and grabbed the banners before they touched the ground. Christian Fleetwood took up the Stars and Stripes, while Corp. Charles Veal, Company D, yanked the regimental standard from the fallen bearer. Then both advanced into the teeth of the storm, brandishing the flags like weapons and calling on their comrades to follow. With Appleton in the lead, most did so, yelling at the top of their lungs.

About halfway between the abatis and the breastworks, Fleetwood and Veal planted the colors and stood side by side, unmoving, defiant, as bullets and shells whistled past. By some miracle, neither man was hit, although the flags were reduced to tattered streamers. The regimental standard alone attracted twenty-two bullets; its staff was so badly shattered that Veal had to use both hands to hold the severed pieces together and keep the banner waving.[30]

For all the gallantry the substitute color-bearers displayed, and despite the determination with which officers and men charged the works, the assault was doomed to failure. The converging fire of Bass's men and their supports methodically decimated the blue ranks. Even so, almost incredibly, a handful of men not only reached the works, but scaled them. Most were blasted at point-blank range or were run through with bayonets. A few, too late sensing the futility of the effort, tried to surrender, but although they threw up their hands, the defenders gunned them down. Confederate accounts of the fight admit that several African-Americans were murdered after giving up.[31]

Once they realized that not enough attackers remained to carry the Rebel line, the 4th's officers ordered everyone to retreat. Those able to do so without exposing themselves to certain death turned toward the *chevaux-de-frise*. Only then did Fleetwood and Veal head for the rear, the colors wrapped around their upper bodies to prevent further damage. As best they could—running, stumbling, crouching, crawling on hands and knees—the men of the 4th made their way to the cover of the abatis. There they huddled as slugs whipped past or thudded into the logs, hoping against hope that reinforcements would appear.

The only unit to come up was the 6th USCI. Instead of covering the 4th, its men launched a second attack, which fared no better than the first. Under repeated volleys from the Confederates, almost all of Colonel Ames's troops were cut down short of their objective. As before, a tiny remnant reached the main line, but none returned to his outfit alive. The 6th's flag-bearers also fell, the colors being passed to a couple of noncommissioned officers, including Fleetwood's friend, Thomas Hawkins, who waved them defiantly through the rest of the fight.[32]

The 6th's retreat, which degenerated into a frantic race for survival, ended the involvement of Duncan's brigade, which this day had lost about 400 men killed, wounded, and missing out of fewer than 700 engaged. Duncan himself had been knocked out of action early in the fight. Having gone in on foot with his old outfit, the colonel had lost his hat to a rifle ball and had seen his uniform perforated by other bullets, before suffering an ankle wound that forced him to limp to the rear. Colonel Ames, who succeeded to the command of the brigade, had escaped from the inferno unscathed.[33]

When the 6th rushed to the rear, supports should have moved up to exploit a sudden diminution of enemy fire. Paine, however, had kept Draper's brigade well back of the firing lines, where most of its men were made to lie down. Holman's brigade had been committed before Duncan's troops quit the field, but it had gone in piecemeal and had been kept so far from the Rebel works that its effect on the fighting was negligible. Nor did the white troops under Terry, to the east, and Foster, to the south and west, render close support. David Birney's strategy was to carry the enemy position with the USCT alone, while the white troops occupied the attention of forces elsewhere along New Market Heights.[34]

Late in the day, the plan worked—thanks partly to the toll taken of the enemy by the 4th and 6th USCI, at least some of whose men disobeyed orders by stopping to fire on Bass's Confederates. After re-forming, Paine struck again, but in greater strength than before, sending forward Draper's three regiments, covered by one of Holman's.

Even with the added weight, the initial effort bogged down short of the farthest point of advance by the 4th. A second charge, launched a half hour later, cleared both lines of abatis, the men pouring through the gaps made by the 4th and 6th. Soon after Draper's lines surmounted the logs, the Confederates, who had stood firm against the earlier attacks, abandoned their line by order of General Gregg and fell back, firing as they went, to Chaffin's Farm. Soon afterward, the crews of the Richmond Howitzers and Rockbridge Artillery limbered up and galloped off, leaving a long section of Richmond's exterior line open to seizure. Cheering USCT occupied the works and the rifle pits beyond, in which they were joined by Terry's men. After hours of desperate struggle and horrific carnage, New Market Heights was in Union hands.[35]

No sooner had Bass's men faded into the distance than members of the 4th who had been cut off from their comrades during the first attack rejoined the other survivors in the outfit. Some went forward to inspect the littered plain in front of the captured works. Officers and men, surgeons

U.S. Colored Troops burying their dead. AUTHOR'S COLLECTION

and hospital attendants succored the many wounded and prepared to bury the many dead, while combing the ground for discarded arms, ammunition, and equipment that could be of use in future battles.

Late in the day, with the field still blooming with corpses, doctors and litter-bearers were joined by visitors from the rear, including a well-mounted Ben Butler and his staff. Years later, in his peculiar oratorical style, the army commander recalled the sights that had greeted his eyes and the impact they had made on his mind and heart:

> There, in a space . . . three hundred yards long, lay the dead bodies of 543 of my colored comrades, slain in the defense of their country, who had laid down their lives to uphold its flag and its honor, as a willing sacrifice. And as I rode along, guiding my horse this way and that, lest he should profane with his hoofs what seemed to me the sacred dead, and as I looked at their bronzed faces upturned in the shining sun, as if in mute appeal against the wrongs of the country for which they had given their lives, and whose flag had been to them a flag of stripes, in which no star of glory had ever shone for them—feeling I had wronged them in the past, and believing what was the future duty of my country to them—I swore to myself a solemn oath: "May my right hand forget its cunning, and my tongue cleave to the roof of my mouth, if ever I fail to defend the rights of the men who have given their blood for me and my country this day and for their race forever." And, God helping me, I will keep that oath.[36]

CHAPTER 8

Seaside Excursion

SOME HOURS AFTER THE BATTLE, PAINE'S DIVISION ADVANCED UP THE NEW Market Road to Laurel Hill Church before turning southwestward to join Ord's troops at Chaffin's Farm. After going into bivouac near Fort Burnham, the officers of the 4th USCI tried to estimate the number of casualties the regiment had suffered this day. At first it was feared that more than 250 men had been killed or wounded, a casualty rate of nearly 60 percent. This figure was advanced by, among other survivors, Captain Wickes, whose Company G had gone into the fight with almost forty officers and men and had come out of it with five. Later calculations placed the casualty count at 178—27 killed, 137 wounded, and 14 missing and presumed captured. While not nearly as high as originally feared, the loss rate was still considerable—more than 40 percent of the total engaged.[1]

Whereas the regiment's only previous full-scale battle, the June 15 attack on Petersburg, had taken a disproportionate toll of noncommissioned officers, on September 29 the casualties had fallen heavily on the commissioned ranks. Most of the officers, including Wickes and Appleton, escaped injury despite having advanced so far that they could have reached out and touched Gregg's works. Among their colleagues, however, Capt. Samuel W. Vannings of Company E had been killed, while five line officers had been wounded: Captain Hill and 1st Lt. J. Murray Hoag (Company B); 1st Lt. Thomas N. Price (C); 1st Lt. Daniel W. Spicer (K); and 2nd Lt. W. Watson Gillingham (I). To this list may be added Colonel Duncan, whose crippling injury would leave him hospitalized for five months. Hill, Hoag, and Price would retake the field following lengthy recuperation, but Spicer's and Gillingham's injuries would compel them to resign their commissions.[2]

Once again the 4th had suffered a heavy loss in noncommissioned officers. Those killed or mortally wounded included 1st Sgt. Nathaniel W. Dorsey (Company B); Sergeants Cyrus Boley and Isaac Harrold (E); 1st

(From left)
Captains Samuel W. Vannings,
Thomas H. Price, and
Albert G. Crawford
LIBRARY OF CONGRESS

Sgt. Augustus A. Norton and Sergeants Allan Torp and Dennis Torp (F); and Corporals James Dawsen (A), William H. Traverse (C), Cornelius Key (F), John H. Dyson (G), John R. Newmon (I), and Andrew Nichols (K). Among the wounded were 1st Sgt. Charles H. Giles (G) and Sergeants John H. Warren (A); Isaac Caulk, George A. Hutchins, and W. E. Matthews (C); Garrison Nicholls (E); Joseph Baker and Charles Linghams (F); Alfred B. Roberts (G); W. G. Buie and J. W. Jenkins (H); J. C. Buchanan (I); and Philip C. Hooper, Henry Johnson, and the towering Grafton Cosley (K). Wounded corporals included James Dawson and Alex Watts (A); George Bond (C); J. G. Johnson (F); Elhawan Buie and Josiah Chew (G); Joseph Haynes and Robert Parker (H); and Andrew Ward (I).[3]

Many of those who fell, as well as several who emerged from the fight without a scratch, had comported themselves, as Duncan wrote, "with unflinching heroism." Five days after the battle, division headquarters asked Major Boernstein to submit a list of those whose behavior he considered worthy of official commendation. While reluctant to name a few when so many had served nobly, in the end he selected four candidates: Lieutenant Hoag, Sergeant Major Fleetwood, Sergeant Hilton, and Corporal Veal.

Capt. Thomas H. Price
U.S. ARMY MILITARY HISTORY INSTITUTE

Boernstein chose well. In saving the colors from capture and dishonor, the noncommissioned officers had demonstrated great gallantry. They had faced danger not only from the front, but also from the rear; a comrade had fired a bullet so close to Fleetwood's head that the hair on his right side had been singed by the powder flash, and his hearing in that ear had been permanently diminished. Of the trio, Boernstein demonstrated special zeal in recommending Hilton, who would die on October 21 of complications from the amputation of his mangled limb, as "a good and faithful soldier, a man." He cited Veal for the efforts he had made to keep the 4th's standard waving despite its splintered condition. And he lauded Fleetwood (if rather condescendingly) as "a highly educated gentleman and . . . one of the many instances of what the African race is capable of being brought to by patient persistent effort."[4]

As for Hoag, he had won Boernstein's high regard for having gone into the battle—in which he lost his left arm—despite a fever. When the 4th had broken camp on the morning of the battle, the lieutenant had told Dr. Mitchell, "I will go on with my regiment," unless forced to remain in camp. The resolve that had carried him through the fight would also carry him—his disability notwithstanding—through the rest of the war, which he would close out as a brevet lieutenant colonel.[5]

The major also acknowledged in general terms the heroic actions of those not initially singled out for honors. Later, Lieutenant Appleton, who had been in the forefront of the assault, encouraging and inspiring the men, was also cited for gallantry. The conduct of all these men told Boernstein that Napoleon's "Old Guard could not have done better" than the 4th USCI on that field of blood and sacrifice. By its determination in the face of adversity, the regiment had won the right to inscribe on its bullet-riddled regimental banner the names "Petersburg," for "gallantry in capturing the line of works and the enemy's guns on the 15th of June," and "New Market Heights," for "gallantry in carrying [i.e., helping carry] the enemy's works at that point on the 29th of September."[6]

Division headquarters collected Boernstein's recommendations, along with those submitted by the commanders of other units involved in the battle, and forwarded them to army headquarters. Butler and a team of subordinates reviewed the composite lists, culled out the names of those they considered most deserving of commendation, and sent them to General Grant. Grant's staff further reviewed the lists, made a few additions and deletions, and presented the final candidates to the War Department.

The 4th USCI heard no more about the matter for several months. In the early spring of 1865, word reached the regiment that the president and the secretary of war had approved Fleetwood, Hilton (posthumously), and Veal to receive Medals of Honor. The award, which had been authorized for enlisted members of the army in July 1862 and for officers the following March, recognized those who went beyond the call of duty in serving their army and their nation.[7]

The medals were delivered by mail to Fleetwood and Veal on April 23. Hilton's was presented to his widow, Harriet, at her Harford County, Maryland, home. Lieutenant Appleton was also declared deserving of the medal—not only for his conduct on September 29, but for leading the June 15 attack on Petersburg as well. For unknown reasons, he did not receive the decoration until 1891. Why Lieutenant Hoag was denied the award also remains unknown.[8]

While the commendation was gratefully received, the Medal of Honor had yet to attain the symbolic value it took on during later years and later wars. Thus Major Boernstein did his best to confer a more tangible award on those whose valor he had cited. In the case of Appleton, Hoag, and Veal, he succeeded. Within two months of the battle in which they had distinguished themselves, Appleton and Hoag won promotions to captain, and Veal to sergeant. Boernstein failed, however, to secure a promotion for another he considered eminently deserving of higher rank—Christian Fleetwood.

Although the government had long banned African-Americans from holding commissions, Secretary Stanton had occasionally violated the rule for his own reasons. In January and February 1865, he did so again, making lieutenants of two sergeants, members of the 54th and 55th Massachusetts (Colored) Volunteers. Hopeful that the secretary would make another exception in Fleetwood's case, several officers of the regiment, including Boernstein, got up a petition that described the sergeant major as a "gentleman and a soldier in every way," one who had proven his fitness to lead "during a daily intercourse extending over considerably more than a year." The signers "earnestly prayed that he might be commissioned to one of the vacancies then existing, and [affirmed] that they would gladly welcome him as one of themselves." Every officer in the outfit signed the petition, which was duly forwarded to Stanton's office—only to be returned, disapproved, several weeks later.[9]

Everyone involved was disappointed by the secretary's action—none more so than Fleetwood himself. In a letter to his former employer, Dr. James Hall, the ranking enlisted man described his feelings in the matter. He was careful to place his disappointment in the context of the overall USCT experience, for he realized how much his promotion would have meant to the cause of racial equality in the ranks:

> From representations made by Col. Birney [during the regiment's formation] and from the position assumed by our friends in Congress you remember we were induced to believe or hope that [as] an evidence of merit and ability to do our duty we should receive promotion, at least to the rank of company & regimental officers. That I have well performed the duties of the office which I have held the past two years it becomes me not to say[,] although I bear a medal conferred for some special acts as a soldier . . . [and] no regiment has performed more active, arduous & dangerous service than the 4th U. S. Col'd Troops. . . .
>
> Upon all our record there is not a single blot, and yet no member of this regiment is considered deserving of a commission or if so cannot receive one. I trust you will understand that I speak not of and for myself individually, or that the lack of the pay or honor of a commission induces me to quit the service. Not so by any means, on the contrary it seems to me that our

continuing to act in a subordinate capacity with no hope of advancement or promotion is an absolute injury to our cause. It is a tacit but telling acknowledgment on our part that we are not fit for promotion & that we are satisfied to remain in a state of marked & acknowledged subserviency.[10]

Fleetwood's disappointment, although deep and long-lived, was lessened by the knowledge that he had won the confidence and esteem of everyone in the 4th USCI. That his petition "was signed by every white officer remaining in the Regiment, from Field officer down to the junior Second Lieutenant" was, he believed, a gesture of recognition "without a parallel" in the annals of the war for the Union. Then, too, army headquarters had awarded him one of the medals that General Butler had ordered struck for presentation to those African-American soldiers who fit the criteria inscribed on its front and back: "U.S. Colored Troops . . . Distinguished for Courage, Campaign before Richmond, 1864." Fleetwood would prize this award almost as much as the better-known medal he would proudly wear, whenever the occasion arose, through the rest of his life.[11]

THE BUTLER MEDAL.

Butler Medal for U.S. Colored Troops. A HISTORY OF THE NEGRO TROOPS IN THE WAR OF THE REBELLION, 1861–65

Lt. William E. Gibson
U.S. ARMY MILITARY HISTORY INSTITUTE

One reason for the zeal with which Boernstein and his subordinates had advanced Fleetwood for promotion was the heavy losses in officers the 4th had suffered at New Market Heights. When he learned he could not advance Fleetwood, Boernstein tried to plug the holes by transferring and promoting four sergeants from outside the 4th, members of two white regiments in the Army of the James with whose personnel he was familiar, the 7th Connecticut and 188th Pennsylvania. He was able to secure the services of only one of his choices, Sgt. (later 2nd Lt.) William E. Gibson of the Pennsylvania outfit, but he appears to have been more successful in making appointments from civil life and in transferring officers from other USC regiments. Late in October, Fleetwood reported that seven new lieutenants had been assigned to the 4th.[12]

Boernstein resorted to other expedients to give individual units the leadership they required. Before October ended, he assigned three of the regiment's lieutenants, including Hoag, to temporary command of Companies C, D, and E, each of which had lost its captain to battle wounds. To preserve company-level experience, Boernstein even consented to retain officers who, in other circumstances, he might have tried to kick out of the army. These included Captain Dillenback, who, after recuperating from the leg wound received on June 15, returned to Company F two days before New Market Heights, but on the morning of the battle reported himself unfit for duty due to "general debility."

Apparently the man recovered quickly, for he rejoined the regiment a few hours after the shooting stopped, only to return to the sick list four days later, when it appeared that another fight was brewing—this time, the stated reason was an attack of neuralgia. Although Dr. Mitchell believed Dillenback's latest illness would pass in less than forty-eight hours, the captain again reported to the hospital, where he remained for several days. When he finally rejoined the 4th, Boernstein greeted him with something less than open arms, but to avoid a rift, he made no comment about the captain's convenient fragility.[13]

If, for a time at least, the regiment lacked able-bodied officers, the rank and file appeared to be in much worse shape. By mid-October, the regiment was officially listed as mustering 344 enlisted men, exclusive of the recruits at Dutch Gap. Indications are that this was an inflated figure, probably inclusive of men assigned to the regiment but absent from it, at least temporarily. It is doubtful that Boernstein could have mustered 200 able-bodied riflemen on short notice. The 4th USCI had become a shadow of its original size.[14]

Its reduced state made it especially difficult for the outfit to shoulder the workload heaped on it in the days and weeks following the bloodletting southeast of Richmond. On September 30, the 4th occupied a section of captured works about a quarter-mile from Fort Burnham. That night, the men were relocated to a more exposed position and forced to erect breastworks of their own, before being moved yet again. The process was repeated on each of the next two days: building works and digging trenches, abandoning them for some reason or handing them over to other troops, then building and digging anew. Periodically, rumors came in of Confederate forces massing in their front; the men would drop their shovels, pick up their Enfields, and stand ready to repel an assault that never came.[15]

The daytime workload was severe enough, but from October 1 through the 14, the 4th was kept alert and under arms through most of the night. The constant labor, the physical and mental stress, and the almost incessant wakefulness took its toll: During the two weeks after the fighting on New Market Heights, dozens of men, along with several officers including Wickes, left the regiment for the hospitals, "worn out & exhausted," and seeking "rest and a little care" beyond the reach of enemy guns. Wickes, for one, spent three weeks flat on his back.[16]

The regiment got some relief from the repetitive, enervating routine when, on October 15, its bivouac was moved some distance to the left and rear. There, in quieter surroundings, the 4th went into fixed camp—pitching tents, clearing land for a drill ground—for the first time since leaving Dutch Gap for Deep Bottom and New Market Heights. Diary entries by Christian Fleetwood over the next week and a half indicate that during this period, the 4th began to recapture the feel and flow of camp life. The pleasantness ended abruptly on the twenty-sixth, however, when the regiment was forced to relocate once again—this time to its former precarious position near Fort Burnham. After marching throughout the day under a warm autumn sun, Fleetwood hoped "to spend the night in peace." Instead, he was awakened several times to post extra guards against a new round of rumored assaults.[17]

Although the weather remained mild while the 4th shuttled to and from Chaffin's Farm, its army was launching its final field operations before going into winter quarters. On October 13, General Terry led two divisions—including one under William Birney, consisting of the USCT who had come over from Meade's army—up the Darbytown Road toward a fresh line of Rebel defenses north of New Market Heights. When Lee reinforced the position, the attack failed miserably, but two weeks later, a large part of the army tried again, this time with Ben Butler himself in command and in cooperation with a new thrust toward the Southside Railroad by the Army of the Potomac. Though it got off to a more promising start, this offensive also bogged down against unexpectedly heavy resistance, forcing the Federals to retrace their steps.[18]

So ended the Virginia campaigns of the Army of the James in 1864. Captain Wickes, just returned from the hospital, summed up the operation of the twenty-seventh in a letter to his father: "Butler's move around to the right did not amount to much. The troops have returned to their old positions and we take up our places again in the left of the line, and settle down again in our little log tents." He thanked the fates that the 4th had been spared participation in the twin failures.[19]

To a man, the 4th hoped it would not have to go into winter quarters in its present insecure position on the advance line. Its wish was granted on November 4, when Paine's headquarters assigned the regiment a reserve role in rear of the line occupied by its corps. Once they reached that position, which was less vulnerable to forays by the defenders of Richmond's intermediate line, the men of the 4th breathed a collective sigh of relief.

Then they began to winterize their tents and build sturdy huts in which to weather the approaching season.[20]

Snug in their new habitation, the men awaited the end of a year that for them had begun on an optimistic note, had degenerated into stalemate and defeat, and had been redeemed by triumphs in other theaters of operations. One result of those dramatic victories was the happy outcome of the presidential race. Late in October, agents from various states visited the Union armies to collect the ballots of those soldiers eligible to vote in the field. The enlisted men of the 4th were denied participation in this process by a government that considered them entitled to only one right—the right to risk their lives in military service. With some exceptions, however, their officers were allowed to cast their vote by proxy.

It can be assumed with confidence that the officers of the 4th voted overwhelmingly to sustain Abraham Lincoln and the war effort. To a man, they appreciated the patient support the commander-in-chief had given his troops even in times of defeat and gloom. Conversely, few had anything good to say of Lincoln's opponent, George B. McClellan. The former commander of the Army of the Potomac had endeared himself to the army through his oft-displayed concern for its welfare, the memory of which meant that he could count on a certain percentage of the soldier vote. Only a few of the 4th's officers had served under "Little Mac," however, and thus most had formed no attachment to the man—certainly none strong enough to impel them to support a candidate running on a platform that called the war a failure and suggested it could be ended quickly and bloodlessly at the negotiating table. To support McClellan was to break faith with comrades who had sacrificed everything in defense of the nation and to proclaim the struggle a gigantic waste of blood and treasure. Many soldiers held McClellan's tacit acceptance of the Democrats' peace plank against him. Alluding to the general's home state, a few weeks before the election Captain Wickes declared it a "disgrace . . . to claim citizenship in the State of New Jersey."[21]

When, on November 8, Lincoln won a decisive victory at the polls—thanks, at least in part, to the soldier vote—the regiment rejoiced. The common sentiment was uncommonly articulated by the 4th's old commander, Colonel Duncan, by then recuperating in New Hampshire following his release from a hospital in Hampton Roads. Duncan, who had returned home just in time to support the Union Party at the polls, rhapsodized over McClellan's repudiation:

> How are the mighty fallen! The once honored, idolized General-in-chief of the armies of the Republic condemned by the

overwhelming rebuke of his loyal & patriotic countrymen to a
retirement never to be interrupted. . . . Fitting reward for the
overweening ambition that was . . . willing even to sink its own
individuality & become the pliant tool of unscrupulous party
leaders! Let us scorn, & then forget [him]![22]

⊁⊹⊱ ⊰⊹⊰

Lincoln's reelection effectively condemned the Confederacy to defeat and
the South to political and economic ruin. Yet Jefferson Davis and his generals refused to concede; they would fight on until physically overwhelmed
or psychologically devastated. That meant that Grant must clamp down
even harder on Petersburg and Richmond, putting added pressure on many
points of the Rebel lines, lengthening and thinning Lee's defenses and
threatening the communication lines that linked his army to the interior of
the Confederacy.

Grant realized, however, that he could not afford to limit his efforts to
middle Virginia. By mid-November, Sherman's victorious armies were
marching from Atlanta to the sea along a route that ran to Savannah and
then north through the Carolinas. While Grant doubted that Sherman's
march would by itself bring the South to its knees, he planned to order the
Westerners to Virginia, there to join the troops of Meade and Butler in
choking the life out of the Confederacy's most strategic cities.[23]

When Sherman turned north, he would cut off enemy coastal defenses
and close most of the seaports, such as Charleston, that continued to connect the Confederacy to the outside world. Yet Grant was not certain that
his trusted lieutenant would have the patience to launch a time-consuming
campaign against the port that every year brought into the Confederacy
$30 million worth of war matériel from England and France. This was
Wilmington, North Carolina, a target of Union forces almost since the
conflict began, one that not even the formidable resources of the North
Atlantic Blockading Squadron had been able to shut down.

Wilmington's strategic value to the South had grown with the succes-
sive capture of other coastal cities. During the last quarter of 1864 alone,
blockade runners out of Liverpool, Nassau, and Bermuda had carried into
the city more than 8.5 million pounds of meat, almost 2 million pounds of
saltpeter, 1.5 million pounds of lead, 520,000 pounds of coffee, 316,000
blankets, 70,000 rifles, 2,639 boxes of medical supplies, almost 100 crates of
revolvers, 43 cannons, and huge quantities of ammunition. The supplies
kept coming because the city sat more than twenty miles from the Atlantic

Interior view of northeast bastion of Fort Fisher, North Carolina, 1865. U.S. ARMY
MILITARY HISTORY INSTITUTE

Ocean, beyond the reach of naval guns. A close-up attack was not possible, for while the sleek blockade runners could easily navigate the shoal- and bar-infested channels of the Cape Fear River on Wilmington's western flank, large warships could not enter safely. Then, too, the gales that frequently lashed the North Carolina coast and the fog that often shrouded the local waters offered additional protection to those who enjoyed the thrill of hauling war-related goods—everything from canteens to canister—under the noses of the blockaders.[24]

A major deterrent to operations against Wilmington was its impressive array of defenses, especially Fort Fisher, a gigantic earthwork near the tip of a peninsula once known as Federal Point—and, since 1861, for obvious reasons, as Confederate Point—about twenty miles below the city. Other works guarded Wilmington's south side, including Fort Anderson; Fort Pender, at Smithville; and Fort Caswell, on Oak Island. But Fisher was by far the most formidable obstacle to anyone approaching Wilmington by land or sea. Defended by a garrison almost 1,000 strong—Regulars and state forces under Col. William Lamb—the fort encompassed 14,500 square feet of interior space divided widthwise by traverses, thick earthen walls that extended twelve feet above its parapets. Both sides of the fort—its 700-yard-long land face to the north and the southward-leading sea face that ran for 2,000 yards along the ocean beach—were studded with a deadly array of artillery. Fisher's forty-four guns included several 6⅜-inch smoothbore cannons and 10-inch Columbiad rifles, as well as a 150-pounder Armstrong rifle imported from England. The garrison was further protected by ditches, palisades, three detached works, and fields stocked with land mines that could be detonated from inside the fort. Little wonder that some called Fisher the "Confederate Goliath" and that others likened it to the Malakoff Tower, the celebrated Russian fortress of the Crimean War.[25]

Grant believed that now, as never before, Wilmington was ripe for the taking. If an amphibious operation could be launched in secrecy, Lee would not have time to reinforce Lamb's garrison or the entrenched camp atop Sugar Loaf, a sand dune four and a half miles north of the fort, where the failed Western commander, Braxton Bragg, commanded a few thousand troops. Grant determined that 6,500 men of Butler's army, including the 4th USCI, would be enough to attack Lamb while also holding off Bragg. To be successful, however, they would require the close cooperation of the blockading squadron formerly under Admiral Lee and now led by the more youthful and enterprising Rear Adm. David Dixon Porter.

To command the land forces, Grant chose Maj. Gen. Godfrey Weitzel, a protégé of Butler's whom Grant had decided to place at the head of the new, all-USCT XXV Army Corps. But the general-in-chief failed to take into account the egotism and determination of Weitzel's superior, who demanded command of the army contingent. Against his better judgment, Grant complied. He realized that Butler had been planning such an operation for several months and had even devised a novel way to launch it. The army leader had recently dredged up a sunken but seaworthy mail packet, the *Louisiana,* which he planned to load with tons of blasting powder connected to a fast-burning fuse. By grounding the vessel, under cover of night, close to Fisher's land face, then detonating the powder by means of a clockwork mechanism, Butler hoped to blast the garrison into surrender without having to assault it. While doubtful that the complex technology would perform as envisioned, Grant could not tactfully deny its proponent command of the mission.[26]

Cold weather having reduced the pace of activity at Petersburg, along the lines below Richmond, and everywhere in between, Grant decreed that the expedition get under way on December 6–7. The 4th USCI received marching orders at midday on the sixth. At dusk, the regiment marched across the rear of Bermuda Hundred, Lieutenant Colonel Rogers in the lead. To the great satisfaction of the regiment, Rogers had returned to it only days before, following the premature closing of his recruiting office in North Carolina. A change in departmental policy had limited his ability to organize USCT units. He hoped to make greater contributions to his regiment and his army in the field.[27]

Near the head of the pontoon bridge at Point of Rocks, the 4th bivouacked for the night under what Christian Fleetwood called a "sprinkled rain." Alive to rumors that a major movement was afoot, that evening the sergeant major left a letter and a copy of a recent photograph with a comrade who would remain behind, with instructions that they be sent to his mother in Baltimore "in case of Accident." This was something he had never done before—perhaps he had a premonition of impending doom.[28]

To be sure, the early stages of the embarkation were rife with omens, and they were all bad. From the start, there was a decided lack of cooperation and mutual support between Butler and his naval counterpart. In contrast to the army, which made quick, efficient preparations to leave Hampton Roads, Porter's flotilla of wooden warships and ironclad gunboats—seventy vessels, in all—took its time loading coal and provisions. From the eighth to the tenth, Butler put his soldiers aboard a small fleet of transports, along with a huge quantity of artillery, horses, supplies of all kinds, and equipment including entrenching tools—Grant had ordered him to lay siege to Fisher if unable to take it by storm. Butler was ready to sail by the afternoon of the tenth, but Porter was not, nor could he say when he would be.[29]

By the tenth, the 4th USCI had been aboard two of Butler's transports—six companies in the *Montauk,* four others in General Paine's flagship, the *Herman Livingston*—for almost two days. On the ninth, the ships had carried the men from City Point to Fort Monroe, retracing a route they had taken almost seven months before. Once in Hampton Roads, they had remained aboard ship with nothing to do but count the number of times the vessels rocked back and forth at anchor. By the morning of the tenth, the men, although ignorant of their destination, were desperate to get under way. Their accommodations were cramped and filthy, and their rations were beginning to run out. Even the coffee served aboard ship was weak and tasteless. Under these conditions, it was easy for the men to get on each other's nerves. Corp. Alex Cassell of Company A was later reduced to the ranks for his role in a fistfight aboard the *Herman Livingston.*[30]

Late on the tenth, the soldiers-turned-sailors experienced even greater discomfort: A gale had sprung up in Hampton Roads, further delaying their departure. For the next two days, they remained cooped in their squalid quarters as high waves crashed into the transports, rocking them to and fro. The men tried to keep their spirits up with music and song, but by the time the gale blew itself out late on the twelfth, everyone was out of sorts. They expressed disgust not only with the delay, but also with the high command, which had permitted them not so much as a few minutes of fresh air on solid ground.[31]

At about 3:00 P.M. on the thirteenth, the transports finally got under way, although when they steamed out of Hampton Roads, Porter and his captains were still readying their ships for the mission. The passengers still lacked a definite idea of where they were heading, but when the troopships steamed up the Chesapeake Bay toward the Potomac River, they began to wonder if they would end up in the Shenandoah Valley. In mid-October, along Cedar Creek, near Newtown, Virginia, Phil Sheridan had defeated his opponent for the third time, this time nearly destroying Jubal Early's army. While it seemed unlikely that Little Phil would continue offensive operations into the winter, the passengers could think of no other explanation for the route being taken.

It turned out that the crafty Butler was feinting to fool enemy observers in Hampton Roads. Not until his flotilla reached Matthias Point, sixty miles up the Potomac from the mouth of the Bay, did he order a retrograde. Early on the fourteenth, the transports were back at Old Point Comfort, leaving the troops completely mystified about the turn of events. Late in the morning, however, after the ships had passed down the coast to Cape Henry, officers spread the word that they were bound for Wilmington, to cooperate with the navy in storming Fort Fisher.[32]

But where was the navy? By the time the transports returned to Hampton Roads, Porter and his fleet were gone. Having gotten under way hours before, the admiral moved south, believing he was trailing Butler's soldiers—the overly secretive army leader had failed to inform his colleague about the feint. This was not the extent of the lack of communication between them. Porter forever insisted he had told Butler that the fleet was going to recoal at Beaufort, eighty-five miles north of Wilmington, and thus would be thirty-six hours late in joining the army off Fort Fisher. Butler claimed to know nothing of Porter's intermediate destination. Thus, when his transports reached the rendezvous site, twenty-five miles off Confederate Point, on the afternoon of the fifteenth, they found only a few of Porter's ships in the area. The officer in command had no information as to Porter's whereabouts or intentions.[33]

The navy failed to show for five days. Butler spent the time sailing about Masonboro Inlet on his sleek little flagship, the *Ben de Ford*. His soldiers enjoyed no such diversion. They whiled away the slow-passing hours fishing, reading, singing, and trying to keep from getting seasick. These half-hearted efforts to stave off boredom failed, and everyone aboard gave himself over to grumbling and cursing. By the seventeenth, Christian Fleetwood was asking, half in despair: "Oh, when will this tiresome floating about end[?] . . . Here we are kept without one thing to relieve the monotony & sameness. 'Rocked in the cradle of the deep' is very good poetry but hang the reality of it."[34]

He was not alone in his anguish and indignation. The same day, an officer in the 5th USCI decided that "either we are not to land here or the expedition is commanded by a lunatic." A few days later, another well-educated sergeant major, a member of a white regiment from New York, wrote his family:

> Day after day we have been tossed drearily on the waves off the bleak coast, out of sight of land, living on raw pork and hardtack, and crowded almost without breathing room into [this] filthy old transport. . . . Had our soldiers been so roughly treated by the rebels, there would be no end to cries of "shame" and the accusation of "barbarity" from the enlightened press. Probably a more mismanaged expedition never left our ports.[35]

The worst was still to come. Porter and the majority of his fleet finally reached the rendezvous on the afternoon of December 19. The admiral rattled off a list of excuses for being late, but none mollified Butler, who, like his men, had begun to seethe with anger. When he learned that Porter had directed that the *Louisiana* be armed and towed toward shore, the army commander edged toward apoplexy. Since Porter knew that Butler's troops were not in a position to exploit the powder boat, it seemed obvious that the admiral intended to claim personal credit for its success. At Butler's demand, Porter had the vessel recalled, but in the end it added to neither man's reputation. On the evening of the twenty-third, the *Louisiana* was sent in again, this time with its arming mechanism activated. The powder detonated much as planned, but the vessel had been grounded too far from the northeast angle of the fort to do maximum damage. The explosion woke up every member of the garrison, but it failed so much as to singe the grass on the parapets of the sea face. The naval officer who had overseen the boat's arming rendered a succinct verdict on the outcome: "There's a fizzle!"[36]

For five days before Porter made contact with Butler off Confederate Point, the coastal weather had been, in Butler's words, "zephyr-like." But almost as soon as the navy arrived, the sea began to run high and rough. Soldiers who had avoided seasickness thus far suddenly became violently ill. Realizing that a gale was coming on, a furious Butler ordered the transports to make for the harbor that Porter had recently departed. While the army headed for safe haven, the navy, which was accustomed to riding out rough weather, remained on station.

The soldiers reached Beaufort only hours before the storm hit. Barely had their ships dropped anchor when the gale began to shake them like a giant fist. For three days, they bobbed and rolled like corks in a tub; at times more than one appeared on the verge of going under. Below decks on the *Montauk* and *Herman Livingston,* men were tossed from one end of the ship to another, along with every item of cargo not securely fastened. The curses of the men suddenly turned to cries of alarm and pleas for deliverance.

The seemingly unflappable Christian Fleetwood took a rather detached view of the crisis, feeling "amused at the sudden conversion of the boys by the storm." The evening of the twenty-first was "a night of prayer for once, quite an agreeable change from the usual swearing." His sentiment was shared by Chaplain Hunter, who led an unusually large group of penitents in asking God to spare them from the perils of the deep. Their prayers were answered the following day, when the seas grew calmer. By then, however, Fleetwood had taken to his sickbed, having finally succumbed to "the effects of yesterdays storm."

By the twenty-third, when the chaplain helped the sergeant major get some fresh air on the *Montauk's* main deck, the gale had blown itself out, with no loss of life among the army. The transports remained in port till late that day, taking on extra provisions and coal. Then they weighed anchor and headed back to Masonboro Inlet.[37]

By 4:00 on the afternoon of the twenty-fourth, soldiers and sailors had again rendezvoused, this time closer to Fort Fisher. By now the powder boat had proven a failure, and Butler realized he had to launch the attack he had hoped to avoid. Already Porter's crews had begun their part in the offensive: Shortly before noon, two lines of wooden ships and ironclads had begun to blast away at Colonel Lamb's earthwork. The men on the transports stared in awe as the heavy naval guns thundered away. Recalling the explosion of the Petersburg mine, Fleetwood thought "the roar of artillery only 2d to July 30."[38]

When, at half past five, the guns fell silent, Porter declared that the garrison had been pounded into submission and suggested that Butler need only land, march inside, and accept Lamb's sword. Though dubious about the effectiveness of the barrage, Butler and his subordinates, including Weitzel, made final plans to land on Confederate Point. As a result of the conference, at 7:00 the next morning, Christmas Day, Porter's ships resumed their shelling in the hope of preventing the Confederates from repairing damage done the previous day. After five hours, the guns again ceased, and Porter made a rather presumptuous statement to his army colleague: "There is not a Rebel within five miles of the fort."[39]

Soon afterward, the army went into action, Butler launching the first of several waves of rowboats. Piloted by Porter's seamen, the boats were crammed with the men of Col. N. Martin Curtis's brigade, part of the newly created XXIV Corps, repository of almost every white unit in the Army of the James. Before the afternoon was over, Paine's USCT division began leaving its transports for the run across the inlet to the landing site, four miles above the fort.

The men of the 4th USCI were among the first African-Americans to cast off. Yet only three companies of the regiment got under way before, without explanation, everyone was ordered to return at once to the *Montauk*. Baffled soldiers were soon back on the deck of their transport, although, as Fleetwood reported, a few "got a drenching in the surf" when making the transition from rowboat to transport deck. Within a few hours, by which time almost every launchboat had returned to the flotilla, the men were asleep in their cramped quarters, none the wiser as to why the attack had been called off.

The mystery deepened when, the next morning, the troopships steamed out of the inlet and headed up the coast to Hampton Roads. By the evening of the twenty-seventh, they were back at Fort Monroe, and the next day, the soldiers were debarking in the rain at Jones Landing. Soon afterward, they reoccupied their old camps, now awash in mud.[40]

By this time, many of the men, including the more inquisitive members of the 4th, had learned why the order to land on Confederate Point had been countermanded. It had come down to a loss of nerve by Butler. Although Curtis's men, upon landing north of the fort, had easily captured Fisher's outworks, along with several hundred defenders, they had found the main garrison—Porter's boast notwithstanding—lightly touched by the navy's cannonade. Few or none of its guns had been disabled, and while much of the palisade had been shot away, its parapets, bastions, and traverses appeared unscathed. When Weitzel, who had been sent ahead to reconnoiter the objective, advised against assaulting a still-intact fortification, Butler readily agreed. Greatly concerned about the rough, high-rising surf, the army leader was predisposed to cease attack preparations. Revealing the extent of his anxiety, he pulled his transports back to sea so quickly that about 800 members of Curtis's brigade were left stranded on the beach.[41]

While Butler sailed for home to report his mission unaccomplished, Porter and his ships remained offshore. They kept up such a heavy fire on the fort that Lamb's men were unable to sally forth and take prisoners. Under cover of the barrage, Porter sent rowboats to rescue the men, although the rough seas prevented him from finishing the task until midday on the twenty-eighth.

Detonated bulkhead of the Dutch Gap Canal, 1865. U.S. ARMY MILITARY HISTORY
INSTITUTE

Once back in Virginia, Butler's troops—none of whom had bathed or
changed clothes in nearly three weeks—expressed disgust at having left
North Carolina empty-handed ("grievously disgruntled," was the way
Fleetwood put it). Butler, however, felt no such dejection—for one thing,
he believed he had a good excuse for aborting the offensive. As he
reminded Grant upon reaching army headquarters, his orders had called on
him to besiege Fort Fisher only if he effected a landing above it. Since so
few of his troops had hit the beach before the surf rose to dangerous
heights, Butler believed that no landing—at least none in any accepted
sense of the term—had taken place. Grant, who lacked his subordinate's
legalistic mind, did not agree, but for a time he did nothing to indicate his
displeasure at Butler's conduct. He allowed the army commander to return
to Bermuda Hundred. As soon as the man left, however, Grant began to
map a second effort against Wilmington, to be directed by someone other
than Butler or Weitzel.[42]

Once back at his own headquarters, Butler contented himself by giving
his account of the mission to friendly reporters and making final prepara-

tions to open Dutch Gap to Union shipping. By now months of back-breaking labor were at an end; all that remained was to blow out the bulk-heads at either end of Farrar's Island. Butler scheduled the detonation for New Year's Day. To mark the occasion, he invited a bevy of army officers, politicians, and newsmen to witness the fruition of his engineering triumph. Precisely on schedule, the powder charges were lit, and the bulk-heads exploded. As tons of earth shot skyward, the crowd exclaimed in wonderment.

The hubbub ceased when most of the flying dirt settled back into place, damming up the gap as before. Months of dredging would be necessary to open the waterway to river traffic. By then the war would be over.[43]

CHAPTER 9

Like Lords and Conquerors

GRANT WAS AWARE, AS HIS POLITICAL SUPERIORS LIKED TO REMIND HIM, that the army could not afford a second failure against Wilmington. When he got up his new expedition, he chose a leader carefully, and he took steps to ensure that preparations to launch would go more smoothly than the first time around. The officer he selected was Alfred Terry. Although a volunteer, not a professional soldier, Terry had experience in amphibious operations; he had a solid combat record; his men admired and trusted him; and he lacked the paranoiac mentality that Butler had displayed in his dealings with the navy. Above all, Grant could count on Terry to follow orders, including the order to occupy Confederate Point and lay siege to Fort Fisher if the earthwork could not be overcome any other way.[1]

The new operation began at high noon on January 3, 1865, with Terry shifting troops from above the James, across Bermuda Hundred, to the landings on the Appomattox. The next day, transportation arrived—a larger fleet of more commodious vessels than had made the first run. When the men of the 4th embarked late that afternoon, their initial disgruntlement, their understandable attitude of here-we-go-again, slowly gave way to a belief that they were going to be treated better this time out. "We have more room," observed a white comrade, "and better ventilation." Moreover, the men did not have to share space below decks with animals and other impedimenta. As Terry later noted, "No horses, wagons, or ambulances were taken; the caissons of the artillery were left behind."[2]

On the other hand, he took additional troops—8,000 instead of the 6,500 Butler had commanded—as well as a portion of a siege train that had been shipped down the Potomac from the government arsenal at Washington, D.C. Terry, however, had secured enough shipping to accommodate the additional resources, ensuring that the soldiers would not have to make room for them. All in all, the passengers agreed that this mission was getting off to a better start. If the weather would cooperate, they could expunge the stain that the first operation had splotched on their army's escutcheon.

As soon as loaded, each vessel made for Hampton Roads. By 9:00 P.M. on the fifth, every transport was anchored off Fort Monroe, and the men were ready to set sail. Terry observed: "The troops were all in heavy marching order, with four days' rations, from the morning of the 4th, in their haversacks, and forty rounds of ammunition in their [cartridge] boxes." That night, the captains of the troopships were ordered to proceed to a rendezvous twenty-five miles off Beaufort. They weighed anchor and got under way at the appointed time, 4:00 A.M. on the sixth.[3]

Eight hours later, one man who had been left on shore—the general whose troops these were—learned that they were his no longer. Just after noon, Benjamin F. Butler, while lolling at his Bermuda Hundred headquarters, was handed a communiqué from Grant announcing that he had been relieved of command of the Army of the James. Before the day was over, "Old Lop Eye" was heading home to Massachusetts to await the receipt of further orders that would never come.[4]

It was perhaps well that the army, especially the African-American portion of it, should not learn of Butler's dismissal until the present mission had ended. The black troops had always regarded him as one of their staunchest friends, in or outside the army. Butler had nurtured them, seeing to it that they received good officers, thorough training, and support resources on a par with those assigned to white units. On the march and in battle, he had tendered them important responsibilities. He had awarded them for their valor. He had even traded white soldiers for an equal number of USCT belonging to another army. Butler may have been no Napoleon, but he had never broken faith with his minority troops, even when it might have been politic to do so. Whatever his faults as a soldier and a person, the blacks of the Army of the James would miss him.

— ◄ ► —

There would be plenty of time for sorrow and regret later; at present, there was an important job for every soldier on this expedition, whatever his race, to do, and do well. One thing they did well was tolerate the long sea voyage and the weather that accompanied it. Off Cape Hatteras, a squall sprang up, rocking and jouncing the vessels and triggering memories of the gales that had menaced the first mission. This time, however, the men rode out the storm without panicking. By the morning of the eighth, the worst was over, and a few hours later the transports arrived safely at the rendezvous point. Once the vessels dropped anchor, Terry was rowed into Beaufort harbor for a get-acquainted session with the navy.

He and Porter hit it off almost immediately. In happy contrast to the Butler-Porter relationship, from the outset Terry and the admiral treated each other with respect and openness, forging a mutually supportive alliance that boded well for the shared enterprise. From the meeting of their minds came a productive plan of attack. On the morning of the twelfth, Porter's men-of-war would renew their bombardment—this time from positions 1,000 yards or less from Fort Fisher's sea face, a distance that would promote accuracy and ensure maximum destructiveness. Other naval vessels, anchored farther north, would cover a landing by all 8,000 of Terry's troops, including the two brigades under Paine.[5]

As soon as the army landed, it would erect heavy works across the peninsula several miles above the garrison. This line would prevent the troops encamped at Sugar Loaf from reinforcing Colonel Lamb. About 6,000 Rebels had gathered in and around the sand dune—not only Bragg's regular force, but also 6,500 additions from Lee's army under Maj. Gen. Robert F. Hoke. These had arrived from Petersburg on December 22 in response to ill-timed reports of Butler's expedition in the New York newspapers. They had remained in position when word came of the Federals' return to Wilmington.[6]

Once Bragg and Hoke had been stymied, Terry would attack Fisher's land face in coordination with Porter's ships. The attack would be a joint effort: While three brigades of white troops struck the northwest angle of the fort, a small contingent of seamen would attack up the beach against the northeast bastion. The sailors' utility was dubious—they would be armed with pistols and cutlasses rather than rifles—but Porter wanted a role in the assault, and Terry, displaying the cooperative spirit, agreed.[7]

Terry's intent to launch his attack using only white troops relegated his USCT to a rear-guard role. Upon landing, Paine's men would build and occupy that line of defense between Sugar Loaf and the garrison. While this position undoubtedly would place the African-Americans, at some point, in conflict with Bragg and Hoke, it would deny them participation in the more critical, more dramatic offensive to the south. Terry's strategy suggested that he did not trust black soldiers on the offensive. If so, his attitude contrasted sharply with that of his predecessor: Butler had intended to use them in the assault on Fisher.

As per Terry's plan, the transports, convoyed by a section of Porter's fleet, sailed from Beaufort on the afternoon of the twelfth. The army spent the night a few miles off Confederate Point as Porter's ships treated Fisher to a devastating cannonade from close-in positions. The guns were still booming the next morning, when the soldiers awakened, grabbed something to eat, and assembled on deck. Minutes later, the men of the 4th USCI and their comrades in Paine's division were again piling into launchboats. Despite a high surf, they made it ashore without difficulty. They alighted near the mouth of Myrtle Sound, a long, shallow stretch of water separated from the ocean by a 100-yard-wide sand spit. The landing site, almost five miles from Fort Fisher, lay about a mile north of the point where Curtis's men had gone ashore on Christmas Day, and not far below Bragg's defenses at Sugar Loaf.[8]

The first troops to land remained in position, confronting Sugar Loaf, until the white troops hit the beach. By 3:00 P.M., more than 8,000 men had been safely deposited on Confederate Point. Already they were poised to attack southward, while also defending against an attack from the north.

But this was not an optimum position from which to safeguard the rear. Originally, Terry had planned to construct a line of works a short distance from Myrtle Sound. The water would anchor the right flank, making unlikely the possibility that Bragg would turn it. An examination of the site, however, revealed that the sound, for a long distance above its head, was too shallow to impede enemy troops at low tide.

Terry decided, instead, to establish a perimeter about a half mile closer to Fisher, where a large pond appeared to provide a barrier to enemy advance. Along with the rest of Paine's division, the 4th USCI was marched to that location and then westward toward the Cape Fear. It was 9:00 P.M. before the USCT reached the river. The long, cautious trek through the darkness went for naught, when Terry discovered the pond to be, in reality, "a sand flat, sometimes covered with water, giving no assistance to the defense of a line established behind it." The men then reconnoitered the area nearer the fort, finding it to be more suited to their purposes. The final choice was a stretch of land only two miles north of the garrison, the right flank of which was anchored by Battery Anderson (or, as the Federals called it, the Flag Pond Battery), a position that Butler's men had captured on December 25.[9]

Already bone-weary from hours of marching and countermarching, the African-Americans were issued entrenching tools and told to start digging. For six hours without respite, they sank shovels into the hard-packed earth of the peninsula, scooping out tons of white sand. Under the critical eyes of Lieutenant Colonel Rogers and Major Boernstein, most of the 4th USCI fashioned rifle pits, while other men, supplied with axes and hatchets, felled scrub pines to supply material for the works themselves.

By 8:00 A.M. on the fourteenth, Terry reported with satisfaction, "a good breast-work, reaching from the river to the sea and partially covered

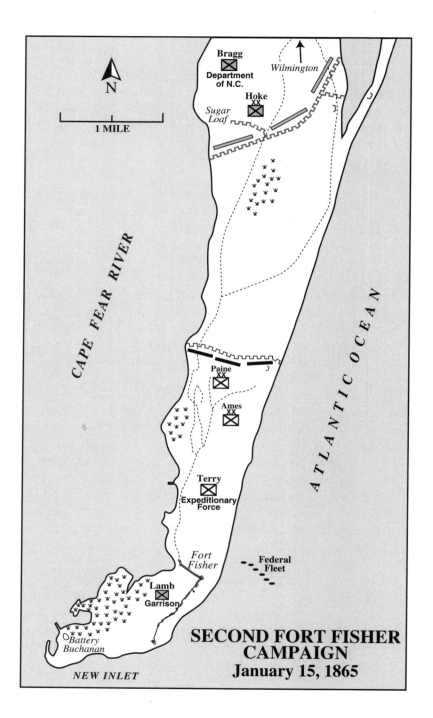

N

1 MILE

Bragg
Department
of N.C.

Wilmington

Hoke
XX

Sugar
Loaf

CAPE FEAR RIVER

ATLANTIC OCEAN

Paine
XX

Ames
XX

Terry
XX
Expeditionary
Force

Fort
Fisher

Federal
Fleet

Lamb
XX
Garrison

Battery
Buchanan

NEW INLET

**SECOND FORT FISHER
CAMPAIGN
January 15, 1865**

by abatis had been constructed and was in a defensible condition. It was much improved afterward, but from this time our foothold on the peninsula was secured." Soon barges were carrying to shore the light artillery component of the expeditionary force. That night, dozens of guns went into position along the works. Most were emplaced near the river; that area, less exposed to the shelling of Porter's ships than the ocean side, was where Bragg and Hoke were most likely to attack.

On the afternoon of the fourteenth, Terry left Paine's division behind and led his white troops into position for the assault on Fisher. Following a meeting with his ranking subordinates, including General Curtis, Terry decided to strike the following day in midafternoon, provided that Porter's guns had knocked enough holes in the recently repaired palisade to provide access to the garrison.[10]

By early evening, with the artillery on line, the men of the 4th had settled down behind their freshly constructed works to try to sleep. Out in the ocean, a few of Porter's gunboats kept up a desultory fire on the garrison, but here on the moonwashed beach, it was quiet and still—ominously so. The men were well aware that although their line was as strong as hours of labor could make it, it was held by only three brigades—their own, Colonel Wright's, and on the far right, stretching as far as the ocean beach, Col. Joseph C. Abbott's four white regiments from Connecticut and New Hampshire. The total force—perhaps 5,000 troops—might find itself, on the morrow, opposed by 8,000 Rebels, including hard-bitten veterans of the Army of Northern Virginia.

This was a scary thought. So, too, was the possibility that, given his presumed bias against using black troops in an offensive role, Terry would be likely to send Abbott's men southward if the rest of the expedition—the three XXIV Corps brigades he had positioned near the fort—failed to capture Fisher. In that event, Paine's troops would face even greater odds in resisting an attack on the Union rear.

❈

If the USCT guarding Terry's rear anticipated big trouble on the fifteenth, they were mistaken—fortunately so. At 8:00, those warships not needed to secure the army's hold on the peninsula again opened on Fisher at close range. The barrage, said Terry, was "magnificent alike for its power and accuracy." The guns did indeed splinter the fort's palisade; they also blew away parts of its earthen walls, while dismounting every cannon but one along the land face. Shortly after 3:00 P.M., when it received a signal from shore, the navy began to concentrate its fire on the southern end of the fort. Minutes later, Terry's leading brigade, Curtis's, charged the northwest angle of the land face, while a force of 2,000 sailors and marines raced up the beach toward the northeast bastion.

Distracted by the navy's attack, Lamb's garrison concentrated its fire on the seamen, enabling Terry's men to sweep over the parapets and through the embrasures. When the Rebels finally confronted them, some of the most ferocious hand-to-hand fighting of the war raged throughout Fisher's interior. When his initial wave bogged down, Terry committed his second brigade, and later, his third. The constantly renewed assault drove Lamb's people from the first four traverses, but then, just before nightfall, it again lost momentum as exhausted attackers sank down behind the positions they had captured, too weary to push farther.[11]

Despite the stubborn resistance of his North Carolinians, by 4:00 Lamb had come to believe that his only hope of holding the fort rested on a successful attack by Bragg on the Union rear. In fact, at that hour, the lead elements of two brigades from Hoke's division were advancing south from Sugar Loaf to test the breastworks Paine's men had thrown up. Already Hoke's superior had received several calls for help, not only from the garrison leader, but also from Lamb's departmental commander, Maj. Gen. William H. C. Whiting (the officer who had failed to attack Butler's rear during the retreat from Drewry's Bluff). Bragg had resisted responding for fear that the gunboats Porter had stationed off Myrtle Sound would break up any advance before it truly got under way. Now, finally, he had been prevailed upon to move, and he had ordered Hoke's men forward.[12]

To the south, the 4th USCI saw lines of Rebel infantry—skirmishers in front, the main body a few hundred feet in rear—emerge from the pine trees south of Sugar Loaf and start toward it. The force expanded in both directions, forming an almost unbroken line stretching the width of the peninsula. At Lieutenant Colonel Rogers's order, the men of the 4th poked the barrels of their Enfields over and through the breastworks, training them on the gray and butternut-colored uniforms moving toward them—but held their fire.

The next few minutes were nerve-wracking. The men of the 4th were not used to remaining unresponsive under provocation—already their works were coming under a skirmish fire. Some in the line feared they would fall before getting off a shot in their own defense. Others hoped—as they did before every fight—that they would not disgrace themselves when the crisis came, allowing their "cowardly legs" to run away with them. Christian Fleetwood recalled the letter he had written his mother and wondered if he would live to retrieve it. But the soldiers of the 4th had become, to a man, disciplined and experienced. They refrained from replying until ordered to do so.

Before them, the Rebels advanced unhurriedly, deliberately, confidently. Everyone in blue could guess what their opponents were thinking: All that stood between them and Fort Fisher was a line of works held mostly by black regiments—one quick thrust and the position would be in Confederate hands, regardless of how many cannons anchored it. Then it was on to Fisher to save the day, the battle, and the city of Wilmington.

But it did not work out that way. The white troops—North Carolinians from the brigades of Brigadier Generals William W. Kirkland and Thomas L. Clingman—drove in the skirmishers posted in advance of the breastworks. Then, closing in, they unleashed a volley at the position before them. The fusillade caused a part of the Union line to waver. Along its east flank, a few of Abbott's troops fell dead and wounded; seconds later, many times as many comrades, although unhurt, abandoned their rifle pits and hastened to the rear.[13]

Shouting in triumph, the Confederates stepped up their pace—only to absorb an extended blast from the other end of the Federal line. Suddenly, it was the attackers who began to stagger. Colonel Ames, Lieutenant Colonel Rogers, and the other commanders having finally given the word, Paine's division had poured an accurate fire into the head of the Rebel line. Beside and behind the USCT, Terry's artillery unleashed rounds of shrapnel and canister—deadly, short-range ammunition that tore holes in the advancing wave. A few men on either side of the 4th's position fell to the enemy fire, but reinforcements stepped up to take their places. The stunned, shot-riddled Confederates did not close up so quickly or so smoothly—their assault had begun to falter.

As the gray line reeled like a drunken sailor, the African-Americans raised their voices in a cheer that dwarfed the Rebel yell the enemy had raised minutes before. The cheering continued as the USCT fired, reloaded, and fired again. The noise was finally drowned out by Porter's offshore gunboats, which began to tear apart the stands of trees that sheltered portions of Hoke's division. One after another, the outsize rounds came howling in on the heads of the enemy. Those that missed human targets struck the beach, filling the air with sand and marsh grass.

The opposition of army and navy proved an unbeatable combination. Less than an hour after they sauntered forth, General Bragg recalled Hoke's troops, some of whom had occupied the trenches abandoned by Abbott's brigade. With apparent reluctance, the troops of Kirkland and Clingman began to retire, firing as they went. When they turned at last to flee, the men of the 4th poured a parting round into them, hurrying them along. Soon the field in front of the works was clear of troops except the dead and wounded. Observing the result of their steadfastness, Paine's men rose up above their works and unleashed another exultant chorus.[14]

The Rebels retreated beyond rifle range, where Hoke had emplaced artillery of his own. For the rest of the day, the opposing cannons carried on the fight, with an occasional salvo from Porter's gunboats thrown in for good measure. With the Union line no longer under threat, Terry was able to detach some of its defenders for service against Fort Fisher, which he did some time after 5:00 P.M. Confirming the suspicions of many, he chose Abbott's white troops, although he supported them closely with the largest USCT regiment on the peninsula, the 27th USCI of Wright's brigade.[15]

The additions provided the margin of victory. Within an hour of being committed to the attack, they drove the remnants of Lamb's garrison out of the fort and onto the beach to the south, where they were trapped and forced to surrender. By 7:00 P.M., the Stars and Stripes were floating over the Confederate Goliath, and the South's most important port was on the verge of being closed—an outcome due as much to the tenacity and courage of the USCT as to any other element of the Army of the James. Dubious racial assumptions aside, Terry had the courage to call the African-Americans' contribution "absolutely essential to our success."[16]

⊶ ≊✦≊ ⊷

When the shooting ceased, Fort Fisher looked like a slaughter pen. Christian Fleetwood, along with other members of the 4th, inspected its interior a few days later. In a letter to his father, the sergeant major spoke of finding "scarcely a square foot of ground without some fragment or unexploded shell." A veteran of several engagements, Fleetwood believed he had seen the worst of war, but he was unprepared for the sights that assailed his eyes as he moved deeper inside the captured earthwork: "Heavy guns bursted, others knocked to pieces as though made of pipeclay, heavy gun carriages knocked to splinters and dead bodies of the rebels lying as they fell with wounds horrible enough to sicken the beholder. Some with half of their heads off, others cut in two, disemboweled and every possible horrible wound that could be inflicted." In the end, his emotions got the best of him: "Oh this terrible war!"[17]

Although he could not have distinguished one from another, Fleetwood was observing not only battle casualties, but also the bodies of men killed in a tragic, and eminently avoidable, accident. The morning after the garrison's surrender, officers had posted guards in those sectors of the fort declared off-limits to the occupiers, especially to prospective looters. Through some mistake, the entrance to the fort's main powder magazine was not sealed off. Incredibly, soldiers and marines bearing torches began to rummage through the boxes of ammunition stored inside. At 7:30 A.M., a tremendous blast shook the fort, hurling sand, debris, and bodies through the air. The force of the explosion was such that within seconds, almost 200 men, including Confederate prisoners, lay dead or dying.[18]

Added to those who had fallen in the attacks, the casualties resulting from the explosion brought the Army of the James's loss on both expeditions to more than 1,000 (a precise count was never arrived at). The navy had added almost 500 casualties to the total, most of them suffered during the doomed attack on the northeast bastion. The Union casualty total was frightful, but it paled in comparison to the approximately 2,300 Confederates who had been killed, wounded, or captured between December 22 and January 15.

The men of the 4th USCI were extremely grateful that their regiment had not contributed to the body count. In fact, the only losses suffered by Paine's division on January 15 were one man killed and four wounded in the 27th USCI. Apparently these occurred when that outfit was moved to the support of Abbott's brigade in the waning hours of the fight.[19]

There was no way to know, of course, how many casualties, if any, the 4th and its comrades would suffer in the days and weeks to come. The city's leading defensive work might have been surmounted, and the navy might have secured a position from which to close the port to blockade runners, but Wilmington itself remained in enemy hands. Terry's troops would have to confront the men under Bragg and Hoke at least once more, and probably more than that, until the Rebels surrendered or fled the area by crossing the Cape Fear. Either outcome would be acceptable to Terry, but either would be difficult to bring about.

At least the casualties Terry had suffered had produced strategic gains. Immediately after Fort Fisher surrendered, Bragg ordered the defenses at the mouth of the Cape Fear, including Forts Caswell, Pender, Campbell, Holmes, and Johnston, evacuated. Their garrisons were removed to the larger and more defensible Fort Anderson, on the west bank of the river. Terry made no immediate advance against Anderson, for he knew that with Hoke's troops within easy reinforcing distance, the garrison was almost as formidable an obstacle as Fisher had been.[20]

Instead of committing himself to an all-out offensive, Terry kept the majority of his troops in and around Fisher, which, in response to advice from Admiral Porter, he sought to restore as a defensive work. In the meantime, he moved to size up the opposition on his side of the river. On January 18, he ordered Colonel Ames to lead the 4th, 6th, and 30th USCI toward Sugar Loaf. Ames was to determine whether Hoke's force remained intact, had crossed the river to reinforce Anderson, or had returned to Virginia. In the end, Terry decided to accompany the column and see for himself.

When the word to march came, Lieutenant Colonel Rogers led the 4th up the peninsula, beyond its battlefield of the fifteenth. About 4:00

P.M., the head of the column drew fire from a contingent of pickets, whom the 4th and some comrades drove back to a well-occupied line of works made of logs and sand. At Ames's order, the march halted, and the men scattered behind whatever cover was available, from which they traded sharpshooter fire with the nearest Rebels. After perhaps a half hour, Terry, who had failed to get a good look at the enemy position due to fading daylight, called off the reconnaissance. Carefully disengaging, the USCT retraced their steps to Fort Fisher. They had lost one man killed and another wounded—none in the ranks of the 4th—while taking an unknown toll of the enemy.[21]

The next morning, Terry launched a second reconnaissance of Sugar Loaf, one he did not accompany. The new effort was conducted by all four of Ames's regiments (the 39th USCI had recently joined the brigade), supported on land by Abbott's brigade and offshore by one of Porter's gunboats. The enlarged column made contact with Hoke's advance early in the afternoon, enabling officers to observe his works in broad daylight. Having advanced up the center and left side of the peninsula, Ames's men, much as on the previous day, dug in and began popping away at the Confederate skirmishers.

For three hours, the 4th and the other USCT kept up a steady fire, pinning down Hoke's main body and enabling Abbott's men to flank it via Myrtle Sound. Covered by the fire of the gunboat, the New Englanders captured some outworks, then penetrated to a point that offered a long, unobstructed view of the enemy line. Several minutes' observation of the force opposing the USCT told Abbott and his subordinates that Sugar Loaf was well defended in terms of both the quality of its works and the number of its occupants. From his own vantage point, General Paine described the position as "quite a strong infantry breast-work, defended from approach by abatis in places; swamps elsewhere, running apparently from Sugar Loaf half a mile to a mile down the river bank; thence easterly toward Myrtle Sound; well manned."

As afternoon merged with evening, the reconnoiterers withdrew to bring the unhappy news to Terry. Gathering darkness enabled the men of the 4th and the rest of the brigade to break contact and retire. They had lost this day one man killed and twelve wounded, including two officers. But the survivors were comforted by the knowledge that again they had withdrawn of their own volition, not through compulsion.[22]

The reports of Paine and Abbott convinced Terry that he would gain nothing by attacking Sugar Loaf with his force on hand; he would await reinforcements before taking on either Hoke's line of defense or Fort Anderson. When General Grant got the news, he decided to display his strong personal interest in Wilmington's capture. In the last week in January, he left the stalemated front outside Petersburg and Richmond and traveled to North Carolina for a conference with Terry and Porter. The meeting produced, or at least refined, a strategy not only for capturing the port city, but also for penetrating the interior of the Tarheel State.[23]

By late January, William T. Sherman's armies were resting in and around Savannah, which they had occupied the previous month. They were about to turn north toward the railroad center at Goldsboro, North Carolina. There Grant wished Terry's troops to make contact with Sherman, reinforcing and resupplying the troops that had carved a path of destruction sixty miles wide from Atlanta to the coast. Grant realized that for Terry to reach Goldsboro, he would have to be reinforced; the lieutenant general had already taken steps to add another corps to the North Carolina theater. Overall command of this force would not go to Terry, even though his capture of Fort Fisher had brought him a brevet major generalship in the volunteer service and the rank of brigadier in the Regular army. The position would go, instead, to Maj. Gen. John M. Schofield, whose XXIII Corps, once an element of Sherman's forces, would join Terry's command (officially designated the X Corps) in a matter of weeks. The combined force would be known as the Department of North Carolina.[24]

By the time the planning conference ended, Schofield's corps was well on its way, by overland march and steamboat, from Tennessee to Virginia. By the last day in January, the entire command had reached Alexandria, although, thanks to delays caused by a frozen Potomac River, its vanguard did not reach Terry's headquarters until February 9.[25]

The combined offensive against Sugar Loaf commenced almost immediately. On the eleventh, the men of the 4th USCI left their camp near Fort Fisher and marched north in regimental strength for the first time in three weeks. The interval had been filled with dreary routine amid the sand dunes and sawgrass of what was known once again, at least among the occupiers, as Federal Point. Only occasionally had the boredom been relieved by fighting—mainly by exchanges of long-range rifle fire with Hoke's pickets. Therefore, like the majority of their African-American and Caucasian comrades, the men of the 4th were looking forward to some activity of purpose.

It came quickly and abundantly. Minutes after moving out, Ames's brigade, which led Terry's advance, encountered a long line of well-entrenched Rebels just south of Sugar Loaf. A major skirmish broke out between the defenders and that part of the brigade that did not include the

4th. In this action, two officers and fourteen men of Paine's division were killed, and seven officers and almost seventy men fell wounded.

For an hour or more, the fighting gyrated back and forth over the whitened earth. The heavy rifle fire pinned down both sides, but being entrenched, the Confederates enjoyed the better position. Not content to remain facedown in the sand, at length Ames brought up the 4th and ordered Lieutenant Colonel Rogers to use as much force as necessary to seize the trench line.

Rogers twirled his sword above his head. The gesture stirred the regiment to its feet in unison, and it went racing toward Sugar Loaf, kicking up clouds of sand. The men came on so fast and with such determination that the startled Rebels fired a parting volley, scrambled out of their holes, and ran. Paine himself noted that the 4th "drove the enemy very handsomely . . . into his main works." Its success enabled the entire division not only to occupy the abandoned pits, but also to stake out a line close enough to Sugar Loaf to hold Hoke's men in place indefinitely. Victory had come at a cost, however: Several members of the 4th had taken wounds, including 1st Lt. Henry G. Mohler of Company B and 2nd Lt. Jacques Noble of Company H. Two months after the fight, both officers were granted medical discharges.[26]

Having helped define the new perimeter, the 4th held a position in advance of it for a week, while other units tried to make headway in other directions. Over the next three days, Terry's white troops, augmented by a XXIII Corps division, tried to outflank Sugar Loaf on the ocean side, only to be foiled by high tides and the quicksand-laden beach in that area. Temporarily conceding failure, Schofield decided to operate, instead, against the far right of Hoke's line. On the sixteenth, while the USCT lashed Hoke with an incessant frontal fire, the new departmental commander crossed two of his divisions, backed by most of Terry's white units, over the Cape Fear and advanced on Fort Anderson. While some of Porter's warships raked the garrison, Schofield sent one division west of the fort and then toward its rear. Before its escape route could be blocked, the garrison evacuated Anderson in the small hours of the nineteenth. The Rebels retreated to Town Creek, eight miles above the fort. Schofield quickly followed and the next day drove the enemy, with heavy loss, from the stream.[27]

Many elements of the combined Union forces shared credit for this outcome; they included the 4th USCI and the other Colored Troops under Paine. By holding Hoke's men on the east side of the Cape Fear, they had ensured Bragg's inability to reinforce Fort Anderson and its outworks. In turn, the fall of Anderson doomed the city of Wilmington by rendering it defenseless.

Soon after sunrise on February 19, the 4th USCI found the Rebel lines in its front strangely silent. Upon inspection, it appeared that Hoke's men had evacuated their works astride the peninsula. When a hasty reconnaissance confirmed the fact, Paine ordered everyone forward, albeit cautiously. Despite his concerns, his men met no opposition. Within minutes, the 4th had occupied the earthworks it had been confronting since landing on Federal Point more than two months before.[28]

The officers and men of the regiment had no time to savor their good fortune; almost as soon as they entered the works, they were ordered in pursuit of the evacuees. The directive came not from Colonel Ames, but from the 4th's old commander, Samuel Duncan, who had rejoined the army the day before. Five months of recuperation from his New Market Heights wound had left Duncan thinner in face and body and a bit unsteady on his still-tender ankle—he admitted to having acquired "an elegant limp." But he was in good spirits, not only happy at being back with his troops, but also thrilled to be sporting shoulder straps that bore the star of a brevet brigadier general of volunteers, a reward for having led his brigade so ably on so many fields.[29]

Duncan's resumption of field service began smoothly enough. Through the balance of the nineteenth, his brigade's northward march proceeded unopposed. The next day, however, his command attracted a brisk fire from Bragg's rear guard. Thereafter, the march continued, but more slowly than before. By about 3:00 in the afternoon, with the head of the brigade within five miles of Wilmington, resistance increased. Snaking forward, scouts from the 4th found an artillery-braced earthwork dead ahead. While the regiment unleashed a continuous fire at its parapets, the 5th USCI was ordered forward on a reconnaissance-in-force. The 5th precipitated a heated skirmish that widened to involve Colonel Wright's brigade. The action inflicted more than fifty Union casualties, including the wounding of Wright himself.[30]

It turned out that the earthwork was defended by at least a half dozen cannons. Wishing to avoid further casualties, and convinced that the position would soon be evacuated, General Paine had the 4th and its comrades erect a new set of breastworks along their most advanced line. The position was held through the rest of the day and well into the twenty-first. As anticipated, that evening the enemy abandoned the field, hauling away its guns. When inspected, the captured post was found to have made such effective use of natural protection that, as Duncan opined, "if well defended, [it] would have made Wilmington almost impregnable."[31]

Again Paine's men occupied the enemy's defenses. They held this latest prize of war throughout the night, aware that with this last barrier gone, they would be inside Wilmington sometime the following morning. Mike Arnold and his comrades discussed the prospect well into the night, asking each other, "How would you like to march through Wilmington tomorrow, February 22d, the anniversary of the birthday of Washington?" The most frequent response: It would be a great day for the Republic, a great day for the African-American people, a great day for the old Army of the James. It would also be, as more than one comrade put it, "the proudest moment of my life."

Arnold described that moment as it unfolded for the men of the 4th USCI:

> The 22d came, and a more lovely day I never saw. By half past six we were on the move . . . and one hour's march brought us on the corporation line of Wilmington, when large volumes of smoke were seen rising in the eastern part of the city. For a time, we thought Hoke had set fire to the city as he went through. But not so. It was the burning of cotton and turpentine at and near the Wilmington and Weldon Railroad. The column halted for a few moments, when the mayor met General Terry, and begged for protection.

> We finally moved, and entered the blockaded city of the Confederacy—the place where all the southern and some of the northern men have made their piles of money—the once [rising] city of the Confederacy, the place noted for its slave market. But now, alas! we march through these fine thoroughfares, where once the slave was forbid[den] being out after nine P.M. . . . Negro soldiers! with banners floating! with their splendid brass bands and drum corps, discoursing the National airs and marches![32]

The very idea of occupying such a historic city—so long an object of the Union armies—was enough to make the men swagger through the streets. "The troops were in the highest spirits," said General Duncan. "They stepped like lords and conquerors." Spirits rose even higher, and pride swelled in the men's chests, when the black people of Wilmington came forth to greet them. "The frantic demonstrations of the negro population," Duncan later recalled, "will never die out of my memory. Their cheers and heartfelt 'God bless ye's' & cries of 'De chains is broke; De chains is broke,' mingled sublimely with the lively shouts of our brave soldiery that welled up as they caught sight of the 'Old Glory' floating again over the dwellings of the loyal citizens."[33]

The extent of the welcome amazed and touched the enlisted men. "Cheer after cheer they gave us," Arnold reported of the city's black residents. "They had prayed long for their deliverance, and the 22d day of February, 1865, realized their earnest hopes. . . . The streets were crowded with them, old and young; they shook hands with the troops, and some exclaimed . . . 'Freedom today!' 'Hurrah for Uncle Abe!'"

On almost every corner, the people tried to force on the passing troops whatever gifts they had to offer—bread and meat, boxes of tobacco, pails of water. A middle-aged woman, tears streaming down her cheeks, broke from the crowd to embrace her son, a corporal in the 4th, whom she had not seen in three years. She beamed with pride at the sight of the young man who "had left his home a slave, but had returned in the garb of a Union soldier, free, a man." A little farther on, the column passed a crowd literally jumping for joy. One of the group, a man who gave his age as ninety-three, explained that he had been too sick to leave his house for seven months, "but hearing the music of the Union troops, it had revived him, and he felt so happy that he came out, and there he stood, with his long white locks and his wrinkled cheeks, saying, 'Welcome, welcome!'"

Although most of the soldiers passed through the city without stopping, a few were assigned to duty as members of the occupation force. Among them was Chaplain Hunter, who, soon after entering, repaired to the city's leading African-American church, Zion Hill A.M.E., whose history dated to the mid-eighteenth century. Since the erection of its present edifice, the congregation had lacked a black pastor—local slave codes decreed that the people, who owned the ground and had financed construction of the church, could not hold services unless a white minister presided.

This state of affairs ended on Sunday, March 5, 1865. At 8:00 that evening, the worshipers—including a few curious whites—assembled to hear the chaplain of the 4th USCI preach the first sermon ever delivered there by an African-American clergyman. Corporal Arnold, who was also in attendance, noted that Hunter strode to the altar "robed in his army uniform," raiment that "failed, I am sure, to please the eye of one or two Secesh Gents, who came, not to hear him preach, but to see what was going to be done by the Negroes." When the guest preacher began to speak, "eloquence never flowed so freely. . . . Few in the church could say their eyes were dry. Mr. Hunter himself was born a slave on this very soil; sixteen years previously he left the state a slave. But now he had come to the land of his birth an officer in the United States Army. Was not that congregation of citizens proud of him . . . ?"

Hunter's text, which he drew from his beloved Book of Psalms, could not have been more appropriate to the occasion: "Sing unto the Lord a new song, for he hath done marvelous things, with his right arm he hath given him the victory."[34]

CHAPTER 10

The Last Long Year

ALTHOUGH MORE THAN TWO MONTHS WOULD PASS BEFORE THE WAR IN North Carolina ended, everything that followed the occupation of Wilmington smacked of anticlimax. As a result of the city's fall, a noose was tightening around the neck of Bragg's army, and breathing air would soon be gone. The situation was much the same in other theaters of operations. By late February, Grant and Meade were getting closer to turning Lee's right and seizing control of his last lifeline. In the Shenandoah, Sheridan was preparing to strike yet again at the pitiful remnant of Early's army, this time with a death blow. And Sherman's legions were approaching the North Carolina line, having departed occupied Charleston, cradle of secession and scene of the war's opening shots.[1]

The forces of the Confederacy had run out of maneuvering room, and nearly out of hope. But their opponents realized that this was no time to let up. On the twenty-second, after passing through Wilmington, Paine's command, preceded by Abbott's brigade, marched ten miles beyond the city. Late in the morning, the head of the column overtook the rear of Bragg's troops just below the northeastern branch of the Cape Fear (also known as the Northeast River), and skirmishing broke out anew. After making a brief stand, the secessionists retreated across the Wilmington and Weldon Railroad bridge over Smith's Creek, which they set afire. To their astonishment, reckless Yankees from Abbott's brigade dashed through the flames, gained the other side, shoved the defenders out of the way, doused the fire with water from the stream, and saved the bridge. The pursuers crossed in force to precipitate a running fight that stretched as far as Northeast Station, nine miles above Smith's Creek.[2]

Abbott's men again struck the Rebel rear just north of the station, as Bragg's main body crossed the river on pontoons at McRee's Ferry. Although the New Englanders tried to disrupt the crossing, they were held too far from the river to do maximum harm. At length, Terry ordered Duncan to break the stalemate. The brevet brigadier selected his old regiment for the job, and he went in beside it as the 4th, supported by a battery, pressed the Rebel right flank. The regiment shoved so mightily that the rear guard abandoned its position and scurried over the floating bridge.

From across the stream, angry Rebels sprayed the 4th's position with rifle balls. In a letter to his prospective fiancée, Julia Jones, Duncan waxed poetic about his reaction: "For a half hour I rode amid the dripping patter of the leaden rain, for a minute and a half amid the thickest of the bursting shower, and yet came out without the smell of fire upon my garments."[3]

After crossing, the Confederates tried to dismantle their bridge, but it fell into the hands of the pursuers, who repaired it the next day. Before the Federals could renew the chase, however, Bragg retreated toward Goldsboro under a full head of steam. There he hoped to add his troops to the remnants of the once-powerful Army of Tennessee, which had escaped from its namesake state to regroup in North Carolina under Joseph E. Johnston.[4]

After a brief attempt to follow, Bragg's opponents let him go. With the Rebels now far from Wilmington, the job assigned to Terry's command was over, at least for a spell. Accordingly, the Federals fell back from the river and went into camp. The 4th and the other USCT remained in and around Northeast Station for three weeks, consolidating their recent gains and allowing other forces to carry on the fighting. Soon after Bragg's retreat, Schofield sent portions of his corps inland to New Bern and Morehead City, preparatory to securing Goldsboro as a rendezvous for Sherman's advancing troops. Early in March, Schofield moved two more divisions toward Kinston. After overcoming the desperate resistance of Bragg, the various wings of the XXIII Corps united, and on the fourteenth they occupied abandoned Kinston. They rebuilt ruined bridges over the Neuse River, crossed on them, and entered Goldsboro, against light opposition, on the evening of March 21.[5]

While Bragg fought and retreated, Johnston made plans to waylay Sherman before he could reach Goldsboro from the south. On March 19, three days after an indecisive clash between one of Sherman's wings and one of Johnston's corps at Averasboro, North Carolina, Johnston encountered the same Union column near Bentonville. For a time, Sherman's men were in danger of overthrow and defeat, but after weathering a series of assaults, they compelled the frustrated Confederates to fall back. Two days later, after an engagement near Mill Creek, Johnston withdrew to Smithfield, minus 2,600 casualties—men he could not afford to lose. Although sporadic fighting continued for another five weeks, Bentonville and Mill Creek essentially ended the war in North Carolina. No longer impeded,

Sherman headed for Goldsboro to link with Schofield and create a force nearly 100,000 strong.[6]

Having spent three weeks enjoying what General Duncan called "a rather lazy life," on March 15 the forces under Terry moved to join the convergence toward Goldsboro. That morning, the majority of the troops who had helped capture Fort Fisher moved northwestward, heading for the line of the Wilmington and Weldon Railroad. "Marching to the roar of Sherman's guns," as Duncan put it, the 4th USCI and the balance of Paine's division reached South Washington on the seventeenth, Island Creek the next day, and the Kenansville vicinity on the nineteenth. The 4th spent the journey passing "thro' pine forests, wading swamps, [and] traversing extensive plantations." Many estates lay in ruins, symbolic of the fate of the Southern economy, but they retained enough prewar symbolism to make the men shudder. Duncan observed, "The blighting influences of slavery are all around me. The institution of slavery is simply damnable. No wonder that the seven vials of wrath are being poured out upon our country because of its tolerance of such an abominable system."[7]

On the twentieth, following a twenty-mile trek, Terry's vanguard, including Duncan's brigade, reached Cox's Bridge on the Neuse, the main gate to Goldsboro. Across the river was a heavy picket, the advance element of the small force guarding the city and its environs. Oblivious to the danger, that night Duncan ferried his brigade over the river aboard pontoons. On the other side, his men began to entrench. After digging what must have seemed like its thousandth line of rifle pits, the 4th helped the rest of Terry's command erect an extensive set of breastworks along the stream.

The USCT held the works until the evening of the twenty-third, when the men of Sherman and Schofield clasped hands in the city. Terry's column had joined, wrote Duncan, "the all-conquering army that is now sweeping like an avalanche over the domains of the rebellion." The following day, he withdrew his brigade from the Neuse and marched to Faison's Depot.[8]

The men remained along the Wilmington and Weldon until April 10. During that time, joyous news reached the camp of the 4th USCI: On the first, the Armies of the Potomac and the James had broken through Lee's right flank at Five Forks; on the second, they had cut the Southside Railroad; and on the third, both Richmond and Petersburg had fallen. Evacuees were heading west, with the troops of Meade and Ord (Butler's successor) baying at their heels. It seemed likely that the fighting in Virginia would be over in a few days—a week, at most.[9]

The vision of impending triumph lightened the men's steps when, early on the tenth, the 4th USCI broke camp at Faison's Depot and headed northwest toward Bentonville. The next day, the outfit passed the recent battlefield, still littered with the flotsam of combat. Four days later, after a series of "easy marches," Terry's column reached the destination Sherman had assigned it, the state capital at Raleigh. The troops went into camp a mile south of the place, excited by the recently received news of Lee's surrender to Grant at Appomattox Court House. Some members of the 4th probably felt pangs of regret that they had not been on hand to contribute to the pursuit that blocked the path and broke the spirit of the Army of Northern Virginia. Even so, the regiment was gratified to learn that thousands of its comrades in the Army of the James, including the USCT division led by the 4th's original commander, William Birney, had played a major role in overtaking Lee and forcing his capitulation.[10]

The 4th and its brothers in Paine's command had not missed out on all the honors. On the morning of the twentieth, the USCT were marched out of camp and through the streets of Raleigh, where they passed in review before Sherman, his ranking subordinates, and his staff. The celebratory nature of the event pleased the regiment, whose only regret was that a large number of its men, lying dead in shallow graves or lying ill in the wards of army hospitals, were not on hand to join in. Christian Fleetwood, for one, was back in Wilmington, where, wracked by typhoid fever, he had been admitted to the U.S. Army General Hospital for Colored Troops. He was still abed a week later when the Medal of Honor he had won for rescuing the colors at New Market Heights reached him. He must have thought it ironic that although he had emerged unscathed from a shower of rifle balls, some miasmic vapor had left him flat on his back and as weak as a baby.[11]

⊷ ⊰⊱ ⊶

The war in North Carolina ended not with a bang, but with two peace parleys. On April 18, Sherman and Johnston met near Durham Station, northwest of Raleigh, and signed a surrender memorandum. Instead of confining himself to military matters, however, Sherman usurped his superiors' prerogatives by setting postwar occupation policy. Only four days before, Abraham Lincoln had been assassinated at Ford's Theater in Washington, and his successor, Andrew Johnson, was in no mood to be conciliatory. He and Secretary of War Stanton rejected the terms Sherman had offered his opponent and nullified the peace agreement.

The administration's action enraged Sherman, but he was forced to abide by it. The generals met again at Durham Station on the twenty-sixth, the day Union troops cornered and killed Lincoln's murderer, John Wilkes

Booth. This time Sherman and Johnston worked out terms acceptable to the president, his war secretary, and General Grant, and hostilities ceased throughout the state.[12]

Johnston's surrender immediately placed the Union forces in North Carolina on occupation duty. Two days after the second peace conference, the men of Paine's command were notified of a pending movement. At 7:00 A.M. on the twenty-ninth, they started back to Goldsboro. The trip appeared to give the high command pause: Now that hostilities were officially ended, it was feared the USCT might break free of wartime restraints to trespass, assault, and loot. Duncan was enjoined to place a guard at virtually every house on his route, "and allow no one to interfere in the slightest degree with the persons or property of the residents." The order indicated the low opinion that their own commanders sometimes entertained of the discipline and deportment of the USCT.[13]

Soon after the regiment reached Goldsboro and set up camp on the city's outskirts, it found itself without its leader. Even before the fighting terminated, Lieutenant Colonel Rogers had submitted his resignation in order to return to Ohio to tend to unspecified "interests at home." The departmental commander, Schofield, accepted the resignation on April 28, and soon afterward Rogers, by then a brevet brigadier general, bade farewell to the officers and men he had commanded so ably for the past twenty months.[14]

Upon his departure, Major Boernstein took over the regiment on a permanent basis—after July 8, as lieutenant colonel. While at Goldsboro, in fact, the 4th experienced a command shake-up, the product of a wave of officer promotions. An omnibus "war service" promotion decree, backdated to March 13, made a brevet colonel of Wareham Hill, who, upon Boernstein's promotion, succeeded to the full rank of major. The same brevet was bestowed upon the hard-working Surgeon Mitchell, while Sidney Mendall and the one-armed James Hoag, a captain since the previous November, won the brevet of lieutenant colonel. Mendall and Hoag thereby joined Captain Parrington, who had been breveted lieutenant colonel at the close of 1864. The same order made brevet majors of the heroic Captain Appleton, as well as Capt. John J. Eberhardt (Company D); First Lieutenants James M. Bradley (C), Horace L. Piper (F), and Zenas F. Wilber (K); and 2nd Lt. Reuben A. Schofield (H). Quartermaster Barnes became a brevet captain, as did 1st Lt. S. Walter Reynolds (H) and Second Lieutenants William H. Greene (B) and John H. McCullough (G).[15]

In the early weeks of occupation duty, regiments experienced sudden, and sometimes frequent, shifts of duty stations. At 5:00 A.M. on June 3, the

Bvt. Capt. S. Walter Reynolds
LIBRARY OF CONGRESS

4th USCI left Goldsboro for New Bern. Soon after camping on the outskirts of that coastal city, some members of the 4th noticed that their new leader seemed to have undergone a change of personality. Although Boernstein had a reputation as a firm but honest leader, within weeks of succeeding Rogers, he developed what appeared to be an inflexible, dictatorial approach to command. On occasion, and without explanation, the little Austrian would confine the entire regiment to camp. When issuing orders restricting access to the city, he would word them in such a manner as to imply that the men were nothing but thieves and rioters. More than once, he took steps to forestall what he interpreted as an impending mutiny. He never revealed the basis of his actions.[16]

Boernstein made a practice of berating the men for crimes real and imagined. On one occasion, he excoriated the regiment for its appearance at guard mounting, which he seemed to take as a personal affront. His remedy was to subject the camp guards to detailed inspections, not only by their company commanders, but also by officers specially detailed for that purpose. At other times, he appeared to carry on vendettas against officers

Bvt. Maj. John J. Eberhardt
LIBRARY OF CONGRESS

he did not admire, especially Lieutenant Holcombe. Early in June, he arrested the subaltern—Boernstein had never forgiven him for reporting himself injured by that shell "rolling over his back" at Dutch Gap—on a trumped-up charge of being AWOL. Two weeks later, Boernstein again ordered the officer arrested, this time for disobedience of orders and "contemptuous conduct towards his superior officer." That same month, when he learned of Holcombe's appointment as captain, Boernstein refused to acknowledge the promotion. Until the day, weeks later, when Holcombe's commission arrived in the mail, Boernstein continued to address him orally, and in writing, by the lower rank. Then, too, he reduced an unusual number of noncommissioned officers, including the estimable John Hance, to the ranks for trivial infractions.[17]

Such erratic behavior made some observers wonder if the new lieutenant colonel was taking out on them his resentment at being passed over for higher rank by brevet. Others attributed his change of personality to drinking—the same vice he condemned, time and again, in published orders. While at New Bern, Boernstein arrested several subordinates for this offense, including Brevet Captain McCullough and Second Lieutenants Harry C. Sherriff (Company C) and Frank Richmond (D). McCullough fought the charge, weathered the storm, and served out his time with the 4th. At Boernstein's urging, however, Sherriff was dropped from the rolls of the regiment and Richmond was cashiered. Of course, if the bottle turned out to be Boernstein's problem as well, sooner or later it would affect his career in the same way.[18]

Those officers and men who did not take kindly to Boernstein's rule doubted they would be rid of him soon. As General Duncan had observed during the 4th's time at Goldsboro, although Sherman's regiments had headed north for a gala review in Washington, D.C., prior to being returned to their home states for muster-out, the X and XXIII Corps had been tabbed for an indefinite tour in North Carolina. He predicted accurately that "the Colored regts. will probably be retained in the service longest of the volunteer forces." The only reprieve the regiment got was short-lived: In July, Boernstein was appointed provost marshal of the local military district. But the lieutenant colonel devoted only part of his time to his additional responsibilities; he refused to delegate his regimental duties to Major Hill.[19]

Boernstein's evident belief that he had to rule with a heavy hand was strengthened by some dramatic incidents that occurred while at New Bern. There the regiment was saddled not only with the usual duties of occupation service, but also with the task of augmenting local law enforcement officials. The men did not always shoulder their police duties effectively. For example, the laxity of enlisted men posted as guards made possible a jailbreak from the Craven Street prison; Boernstein personally headed the panel that investigated the escape and punished those responsible.[20]

On a few occasions, members of the regiment did violence to local citizens, especially merchants who discriminated against them or subjected them to racial slurs. One day when off-duty, Pvt. Landin Edmunds of Company B accompanied two comrades to a downtown saloon. Apparently the trio took their Enfields with them, for, as one man recounted, Edmunds "thought he was not waited on quick enough, and had some words with him [the saloonkeeper] and shot him." When local authorities arrived, the assailant may have compounded his crime by resisting arrest. Assuredly, Boernstein came down hard on Edmunds, although his punishment is unknown.[21]

As a result of these and other, similar, if less violent, incidents, Boernstein blasted the regiment for the "considerable ill-feeling manifested by the men of the command towards the civil authorities. Insults and threats of the gravest character have been uttered towards men who were simply doing their duty. Even violence has been done by soldiers of this command against those who represent the law. Such a state of things can not and will not be tolerated in this regiment." One remedy was to bar enlisted men from visiting the city without a pass from the lieutenant colonel himself or from the local provost marshal. Also, he curtailed the popular practice by which some officers resided not in camp but in New Bern; in the future, the "officers' mess would be the men's mess."[22]

One possible reason for the occasional lawlessness the 4th displayed was the men's growing boredom with occupation duty. Life at New Bern became even bleaker after popular officers such as Captain Wickes and Assistant Surgeon Wharry sent in their resignations, Wickes in order to resume his studies at Harvard, Wharry to return to private medical practice. Wharry's departure was ill timed, for the regiment's medical staff was already overtaxed. The many diseases endemic to coastal North Carolina in spring and summer contributed to a lengthy sick list. At times, no more than a couple hundred men were well enough to pull duty.[23]

The resignation the men regretted most was that of Chaplain Hunter, who left the regiment on July 19 to return to his ministry in Baltimore. With his leave-taking, not only did regular religious services cease, so too did the education classes Hunter had kept up for the benefit of the men of the 4th as well as for local African-American children and adults.[24]

With Hunter gone, some of the regiment's spirit seemed to die, while complaints increased. As summer ended, one semiliterate member of the 4th—doubtless one of Hunter's students—made bold to address a list of grievances to Secretary of War Stanton:

> [The 4th] came out in 1[8]63 as Vlent hearted men for the Sacke of our Surffring Courntury & Sibnce that time things has changs a Round. . . . Ever Since we have bin a Laying here at this awlfull & Deserble & Forceaken Place We have bin a Surffring in Terrable condision. We hvent a 150 men for Duty & the officers are a Reporting 400 men for Duty & they cant Rates a Relefe of guard. We have men that bin on Duty now fo Near Two months havent bin Releve from guard & when we Put men on guard in Town we hafto Leve them there for a Weeke at a Time & I Know that it tis not milertary to Keepe men on guard Longer [than] 48 Hours at the Longes. & we have bin a careing has high as five & Six men to the Hosopital in a Day. . . . We have come out Like men & we Expected to be Treated as men but we have ben treated more Like Dogs then men.

The soldier went on to criticize the 4th's current venue (a man could not go "a Houndred yards from camp without getting into a Swamp"), the unhealthiness of the region ("We are Surounded with Ponds chills & fevers & Deseasses of Every Kind"), and the "Duble prices" charged by the sutler. He suggested no specific remedies for the problems he and his comrades encountered on a daily basis, nor is it likely he expected his complaints to result in improved conditions. It appears that he merely wished to get certain things—quite a few things—off his chest.[25]

Presumably by coincidence, the regiment underwent major changes ten days after the unknown complainant wrote Edwin Stanton. On October 10, the 4th was ordered to strike camp, turn in its tents, and assemble at the local steamboat landing. Within hours, it was on its way down the Neuse River and out into the ocean. Five days later, a much-interrupted journey on the high seas ended with the 4th in Alexandria, Virginia. From there the men trekked overland to what would be their last duty station in the army, the defenses of Washington, D.C.

Samuel Duncan had been prescient when predicting that the Colored Troops would be kept in service longer than most of their white comrades. By the end of 1865—five months after the XXIV Corps had officially ceased to exist—only a handful of Caucasian regiments in the Army of the James remained in the field, most of them on Reconstruction duty in middle Virginia. These units would be mustered out the following January and February. Much of the army's USCT strength, however, would be kept on active duty for almost another year.[26]

The War Department had decided it needed a ready reserve of volunteers to augment the still-minuscule Regular army in event of a crisis. Unrepentant Rebels in the Deep South might rise up, requiring troops to suppress them on a scale short of all-out hostilities. Then, too, war clouds appeared to be hovering on America's southern flank. While North and South had been fighting each other, the French had invaded Mexico, installing a puppet government in Mexico City in violation of the Monroe Doctrine. As a result, many of the 4th's old comrades in the XXV Army Corps were now patrolling the Rio Grande, showing the flag for benefit of the French and their local allies and giving covert assistance to Mexican nationalists.[27]

The War Department knew that if it were to keep white volunteers in service well beyond their appointed term of "three years or the duration of the war," it risked the wrath of voters and their political representatives.

Not surprisingly, the War Office preferred to alienate African-Americans troops, few of whom could vote and even fewer of whom wielded political power. Moreover, many black soldiers—especially former slaves—had no homes to return to once they left the service. They would be unlikely to object to being kept on the army's payroll indefinitely.

The army resisted committing too much of its strength to a single venue, such as south Texas. Instead, it desired to concentrate a certain amount of its manpower—especially the African-American portion of it— in Washington, where it would be available for short-notice deployments to trouble spots anywhere in the country. Thus, on the fifteenth of October, the men of the 4th USCI were distributed among several of the twenty-some forts that encircled the District of Columbia, most of which had been constructed during the war.

Lieutenant Colonel Boernstein and Major Hill established regimental headquarters at Fort Slocum, on the northern edge of the District. At the same time, Companies A and I were assigned to Fort Sumner, Company B to Fort Totten, Companies C and H to Fort Stevens (where, in July 1864, Abraham Lincoln had come under enemy fire when observing a near-successful attack on the capital by Jubal Early's Confederates), Company D also to Fort Slocum, Company E to Fort Lincoln, Company F to Fort Mahan, and Companies G and K to Fort Reno. The following month, Company I left its new post to garrison Fort Stanton, and in December, four of the other units switched locations. With these exceptions, the initial duty-station assignments prevailed for the duration of the regiment's seven-month service in Washington.[28]

By all accounts, this was a trying period for officers and men alike—at least, those who wanted out of the service. For one thing, the army had curbed its eagerness to accept officer's resignations. Throughout the regiment's stint in the capital, it appears that only one commissioned officer, 2nd Lt. George Sells of Company A, was permitted to resign and go home. Noncommissioned officers and private soldiers lacked the opportunity to apply for discharge on grounds other than disability due to wounds or illness.[29]

The more dedicated soldiers did not try to leave the army, even when truly ill. In fact, when Christian Fleetwood was returned to the hospital after a recurrence of typhoid fever, he fled his sickbed the very day he was admitted, walked back to Fort Slocum, and resumed his duties. Because he had left the hospital without permission, for a time the sergeant major was officially listed as a deserter. When his case was looked into, however, the charge was removed from his record.[30]

Fleetwood's steadfastness, his habit of doing his duty without cavil or complaint, was very much the exception to the rule in the 4th USCI.

Officers of the 4th U.S. Colored Infantry, at Fort Slocum, D.C., ca. October 1865. U.S. ARMY MILITARY HISTORY INSTITUTE

Throughout their garrison tour, most of the men declared their distaste for one aspect or another of their service. They muttered and grumbled about hardships real or fancied, including the dull, onerous routine; their confinement to damp, drafty, and generally unhealthy quarters; and the difficulty of obtaining leave to visit their homes, even though Baltimore lay only fifty miles to the north.

The men had at least one thing to cheer about. Within six weeks of arriving in Washington, they were relieved of a major source of discontent—Augustus Boernstein. This came about as a result of the lieutenant colonel's mistaken belief that in Washington, as in North Carolina, his authority extended to the local constabulary. Only a day or so after establishing himself at Fort Slocum, Boernstein broke up an altercation between some of his men and a few African-American residents of the district. He tried to take into custody a civilian who had assaulted his troops, but the man took refuge with a member of the Metropolitan Police. According to a legal deposition, when the policeman refused to surrender the assailant, Boernstein "did with oaths and threats of violence, demand the delivery of said colored man to his hands."

Enlisted men of Company E, 4th U.S. Colored Infantry, at Fort Lincoln, D.C.,
ca. October 1865. U.S. ARMY MILITARY HISTORY INSTITUTE

Such behavior could have damaged Boernstein's career, but he brought greater trouble upon himself a week later by getting drunk at a bar near the local Soldiers' Home and then displaying his condition before several enlisted men. After that, he mounted his horse—rather unsteadily, one assumes—and rode through the streets of the city at top speed, "endangering the lives of passers upon the said highway" and calling "attention to his drunken condition." It was bad enough that he frightened private citizens, but he made the fatal mistake of nearly running down the army's surgeon general.

On December 1, Boernstein was arraigned before a general court martial on five charges: drunkenness to the prejudice of good order and military discipline, conduct to the same end, conduct unbecoming an officer and a gentleman, violation of the Thirty-second Article of War (relative to his attempt to overawe civilian authority), and use of contemptuous and disrespectful language against the president (when the policeman had explained by whose authority he had taken custody of the assailant, Boernstein supposedly exclaimed: "God damn the President of the United States, and the whole police force!").

The accused was found guilty of four of the charges, being acquitted—apparently on a technicality—of violating the Thirty-second Article. The court ordered him dismissed from the service, a sentence duly carried out. So ended a career marked by gallantry in combat and erratic, self-defeating behavior off the battlefield.[31]

Fortunately for the 4th USCI, one week before Boernstein's sentence was handed down, it reacquired a commander who enjoyed the respect and esteem of the entire outfit.

After the close of hostilities in North Carolina, Samuel Duncan had been named commander of the District of New Bern, a desk job that insulated him from the day-to-day activities of his brigade. Early in September, he had taken leave of the army to return home to attend to personal business—including proposing marriage to Julia Jones. Having won the hand of his beloved, he had returned to New Bern on the very day the 4th left the city for Washington.[32]

Duncan, who by now had been advanced to brevet major general of volunteers, believed the regiment had been sent north as a prelude to muster-out. Because he still held the full rank of colonel, he would have to leave the service at the same time as the 4th. Thus he requested relief from district command, that he might join the outfit in the Washington defenses. On November 23, after much delay, he reached the capital and resumed command of the outfit for the first time in a year and a half. He found, to his delight, that muster-out was not imminent. He had no immediate prospect of civilian employment—he would not, or could not, return to Dartmouth—and he needed his army pay to finance his wedding.[33]

At first everyone regarded Duncan's leadership as a welcome change from the Boernstein regime. Many of his early actions were universally popular. He cleared the names of many who, like Fleetwood, had been erroneously identified as deserters. He refused to order the arrest of conscripts who failed to join the regiment, arguing that many simply had failed to receive their draft notices. Early in 1866, through his efforts, the regiment regained its fine band, which Duncan ordered to play at regimental headquarters for at least a half hour each afternoon, as well as during reveille, retreat, and taps. He gave the unscrupulous Sutler Cooper his comeuppance, levying on him a merchandise tax in excess of $800, most of which went into the Regimental Fund. And on those occasions when forced to discipline or punish wrongdoers, he appeared to do so reluctantly. When, for instance, he reduced to the ranks Sgt. Elijah Ash of Company F for going AWOL and disobeying orders, Duncan publicized his regret at "the necessity for making such an example of so capable a soldier." This gesture would have been alien to his predecessor.[34]

Early in the new year, however, Duncan was forced to rule with a heavier hand. At this juncture, nearly a year after Lee's surrender, the men were becoming not only bored and restless, but also angry and unruly. Their unhappiness over their prolonged service showed itself in incidents of flagrant disobedience and even near-mutiny—drastic behavior of the sort Boernstein had taken draconian measures to preempt. To keep the situation in hand, Duncan resorted to swift and severe action. January and February witnessed a noticeable increase in the number of enlisted men punished for being absent without leave, refusing to obey lawful orders, and exhibiting conduct prejudicial to good order. The period also coincided with an increase in the number of noncoms who lost their stripes for various offenses. The regiment's bad behavior culminated in six enlisted men of Company F being court-martialed for inciting to mutiny. Sgt. Charles Linghams, Corp. William Matthews, and Privates Joseph Carroll, William Clayton, William Hall, and John Steward were sentenced to three months' hard labor in ball and chain.[35]

After the mutineers were removed from the regiment, the unrest in the ranks appeared to diminish—so much so that early in March, Duncan felt able to take another extended leave in New Hampshire. Before departing, he had the satisfaction of learning that two members of Company A, Privates Thomas Dodson and Arthur Simmons, had been assigned to the elite unit that guarded the White House and its occupants.[36]

The 4th USCI served out its final two months of garrison duty in relative tranquillity. Upon his return from leave in April, Duncan learned that preparations were under way for the 4th's muster-out. The War Department had decided that some USCT outfits could be dispensed with without endangering the republic. Accordingly, late that month, the officers closed out the accounts of their companies and took a final inventory of weapons, equipment, and supplies. By mid-April, the regiment had been relieved of duty in the District of Washington. As of month's end, the companies had been removed from their posts and grouped at the local Soldiers' Rest.[37]

There the formal process of mustering out the regiment took place on the morning of May 4, 1866. A few days later, the men were returned by train to Baltimore, where, on or about the tenth of the month, they received their discharge papers. Thereupon every enlisted man, with the apparent exception of the two privates posted to the White House, became, once again, a civilian. For a few soldiers, the transition was temporary; they returned to active duty two months later, when the army was expanded to include four regiments (two of infantry and two of cavalry) composed of black enlisted men. That veterans of the war should so quickly return to a life that had so often discomfited and frustrated them is not surprising: African-Americans, no matter where they resided, enjoyed limited occupational opportunities, and few had employable skills beyond those they had acquired while in uniform.[38]

Given the pervasive racial discrimination of American society, relatively few of those who left the 4th USCI prospered, professionally or financially, in civilian life. Most returned to unskilled or semiskilled jobs as laborers, cooks, bricklayers, longshoremen, waiters—the same low-paying occupations they had quit when joining the army. The more talented and accomplished veterans did better. Both Christian Fleetwood and Michael Arnold acquired jobs as clerks and bookkeepers and settled comfortably into middle-class black society.[39]

Perhaps not surprisingly, of them all Fleetwood appears to have enjoyed the most varied, productive, and remunerative postwar career. For a time during the war, he had considered making soldiering his profession. Thoughts of joining the regular army had died in late 1864, however, when he failed to gain the commission the officers of his regiment believed him entitled to. In later months, he came to doubt that the military offered the best way of life for members of his race. As he explained to his former employer in June 1865:

> A double purpose induced me and most others to enlist, to assist in abolishing slavery and to save the country from ruin. Something in furtherance of both objects we have certainly done and now it strikes me that more could be done for our welfare in the pursuits of civil life. I think that a camp life would be decidedly an injury to our people. No matter how well & faithfully they may perform their duties they will shortly be considered as "lazy nigger sojurs" [and] as drones in the great hive.[40]

After his discharge, the erstwhile sergeant major began a job search that took him to Columbus, Ohio, where he landed a bookkeeping position in a wholesale grocery firm. When the company folded in 1867, he returned east to settle in Washington, D.C., where he entered government service, first as a clerk for the United States Supreme Court, then as an employment agent in the Freedmen's Bureau. Both jobs were of short duration; later that same year, he returned to the private sector as a sales assistant for a realty company. He landed more steady employment when, in 1867, he accepted a clerkship in the office of the registrar of the District of

*Christian A. Fleetwood after the
war, wearing Medal of Honor*
LIBRARY OF CONGRESS

Columbia. Two years later, he transferred to a job in the district's tax collection bureau. In 1871, he began a ten-year stint as a bookkeeper in the Washington branch of the Freedmen's Savings and Trust Company. In 1881, he returned to clerking, this time in the War Department. He remained in that position until his death in the capital on September 28, 1914.

In November 1869, Fleetwood married Sarah Iredell of Washington, one of the first registered nurses of African-American ancestry in the District of Columbia, as well as an accomplished musician. The couple reared two children, who became teachers in the Washington, D.C., school system. In later years, it was said of the Fleetwoods that they "led an active social life, always in the best society." At their Fifteenth Street home, the couple entertained leading lights of the military, political, and literary worlds, including the civil-rights spokesman Frederick Douglass, the future U.S. senator and Pulitzer Prize–winning biographer William Cabell Bruce, the poet Paul Lawrence Dunbar, and "other interesting people."

Despite the disappointments he experienced on active duty, Fleetwood never lost his interest in things military. In 1880, at the request of a group of young men who had formed an infantry organization, he became captain of the militia unit that evolved from it. Known as the Washington Cadet Corps, the unit grew under his leadership to form a battalion, four companies strong, "fully officered and uniformed and having their own brass band of thirty pieces, able to parade two hundred rifles at a couple hours' notice." Under now-Major Fleetwood, the battalion became, in 1887, the first National Guard unit in the nation to be composed exclusively of African-Americans. Under his efficient supervision, it won several drill competitions and in 1898 provided the nucleus of an all-black regiment that, when the Spanish-American War ended, was being considered for service in Cuba or the Philippines.[41]

Postwar accomplishments notwithstanding, virtually every member of the 4th United States Colored Infantry considered his service from 1863 to 1866 to be the most exciting and important period of his life. In after years, the regiment's war record was a never-ceasing source of pride to its veterans—and with good reason. Like many another volunteer regiment, the 4th had erred on and off the battlefield in ways that cost it casualties and perhaps also some measure of self-confidence. But like other regiments, it overcame inexperience and not only rose above its mistakes, but profited from them as well. The outfit also surmounted obstacles that white regiments did not face, including the necessity of molding freemen, freedmen, and fugitive slaves into a cohesive fighting force.

Because it did overcome and surmount these barriers, the 4th had numerous successes to its credit. It had helped capture well-defended batteries during the initial attack on Petersburg, two of which it seized wholly on its own. The regiment had sacrificed itself during a forlorn-hope assault at New Market Heights, but despite suffering heavily, it had softened up Richmond's exterior defense line so that later attacks, in greater strength, carried the position. The 4th had ably guarded the rear of the corps that attacked Fort Fisher, a feat the expeditionary commander considered essential to victory. It had played a large role in forcing the evacuation of Wilmington, North Carolina, and had delivered the blow that sent Bragg's Confederates fleeing across the Cape Fear River. Moreover, it had shown its mettle in numerous smaller engagements, skirmishes, raids, punitive expeditions, and scouting missions.

In so doing, the 4th had confounded soldiers on both sides who believed that the Colored Troops would fight poorly, if at all. Perhaps more significantly, it had overcome the prejudice and discrimination it suffered at the hands of its own army, while allaying the suspicions and doubts of its commanders. It had also quieted those whites who seemed unable to praise African-American soldiers without exaggerating their abilities. In truth, the men of the 4th USCI did not outperform the white soldiers who fought beside them or opposed them across the firing lines—rather, they performed just as well. That was all the regiment had intended to prove.

Although the 4th USCI had many achievements on its record of two and a half years' service, one continues to stand out above the rest. The racist society of the era had given the regiment—and every other USCT unit—a single opportunity to make a point about racial equality. The men of the 4th, at least, had made the most of that opportunity. By proving themselves the equals of white soldiers, they had proven themselves the equals of white men.

NOTES

ABBREVIATIONS USED IN NOTES

A-A	*Anglo-African*
AGO	Adjutant General's Office
B&L	*Battles and Leaders of the Civil War*
CR	*Christian Recorder*
CSR	Compiled Service Record
DCL	Dartmouth College Library
GO	General Order
LC	Library of Congress
M, R	Microcopy, Roll
MHS	Maryland Historical Society
MOLLUS	Military Order of the Loyal Legion of the United States
MSS	Correspondence/Papers
NA	National Archives
NHHS	New Hampshire Historical Society
NIMSUS	*The Negro in the Military Service of the United States*
OR	*War of the Rebellion: A Compilation of the Official Records of the Union and Confederate Armies*
RG, E	Record Group, Entry
SO	Special Order
USAMHI	U.S. Army Military History Institute

CHAPTER 1

1. Christian A. Fleetwood diary, June 20, 1863, Fleetwood MSS, LC; Christian A. Fleetwood to his father, June 23, 1863, Carter G. Woodson MSS, LC.
2. "A Short Biography of Christian Abraham Fleetwood," 1, Fleetwood MSS; James H. Whyte, "Maryland's Negro Regiments—How, Where They Served," *Civil War Times Illustrated* 1 (July 1962): 42.
3. "Biography of Christian Abraham Fleetwood," 2–3.

4. Ibid.; *Lyceum Observer,* June 5, 1863, copy in Fleetwood MSS.

5. E. B. Long and Barbara Long, *The Civil War Day by Day: An Almanac, 1861–1865* (Garden City, N.Y.: Doubleday & Co., 1971), 267–68.

6. Edwin B. Coddington, *The Gettysburg Campaign: A Study in Command* (New York: Charles Scribner's Sons, 1968), 3–9; Wilbur S. Nye, *Here Come the Rebels!* (Baton Rouge: Louisiana State University Press, 1965), 24–25, 28, 61.

7. Coddington, *Gettysburg Campaign,* 103–13.

8. Christian A. Fleetwood diary, June 20, 1863; Christian A. Fleetwood to his father, June 23, 1863, Carter G. Woodson MSS.

9. Coddington, *Gettysburg Campaign,* 198–99, maps 1, 12.

10. Robert C. Schenck to Abraham Lincoln, June 30, 1863, *NIMSUS,* reel 2.

11. John W. Blassingame, "The Recruitment of Negro Troops in Maryland," *Maryland Historical Magazine* 58 (March 1963): 20; John W. Blassingame, "The Recruitment of Colored Troops in Kentucky, Maryland and Missouri, 1863–1865," *Historian* 29 (August 1967): 533–35.

12. Joseph T. Glatthaar, *Forged in Battle: The Civil War Alliance of Black Soldiers and White Officers* (New York: Free Press, 1990), 4; Noah Andre Trudeau, *Like Men of War: Black Troops in the Civil War, 1862–1865* (Boston: Little, Brown & Co., 1998), 10–11.

13. Hondon B. Hargrove, *Black Union Soldiers in the Civil War* (Jefferson, N.C.: McFarland & Co., 1988), 88; Fred A. Shannon, "The Federal Government and the Negro Soldier, 1861–1865," *Journal of Negro History* 11 (1926): 565–67; Albert E. Cowdrey, "Slave into Soldier: The Enlistment by the North of Runaway Slaves," *History Today* 20 (October 1970): 708.

14. Shannon, "Federal Government and Negro Soldier," 568–73; Trudeau, *Like Men of War,* 12–17.

15. Glatthaar, *Forged in Battle,* 9–10; Trudeau, *Like Men of War,* 18–20.

16. Trudeau, *Like Men of War,* 23–34; Hargrove, *Black Union Soldiers,* 97–103.

17. Trudeau, *Like Men of War,* 13–15, 19, 71–73, 92–93.

18. *OR,* III, 3: 215–16; Blassingame, "Recruitment of Negro Troops in Maryland," 20–21; Hargrove, *Black Union Soldiers,* 103–9.

19. Trudeau, *Like Men of War,* 34–46, 71–90.

20. Brainerd Dyer, "The Treatment of Colored Union Troops by the Confederates, 1861–1865," *Journal of Negro History* 20 (1935): 273–86; James G. Hollandsworth, Jr., "The Execution of White Officers from Black Units by Confederate Forces during the Civil War," *Louisiana History* 35 (Fall 1994): 475.

21. Robert C. Schenck to Abraham Lincoln, July 4, 1863, *NIMSUS,* reel 2; Ira Berlin, Joseph P. Reidy, and Leslie S. Rowland, eds., *Freedom: A Documentary History of Emancipation, 1861–1867,* ser. II, vol. 1, *The Black Military Experience* (New York: Cambridge University Press, 1982), 197–98.

22. Gerald S. Henig, *Henry Winter Davis, Antebellum and Civil War Congressman from Maryland* (New York: Twayne Publishers, 1973), 196–97; Edwin M. Stanton to William Birney, July 5, 1863, *NIMSUS,* reel 2; William Birney to Edwin M. Stanton, July 5, 1863, ibid.; Edwin M. Stanton to Robert C. Schenck, July 6, 1863, ibid.; *OR,* III, 3: 470–71.

23. William Birney to Edwin M. Stanton, July 5, 1863, *NIMSUS,* reel 2.

24. Berlin, Reidy, and Rowland, *Freedom,* II, 1: 199; Shannon, "Federal Government and Negro Soldier," 581.

25. Berlin, Reidy, and Rowland, *Freedom,* II, 1: 224–26; George Rogers to Benjamin F. Butler, July 23, 1864, Reg. MSS, 4th USCI, RG-94, NA; *CR,* April 16, 1864.

26. Christian A. Fleetwood diary, June 25, July 7, 8, 1863.

27. *Baltimore Sun,* July 28, August 8, 29, 1863.

28. Ibid., August 1, 1863; Berlin, Reidy, and Rowland, *Freedom,* II, 1: 198–200.

29. *Baltimore Sun,* August 8, 29, 1863; William Birney to C. W. Foster, August 26, 1863, *NIMSUS,* reel 2; C. W. Foster to William Birney, September 9, 1863, ibid.; Berlin, Reidy, and Rowland, *Freedom,* II, 1: 203–5.

30. Whyte, "Maryland's Negro Regiments," 41; Blassingame, "Recruitment of Colored Troops in Kentucky, Maryland and Missouri," 534–36; Blassingame, "Recruitment of Negro Troops in Maryland," 21.

31. Blassingame, "Recruitment of Negro Troops in Maryland," 22–23; *OR,* III, 3: 695–96; Hugh L. Bond to Edwin M. Stanton, August 15, 1863, *NIMSUS,* reel 2; Joseph Holt to Edwin M. Stanton, August 20, 1863, ibid.; Edwin M. Stanton to Abraham Lincoln, October 1, 1863, ibid.; Berlin, Reidy, and Rowland, *Freedom,* II, 1: 200–3; William Birney to William Chapman, August 28, 1863, USAMHI.

32. Berlin, Reidy, and Rowland, *Freedom,* II, 1: 214–15; Whyte, "Maryland's Negro Regiments," 41; Peter W. Crain to Andrew Johnson, August 9, 1866, MHS.

33. *CR,* March 12, 16, 1864.

34. *Record-Times* (Harford County, Md.), May 3, 1934.

35. *OR,* III, 3: 216; John W. Blassingame, "The Selection of Officers and Non-commissioned Officers of Negro Troops in the Union Army, 1863–1865," *Negro History Bulletin* 30 (January 1967): 8–11; Keith P.

Wilson, "Thomas Webster and the Free Military School for Applicants for Command of Colored Troops," *Civil War History* 29 (1983): 101–22; John H. Taggart, *Free Military School for Applicants for Commands of Colored Troops* (Philadelphia: King & Baird, 1863), 3–8.

36. Bell I. Wiley, "Billy Yank and the Black Folk," *Journal of Negro History* 36 (1951): 49–52; "Roster of Commissioned Officers of the 4th Regt. of U.S.C.T. for the Month of March 1865," Reg. MSS, 4th USCI, RG-94, NA; *CR,* August 20, 1864; SO #12, HQ 4th USCI, January 18, 1866, Reg. Order/Letter Books, 4th USCI, RG-94, NA; *A-A,* September 10, 1864.

37. Reg. Descriptive Book, 4th USCI, RG-94, E-112/115, NA; John W. Blassingame, "Negro Chaplains in the Civil War," *Negro History Bulletin* 27 (October 1963): 23; Edwin S. Redkey, "Black Chaplains in the Civil War," *Civil War History* 33 (1987): 350; Samuel A. Duncan to his mother, October 18, 1863, Duncan MSS, NHHS.

38. Christian A. Fleetwood diary, July 30, 1863.

39. Ibid., August 17, 19, 22, 1863.

CHAPTER 2

1. Christian A. Fleetwood diary, September 22, 1863 (recounting events of September 17).

2. Samuel A. Duncan to his mother, September 21, 1863, Duncan MSS, NHHS.

3. Mark Mayo Boatner, *The Civil War Dictionary* (New York: David McKay Co., 1959), 65, 251; Ezra J. Warner, *Generals in Blue: Lives of the Union Commanders* (Baton Rouge: Louisiana State University Press, 1964), 35; biographical sketch of Samuel A. Duncan in index to Duncan MSS, NHHS.

4. Samuel A. Duncan to anon., July 30, 1863, Duncan MSS, NHHS.

5. *A Memorial of the Great Rebellion: Being a History of the Fourteenth Regiment New Hampshire Volunteers . . .* (Boston: Rand, Avery & Co., 1882), 43; J. W. Patterson to Samuel A. Duncan, August 7, 1863, Duncan MSS, DCL.

6. Samuel A. Duncan to Julia Jones, September 6, 1863, NHHS.

7. *Memorial of the Great Rebellion,* 43; Samuel A. Duncan to his mother, August 15, 30, 1863, Duncan MSS, NHHS.

8. Samuel A. Duncan to his mother, September 21, 1863, Duncan MSS, NHHS.

9. Reg. Descriptive Book, 4th USCI, RG-94, E-112/115, NA.

10. Samuel A. Duncan to his mother, October 18, 1863, Duncan MSS, NHHS.

11. John G. Foster to Henry W. Halleck, September 23, 1863, *NIMSUS*, reel 2; John G. Foster to Edwin M. Stanton, September 25, 1863, ibid.; SO #429, AGO, September 25, 1863, Reg. MSS, 4th USCI, RG–94, NA; Christian A. Fleetwood diary, September 26, 1863.

12. Thomas Adrian Wheat, *A Guide to Civil War Yorktown* (Knoxville, Tenn.: Bohemian Brigade Bookship & Publishers, 1997), 1–9.

13. Christian A. Fleetwood diary, September 28, 29, 1863.

14. Ibid., September 29–October 1, 1863.

15. Wheat, *Guide to Civil War Yorktown,* 5–8; Stephen W. Sears, *To the Gates of Richmond: The Peninsula Campaign* (New York: Ticknor & Fields, 1992), 59–66.

16. Henry L. Swint, *"Dear Ones at Home": Letters from Contraband Camps* (Nashville, Tenn.: Vanderbilt University Press, 1966), 107–8, 120–21.

17. Isaac J. Wistar, *Autobiography of Isaac Jones Wistar, 1827–1905: Half a Century in War and Peace* (Philadelphia: Wistar Institute, 1937), 446.

18. Samuel A. Duncan to his mother, October 18, 1863, Duncan MSS, NHHS.

19. Ibid.; *Cavalier* (Williamsburg and Yorktown, Va.), September 28, 1863; GO #2, HQ 4th USCI, October 7, 1863, Reg. Order/Letter Books, 4th USCI, RG–94, NA.

20. Samuel A. Duncan to his mother, October 18, 1863, Duncan MSS, NHHS; Christian A. Fleetwood diary, January 30, 1864.

21. *Cavalier,* September 28, 1863; GO #3, HQ 4th USCI, Reg. Order/Letter Books, 4th USCI, RG–94, NA. The graves of the 4th's soldiers in the cemetery at Yorktown are #1171 (Owens, died February 22, 1864) and #1358 (Banks, died March 28, 1864).

22. GO #7, HQ 4th USCI, November 24, 1863 (reissue of an earlier order, n.d.), Reg. Order/Letter Books, 4th USCI, RG–94, NA.

23. Sears, *To the Gates of Richmond,* 348.

24. Joseph G. Bilby, *Civil War Firearms: Their Historical Background, Tactical Use and Modern Collecting and Shooting* (Conshohocken, Pa.: Combined Publishing, 1996), 45–47.

25. Grady McWhiney and Perry D. Jamieson, *Attack and Die: Civil War Military Tactics and the Southern Heritage* (University: University of Alabama Press, 1982), 48–58.

26. Claimant's deposition by William Henry, November 2, 1900, Pension File of Joshua DeCoursey, RG–15, NA; Carded Medical Record of Alfred M. Brigham, RG–94, E–534, box 3508, NA.

27. *Record-Times,* May 3, 1934.

28. Christian A. Fleetwood diary, October 4, 1863; Samuel A. Duncan to his mother, October 18, 1863, Duncan MSS, NHHS.

29. Christian A. Fleetwood diary, October 18, 19, Nov. 1, 3, 7, 16, 1863; James M. Paradis, *Strike the Blow for Freedom: The 6th United States Colored Infantry in the Civil War* (Shippensburg, Pa.: White Mane Books, 1998), 40–41.
30. Reg. Descriptive Book, 4th USCI, RG-94, E-112/115, NA; Personnel Return for October 1863, CSR of John H. Hance, RG-94, NA; SO #39, HQ 4th USCI, October 6, 1863, Reg. Order/Letter Books, 4th USCI, RG-94, NA; John W. Mitchell to Lorenzo Thomas, November 27, 1863, CSR of G. Michael Arnold, RG-94, NA.
31. Christian A. Fleetwood diary, October 10, 11, 1863; Reg. Descriptive Book, 4th USCI, RG-94, E-112/115, NA; SO #41, HQ 4th USCI, October 11, 1863, Reg. Order/Letter Books, 4th USCI, RG-94, NA.
32. *CR,* March 12, 1864; Samuel A. Duncan to his father, January 6, 1864, Duncan MSS, DCL.
33. Swint, *"Dear Ones at Home,"* 107, 111.
34. *OR,* I, 29, pt. 1: 205–6.
35. Samuel A. Duncan to Stephen R. Reynolds, October 4, 1863, Reg. Order/Letter Books, 4th USCI, RG-94, NA.
36. *OR,* I, 29, pt. 1: 206–8.
37. Christian A. Fleetwood diary, October 6, 1863.
38. *OR,* I, 29, pt. 1: 206–7; Christian A. Fleetwood diary, October 8, 1863; *Cavalier,* October 12, 1863.
39. Samuel A. Duncan to his mother, October 18, 1863, Duncan MSS, NHHS.
40. Samuel A. Duncan to Julia Jones, November 20, 1863, ibid.

CHAPTER 3
1. Samuel A. Duncan to his mother, October 18, 1863, Duncan MSS, NHHS.
2. Long and Long, *Civil War Day by Day,* 438–42.
3. Patricia L. Faust, ed., *The Historical Times Illustrated Encyclopedia of the Civil War* (New York: Harper & Row, 1986), 136–38, 764–65.
4. Christian A. Fleetwood diary, October 19, 20, 23, November 21, December 10, 26, 1863, January 7, 8, 30, May 10–14, 1864.
5. SO #28, HQ 4th USCI, September 12, 1863, Reg. Order/Letter Books, 4th USCI, RG-94, NA; SO #48, HQ 4th USCI, November 5, 1863, ibid.
6. GO #5, HQ 4th USCI, February 1, 1864, Reg. Order/Letter Books, 4th USCI, RG-94, NA; Francis A. Lord, *Civil War Sutlers and Their Wares* (New York: Thomas Yoseloff, 1969), 112.
7. Christian A. Fleetwood diary, November 6, 7, 20, 1863.

8. Ibid., October 31, November 30, 1863; *CR,* April 16, 1864.

9. *A-A,* August 6, 1864.

10. Marilyn Elizabeth Bowie, "An Analytical History of the Fourth and Sixth Infantries of the United States Colored Troops in the Civil War" (Master's thesis, Howard University, 1969), 22–23; *New Regime* (Norfolk, Va.), March 2, 1864.

11. Christian A. Fleetwood diary, October 27, November 3, 20, 1863, January 1, 1864.

12. Ibid., October 27, 1863; *A-A,* September 10, 1864.

13. Faust, *Historical Times Encyclopedia,* 133–35.

14. *A-A,* December 12, 1863.

15. SO #47, HQ 4th USCI, October 31, 1863, Reg. MSS, 4th USCI, RG-94, NA; Christian A. Fleetwood diary, November 8–11, 1863; Samuel A. Duncan to Julia Jones, November 20, 1863, Duncan MSS, NHHS.

16. *New York Times,* November 3, 1863; *New York Tribune,* November 9, 1863; *OR,* I, 29, pt. 2: 397, 447, 494–95.

17. Christian A. Fleetwood diary, December 9, 1863; Edward G. Longacre, *Army of Amateurs: General Benjamin F. Butler and the Army of the James, 1863–1865* (Mechanicsburg, Pa.: Stackpole Books, 1997), 50–55.

18. "Government of the Contrabands: General Butler's Order," in Frank Moore, ed., *The Rebellion Record: A Diary of American Events* (12 vols. New York: various publishers, 1861–68), 8: 261–64.

19. *Cavalier,* December 21, 1863.

20. Ibid.; Christian A. Fleetwood diary, December 16, 1863.

21. Samuel A. Duncan to his father, January 6, 1864, Duncan MSS, DCL.

22. Christian A. Fleetwood diary, December 25, 1863; Samuel A. Duncan to his father, January 6, 1864, Duncan MSS, DCL.

23. Christian A. Fleetwood diary, January 1, 1864; Samuel A. Duncan to his father, January 6, 1864, Duncan MSS, DCL.

24. Christian A. Fleetwood diary, December 31, 1863.

25. Ibid., January 11, 1864; Samuel A. Duncan to his brother, January 18, 1864, Duncan MSS, DCL; *CR,* January 30, 1864; Record of Events, Co. D, 4th USCI, M-594, R-206–7, NA.

26. Christian A. Fleetwood diary, January 12, 1864; Samuel A. Duncan to his brother, January 18, 1864, Duncan MSS, DCL.

27. Christian A. Fleetwood diary, January 12, 1863; *CR,* January 30, 1864.

28. Personnel Return for January 1864, CSR of Samuel A. Duncan, RG-94, NA; Christian A. Fleetwood diary, January 20, 1864; *CR,* January 30, 1864; Versalle F. Washington, *Eagles on Their Buttons: A Black Infantry Regiment in the Civil War* (Columbia: University of Missouri Press, 1991), 32–37.

29. Personnel Returns for January–February 1864, CSR of George Rogers, RG-94, NA.

30. Reg. Descriptive Book, 4th USCI, RG-94, E-112/115, NA; *Official Army Register of the Volunteer Force of the United States Army for the Years 1861,' '62, '63, '64, '65: Part VIII . . . U.S. Colored Troops* (Washington, D.C.: Adjutant General's Office, 1867), 172; L. Allison Wilmer, J. H. Jarrett, and George W. F. Vernon, comps., *History and Roster of Maryland Volunteers, War of 1861–5,* 2 vols. (Baltimore: Guggenheimer, Weil & Co., 1899), 2: 134, 141; SO #5, HQ 4th USCI, January 27, 1864, Reg. MSS, 4th USCI, RG-94, NA.

31. GO #3 HQ 4th USCI, January 17, 1864, Reg. Order/Letter Books, 4th USCI, RG-94, NA; *Official Army Register: Part VIII,* 172; Reg. Descriptive Book, 4th USCI, RG-94, E-112/115, NA; Seth W. Maltby to Benjamin F. Butler, March 14, 1864, Butler MSS, LC.

32. Charles A. Brown to Benjamin F. Butler, March 30, 1864, Butler MSS, LC.

33. Ibid.; Reg. Descriptive Book, 4th USCI, RG-94, E-112/115, NA; SO #37, AGO, April 4, 1864, Reg. MSS, 4th USCI, RG-94, NA.

34. *OR,* I, 51, pt. 1: 1282–84; Longacre, *Army of Amateurs,* 15–16.

35. *OR,* I, 33: 146; Christian A. Fleetwood diary, February 4–6, 1864; Record of Events, Co. D, 4th USCI, M-594, R-206–7, NA.

36. *New Regime,* March 16, 1864; Longacre, *Army of Amateurs,* 19.

37. *OR,* I, 33: 146–48; Wistar, *Autobiography,* 426–30; Benjamin F. Butler, *Autobiography and Personal Reminiscences of Major-General Benj. F. Butler: Butler's Book* (Boston: A. M. Thayer & Co., 1892), 619–21.

38. Christian A. Fleetwood diary, February 6, 7, 1864.

39. Deposition by anon., n.d., Pension File of Isaiah P. Murdock, RG-15, NA.

CHAPTER 4

1. Christian A. Fleetwood diary, February 13, 1864; *OR,* I, 33: 1055.

2. Edward G. Longacre, "Brave Radical Wild," *Civil War Times Illustrated* 19 (June 1980): 8–11; Richard Reid, "General Edward A. Wild and Civil War Discrimination," *Historical Journal of Massachusetts* 13 (January 1985): 14–17.

3. Faust, *Historical Times Encyclopedia,* 417.

4. Christian A. Fleetwood diary, March 1–4, 1864; Alfred M. Brigham to "My Dear Caroline," February 6, 1864, Brigham MSS, Robert W. Woodruff Lib., Emory Univ., Atlanta; Samuel A. Duncan to Julia Jones, May 7, 1864, Duncan MSS, NHHS.

5. Christian A. Fleetwood diary, March 4, 5, 1864.

6. Ibid., March 6, 1864; Alfred M. Brigham to "My Dear Caroline," February 6, 1864, Brigham MSS.
7. Christian A. Fleetwood diary, March 9, 1864; *OR*, I, 33: 240–41.
8. *OR*, I, 33: 241–45.
9. Christian A. Fleetwood diary, March 11, 12, 1865; *OR*, I, 33: 243.
10. Christian A. Fleetwood diary, March 17, 1864; Bowie, "Analytical History of the Fourth and Sixth Infantries," 60–61.
11. *OR*, I, 33: 254–55.
12. Ibid., 255; Christian A. Fleetwood diary, March 19, 20, 1864.
13. *OR*, I, 33: 254, 256.
14. Christian A. Fleetwood diary, April 4, 5, 1864; Long and Long, *Civil War Day by Day*, 473.
15. *Cavalier,* April 11, 1864.
16. *OR*, I, 33: 861; *New Regime,* April 2, 1864; William Farrar Smith, "Butler's Attack on Drewry's Bluff," *B&L* 4: 206–7.
17. Longacre, *Army of Amateurs,* 33–39.
18. *A-A,* April 23, 1864.
19. Christian A. Fleetwood diary, April 9–11, 1864; *Cavalier,* April 11, 1864; Edward W. Hinks to R. V. Dubois, April 11, 1864, Reg. MSS, 4th USCI, RG-94, NA.
20. Alfred M. Brigham to "My Dear Caroline," April 29, 1864, Brigham MSS.
21. *Record-Times,* May 3, 1934.
22. Christian A. Fleetwood diary, April 11, 12, 25, 1864.
23. Ibid., April 25, 26, 1864.
24. Ibid., April 26, 1864; *OR*, I, 33: 1055; Faust, *Historical Times Encyclopedia,* 362–63.
25. Alfred M. Brigham to "My Dear Caroline," April 29, 1864, Brigham MSS; George Rogers to R. S. Davis, April 23, 1864, Reg. MSS, 4th USCI, RG-94, NA; SO #23, HQ 4th USCI, April 29, 1864, Reg. Order/Letter Books, 4th USCI, RG-94, NA; GO #18, HQ Hinks's Division, May 2, 1864, copy in CSR of James H. Wickes, RG-94, NA.
26. Alfred M. Brigham to "My Dear Caroline," April 29, 1864, Brigham MSS.
27. *New York Times,* May 8, 1864; Smith, "Butler's Attack on Drewry's Bluff," 207; *OR*, I, 33: 795; 36, pt. 2: 25, 326–27, 345, 391–93; William Glenn Robertson, *Back Door to Richmond: The Bermuda Hundred Campaign, April–June 1864* (Newark: University of Delaware Press, 1987), 35, 55–56.
28. Alfred M. Brigham to "My Dear Caroline," May 6, 1864, Brigham MSS; Samuel A. Duncan to Julia Jones, May 7, 1864, Duncan MSS, NHHS.

190 A REGIMENT OF SLAVES

29. Edward Simonton, "The Campaign up the James River to Petersburg," in *Glimpses of the Nation's Struggle* (Minnesota MOLLUS), 5: 481–82; "Operations in Virginia: General Butler's Despatch," in Moore, *The Rebellion Record,* 11: 494.

30. Samuel A. Duncan to Julia Jones, May 7, 1864, Duncan MSS, NHHS; *A-A,* May 21, 1864.

31. Christian A. Fleetwood diary, May 5, 1864; Joseph J. Scroggs diary, May 5–7, 1864, USAMHI; *OR,* I, 36, pt. 2: 21–22, 165, 430, 432.

32. *A-A,* May 21, 1864.

33. Faust, *Historical Times Encyclopedia,* 51–52; P. G. T. Beauregard, "The Defense of Drewry's Bluff," *B&L* 4: 195–97.

34. Robertson, *Back Door to Richmond,* 76–91; Beauregard, "Defense of Drewry's Bluff," 197–200.

35. Christian A. Fleetwood diary, May 6–9, 1864.

36. *OR,* I, 36, pt. 2: 165–66; Robertson, *Back Door to Richmond,* 115; Joseph J. Scroggs diary, May 9, 1864; Christian A. Fleetwood diary, May 8, 9, 1864.

37. Butler, *Butler's Book,* 645–47; Longacre, *Army of Amateurs,* 81–83.

38. Samuel A. Duncan to Julia Jones, May 22, 1864, Duncan MSS, NHHS; Record of Events, Co. A, 4th USCI, M-594, R-206–7, NA; *A-A,* May 21, 1864.

39. Samuel A. Duncan to Julia Jones, May 22, 1864, Duncan MSS, NHHS; Christian A. Fleetwood diary, May 18, 1864.

40. Samuel A. Duncan to Julia Jones, May 22, 1864, Duncan MSS, NHHS; *OR,* I, 36, pt. 2: 169–70, 904–5; *A-A,* June 4, 1864.

41. *OR,* I, 36, pt. 2: 169; *A-A,* June 4, 1864.

CHAPTER 5

1. Beauregard, "Defense of Drewry's Bluff," 198–204; Smith, "Butler's Attack on Drewry's Bluff," 209–11; William Farrar Smith, *From Chattanooga to Petersburg under Generals Grant and Butler: A Contribution to the History of the War, and a Personal Vindication* (Boston: Houghton, Mifflin & Co., 1893), 151, 163–64; Robertson, *Back Door to Richmond,* 170–215; Herbert M. Schiller, *The Bermuda Hundred Campaign: Operations on the South Side of the James River, Virginia—May, 1864* (Dayton: Morningside House, 1988), 229–92.

2. Robertson, *Back Door to Richmond,* 217–33; Schiller, *Bermuda Hundred Campaign,* 293–316; Ulysses S. Grant, *Personal Memoirs of U. S. Grant* (2 vols. New York: Charles L. Webster & Co., 1885–86), 2: 151–52.

3. *OR,* I, 36, pt. 2: 269–72; pt. 3: 244; Simonton, "Up the James River to Petersburg," 482–83; "Operations in Virginia: Butler's Despatch," 504; Christian A. Fleetwood diary, May 26, 1864.

4. *A-A,* June 4, 1864.

5. Christian A. Fleetwood diary, May 27, 1864; *OR,* I, 36, pt. 1: 234–35, 243–44, 278; Butler, *Butler's Book,* 671–72.

6. Christian A. Fleetwood diary, May 28, 1864; *OR,* I, 36, pt. 3: 234.

7. Record of Events, Co. A, 4th USCI, M-594, R-206–7, NA; Christian A. Fleetwood diary, May 29, 1864.

8. *OR,* I, 36, pt. 3: 420–23; Paradis, *Strike the Blow for Freedom,* 50.

9. *A-A,* June 18, 1864.

10. *OR,* I, 36, pt. 3: 422–23.

11. Christian A. Fleetwood diary, May 31, 1864; *A-A,* June 18, 1864.

12. AGO to Jarrett Morgan, July 12, 1883, CSR of Morgan, RG-94, NA; Claimant's Affadavit, Jarrett Morgan, September 26, 1887, Pension File of Morgan, RG-15, NA.

13. *Record-Times,* May 3, 1934.

14. Christian A. Fleetwood diary, June 2, 1864.

15. Ibid., June 2, 3, 1864; Alfred M. Brigham to "My Dear Caroline," June 11, 1864, Brigham MSS.

16. Christian A. Fleetwood diary, June 3, 1864; Faust, *Historical Times Encyclopedia,* 149–50.

17. *OR,* I, 36, pt. 3: 420–21; Benjamin F. Butler, *Private and Official Correspondence of Gen. Benjamin F. Butler during the Period of the Civil War,* comp. by Jessie Ames Marshall (6 vols. Norwood, Mass.: Plimpton Press, 1917), 4: 304, 313.

18. Longacre, *Army of Amateurs,* 125–26.

19. Christian A. Fleetwood diary, June 7, 1864.

20. *OR,* I, 36, pt. 2: 275–77, 287; pt. 3: 708; Butler, *Butler's Book,* 672, 677.

21. *OR,* I, 36, pt. 2: 277–78, 288, 292–93, 295, 299, 302–6, 308, 310, 314; Quincy A. Gillmore to Edward W. Hinks, June 18, 1864, Hinks MSS, Mugar Memorial Library, Boston University; Butler, *Private and Official Correspondence,* 4: 331, 351–52; Butler, *Butler's Book,* 678; *Petersburg Express,* June 10, 1864.

22. *OR,* I, 36, pt. 2: 283–87, 290–91; 40, pt. 3: 417–18; David B. Birney to Benjamin F. Butler, July 16, 1864, Butler MSS; William Birney, *General William Birney's Answer to Libels Clandestinely Circulated by James Shaw, Jr. . . .* (Washington, D.C.: Stanley Snodgrass, 1878), 5.

23. *OR,* I, 36, pt. 3: 766–67; 40, pt. 1: 705; 51, pt. 1: 1262; Smith, *From Chattanooga to Petersburg,* 22–23, 123.

24. Christian A. Fleetwood diary, June 13, 1864; Alfred M. Brigham to "My Dear Caroline," June 11, 1864, Brigham MSS.
25. Christian A. Fleetwood diary, June 14, 1864; *OR,* I, 40, pt. 2: 44–45.
26. *OR,* I, 40, pt. 1: 303–4, 705.
27. Ibid., 721, 724; 51, pt. 1: 265; *Record-Times,* May 3, 1934.
28. *OR,* I, 40, pt. 1: 721; 51, pt. 1: 265.
29. Ibid., 40, pt. 1: 721, 724; 51, pt. 1: 265.
30. Ibid., 266.
31. Christian A. Fleetwood diary, June 15, 1864; Christian A. Fleetwood to Robert Hamilton, June 28, 1864, Carter G. Woodson MSS; *A-A,* July 9, August 13, 1864; *OR,* I, 40, pt. 1: 721; 51, pt. 1: 266.
32. Christian A. Fleetwood diary, June 15, 1864; Christian A. Fleetwood to Robert Hamilton, June 28, 1864, Carter G. Woodson MSS; *A-A,* July 9, August 13, 1864.
33. *OR,* I, 40, pt. 1: 237; 51, pt. 1: 266; "Casualties in the 4th U.S.C.T. on the 15th, 16th, 19th June, 1864," Reg. MSS, 4th USCI, RG-94, NA; *Official Army Register: Part VIII,* 172; *A-A,* July 9, 1864.
34. *OR,* I, 40, pt. 1: 725; 51, pt. 1: 266; Washington, *Eagles on Their Buttons,* 42–43.
35. *OR,* I, 40, pt. 1: 722; William Farrar Smith to James F. Rhodes, October 30, 1900, Smith MSS, Vermont Hist. Soc., Montpelier.
36. *OR,* I, 51, pt. 1: 266.
37. Ibid., 40, pt. 1: 722, 724; 51, pt. 1: 267; Paradis, *Strike the Blow for Freedom,* 55.
38. Christian A. Fleetwood diary, June 15, 1864; Christian A. Fleetwood, *The Negro as a Soldier . . .* (Washington, D.C.: Howard University Printing Co., 1895), 14; *OR,* I, 51, pt. 1: 267–68.
39. *OR,* I, 40, pt. 1: 725; 51, pt. 1: 267–68; Paradis, *Strike the Blow for Freedom,* 55–56.
40. *OR,* I, 40, pt. 1: 723.

CHAPTER 6
1. *A-A,* July 9, 1864.
2. Smith, *From Chattanooga to Petersburg,* 24–25; Samuel A. Duncan to William Farrar Smith, April 17, 1866, Smith MSS; William F. Smith to James F. Rhodes, October 30, 1900, ibid.
3. Smith, *From Chattanooga to Petersburg,* 25, 93, 101, 108–10; William Farrar Smith, "The Movement against Petersburg, June, 1864," in *Papers of the Military Historical Society of Massachusetts* (14 vols. Boston: various publishers, 1895–1918), 5: 79, 93–94, 96; *OR,* I, 40, pt. 1: 305; pt. 2: 59–60, 75.

4. *OR,* I, 40, pt. 1: 683–84, 686, 690; pt. 2: 98–99, 101, 106–7, 110–11; P. G. T. Beauregard, "Four Days of Battle at Petersburg," *B&L* 4: 540–41; Butler, *Private and Official Correspondence,* 4: 384–85, 387–89, 395; *New York Times,* June 21, 1864.

5. Christian A. Fleetwood diary, June 16, 1864.

6. Ibid., June 17, 1864.

7. Ibid., June 18, 1864.

8. *A-A,* July 9, August 13, 1864.

9. *OR,* I, 40, pt. 1: 714; pt. 2: 90, 112, 118, 140–41, 144, 176, 203–5, 662–63; 51, pt. 1: 268, 1257–58; pt. 2: 1078; Smith, "Movement against Petersburg," 160–61; Beauregard, "Four Days of Battle," 541–44; *Petersburg Express,* June 18, 1864.

10. Christian A. Fleetwood diary, June 19, 1864.

11. *OR,* I, 40, pt. 2: 225, 555; *A-A,* August 13, 1864.

12. Christian A. Fleetwood diary, June 20, 21, 1864; *A-A,* July 9, 1864.

13. *OR,* I, 40, pt. 1: 169, 677; pt. 2: 157, 209, 222, 227, 232–33, 262, 264; Richard J. Sommers, *Richmond Redeemed: The Siege at Petersburg* (Garden City, N.Y.: Doubleday & Co., 1981), 6, 14; Generals' Reports of Service, War of the Rebellion, 1863–65, 10: 202, RG-94, E-160, NA.

14. Christian A. Fleetwood diary, June 23–25, 1864; *OR,* I, 40, pt. 2: 429.

15. Long and Long, *Civil War Day by Day,* 528–29.

16. Christian A. Fleetwood diary, June 28, 29, 1864.

17. Ibid., July 9, 1864; Reg. Descriptive Book, 4th USCI, RG-94, E-112/115, NA; *A-A,* September 10, 1864.

18. *A-A,* July 30, September 10, 1864.

19. *New York Times,* June 28, 1864.

20. Christian A. Fleetwood diary, July 19, 1864; Personnel Returns for July–August, 1864, CSR of James H. Wickes, RG-94, NA; Claimant's Deposition by Sidney J. Mendall, n.d., Pension File of Wareham C. Hill, RG-15, NA.

21. A. S. Boernstein to Solon A. Carter, October 24, 1864, Reg. Order/Letter Books, 4th USCI, RG-94, NA; A. S. Boernstein to AGO, n.d., ibid.

22. A. S. Boernstein to Edward W. Smith, October 29, 1864, Reg. Order/Letter Books, 4th USCI, RG-94, NA; A. S. Boernstein to A. N. Buckman, May 23, 1865, ibid.

23. AGO to George Rogers, September 2, 1864, CSR of George Rogers, RG-94, NA; SO #249, AGO, copy in ibid.; Personnel Returns for July-October 1864, ibid.; *A-A,* September 10, 1864.

24. *CR,* August 20, 1864.

25. George Rogers to R. S. Davis, July 22, 1864, Reg. MSS, 4th USCI, RG-94, NA; *Official Army Register: Part VIII,* 172.

26. Christian A. Fleetwood diary, July 28, 1864.

27. Ibid., July 21, 23, August 16, 21, 29, September 6, 9, 15, 16, 18, 21, 1864.

28. *National Tribune,* October 8, 1891.

29. Christian A. Fleetwood diary, August 7, 11–13, 21, 22, 27, September 2, 4, 6, 1864.

30. Ibid., July 10, 20, 21, 26, 1864; *A-A,* July 30, 1864; *New York Herald,* May 14, 27, 1864.

31. Christian A. Fleetwood diary, July 15, 23, 1864.

32. *OR,* I, 42, pt. 2: 779; pt. 3: 619, 702, 716–18.

33. Henry Pleasants and George H. Straley, *Inferno at Petersburg* (Philadelphia: Chilton Book Co., 1961), 46–70.

34. Ibid., 104–14.

35. Longacre, *Army of Amateurs,* 166–67, 176–81; Warner, *Generals in Blue,* 349–50; *OR,* I, 40, pt. 3: 122, 144.

36. *OR,* I, 40, pt. 3: 631–34, 698–99, 706, 719; *New York Times,* August 1, 1864.

37. Christian A. Fleetwood diary, July 30, 1864; Affidavit of Christian A. Fleetwood, June 24, 1893, Pension File of G. Michael Arnold, RG-15, NA; Declaration for Invalid Pension, Sep. 15, ——, ibid.

38. *OR,* I, 40, pt. 1: 659, 699–702, 704, 707–8; pt. 3: 687, 715.

39. Ibid., pt. 1: 699–702, 704; pt. 3: 676–77.

40. Christian A. Fleetwood diary, July 30, 1864; Samuel A. Duncan to Julia Jones, October 22, 1864, Duncan MSS, NHHS.

CHAPTER 7

1. Reg. Descriptive Book, 4th USCI, RG-94, E-112/115, NA; Record of Events, Co. B, 4th USCI, July–August 1864, M-594, R-206–7, ibid.

2. Christian A. Fleetwood diary, August 1–4, 1864; *OR,* I, 42, pt. 1: 110; pt. 2: 16, 37–38.

3. *A-A,* September 10, 1864.

4. Christian A. Fleetwood diary, August 4–8, 1864.

5. *OR,* I, 42, pt. 1: 108; Faust, *Historical Times Encyclopedia,* 362–63.

6. Warner, *Generals in Blue,* 354–55; James H. Wickes to Hugh Bond, August 26, 1864, Wickes MSS, MHS.

7. *OR,* I, 42, pt. 1: 110; pt. 2: 622; Record of Events, Co. B, 4th USCI, M-594, R-206–7, NA; Christian A. Fleetwood diary, August 17, 1864.

8. Ulysses S. Grant, "General Grant on the Siege of Petersburg," *B&L* 4: 575; *OR,* I, 40, pt. 1: 691; pt. 3: 570–71; 42, pt. 1: 657–59; *New York Herald,* July 16, 1864; *New York Times,* September 10, 1864.

9. *OR,* I, 42, pt. 1: 657–59; *New York Tribune,* August 16, 1864; *Army and Navy Journal,* August 20, 1864; Butler, *Private and Official Correspondence,* 5: 26.

10. *CR,* August 20, 1864.

11. James H. Wickes to Hugh Bond, August 26, 1864, Wickes MSS, MHS.

12. Ibid.; Longacre, *Army of Amateurs,* 193–95.

13. *OR,* I, 40, pt. 1: 665–66; 42, pt. 2: 158, 160; *New York Tribune,* August 16, 1864; *New York Herald,* August 16, 1864.

14. James H. Wickes to Hugh Bond, August 26, 1864, Wickes MSS, MHS.

15. George Rogers to R. S. Davis, August 1, 1864, Reg. MSS, 4th USCI, RG-94, NA.

16. Christian A. Fleetwood, August 15, 1864; William H. Hunter to Samuel A. Duncan, September 16, 1864, Duncan MSS, DCL.

17. Samuel A. Duncan to C. W. Foster, August 31, 1864, Reg. MSS, 4th USCI, RG-94, NA.

18. Reg. Descriptive Book, 4th USCI, RG-94, E-112/115, NA; A. S. Boernstein to Edward W. Smith, October 29, 1864, Reg. MSS, 4th USCI, RG-94, NA.

19. Butler, *Personal and Official Correspondence,* 4: 544–45; *OR,* I, 40, pt. 1: 308–12, 367, 383, 692–93, 744; pt. 3: 401, 417–18, 435, 546, 573–74, 584–85, 588–89, 619–21, 630–34, 674; 42, pt. 1: 692, 698, 709–10, 718, 724, 727, 738, 744–45, 751, 754, 757, 770, 785, 789; pt. 2: 136, 150, 163, 186; *New York Times,* August 1, 1864; Birney, *General Birney's Answer,* 5; Oliver Willcox Norton, *Army Letters, 1861–1865: Being Extracts from Private Letters to Relatives and Friends from a Soldier in the Field . . .* (Chicago: O. L. Deming, 1903), 219.

20. Faust, *Historical Times Encyclopedia,* 260–61, 835.

21. Butler, *Personal and Official Correspondence,* 5: 136, 154, 300–301; *New York Tribune,* October 5, 1864.

22. Butler, *Personal and Official Correspondence,* 5: 171–83; *OR,* I, 42, pt. 2: 1058–59, 1082–88.

23. *OR,* I, 42, pt. 1: 110, 793, 798, 805, 811; AGO to R. B. Scott, January 5, 1882, Pension File of Scott, RG-15, NA.

24. A. S. Boernstein to Edward W. Smith, October 14, 1864, Reg. MSS, 4th USCI, RG-94, NA; Christian A. Fleetwood diary, September 28, 29, 1864.

25. Sommers, *Richmond Redeemed,* 17–18, 31–33.

26. Ibid., 35–36; Longacre, *Army of Amateurs,* 212–15.

27. Sommers, *Richmond Redeemed,* 30, 33–34.

28. Ibid., 33, 36.

29. Ibid., 34–35; Record of Events, Co. B, 4th USCI, M-594, R-206–7, NA; Fleetwood, *Negro as a Soldier,* 15; James H. Wickes to his father, October 2, 4, 1864, Wickes MSS, Boston Pub. Lib.; James H. Wickes to Hugh Bond, October 7, 1864, Wickes MSS, MHS; A. S. Boernstein to Solon A. Carter, November 26, 1864, Reg. Order/Letter Books, 4th USCI, RG-94, NA.

30. Christian A. Fleetwood diary, September 29, 1864; A. S. Boernstein to Solon A. Carter, October 4, 1864, Reg. Order/Letter Books, 4th USCI, RG-94, NA.

31. Sommers, *Richmond Redeemed,* 35.

32. Ibid.; Paradis, *Strike the Blow for Freedom,* 71–74.

33. Reg. Descriptive Book, 4th USCI, RG-94, E-112/115, NA; Samuel A. Duncan to Julia Jones, October 22, November 24, 1864, Duncan MSS, NHHS; Fleetwood, *Negro as a Soldier,* 17.

34. Sommers, *Richmond Redeemed,* 35–36; Barry Popchock, "A Shower of Stars at New Market Heights," *Civil War Magazine* 46 (August 1994): 36.

35. Sommers, *Richmond Redeemed,* 36–38; Popchock, "Shower of Stars," 37–38.

36. Fleetwood, *Negro as a Soldier,* 15; Butler, *Butler's Book,* 741–42.

CHAPTER 8

1. *OR,* I, 42, pt. 1: 110, 136; Christian A. Fleetwood diary, September 30, 1864; James H. Wickes to his father, October 2, 1864, Wickes MSS, Boston Pub. Lib.

2. Reg. Descriptive Book, 4th USCI, RG-94, E-112/115, NA; A. S. Boernstein to Solon A. Carter, October 24, 1864, Reg. Order/Letter Books, 4th USCI, RG-94, NA.

3. *A-A,* November 12, 1864.

4. Samuel A. Duncan to Julia Jones, October 22, 1864, Duncan MSS, NHHS; A. S. Boernstein to Solon A. Carter, October 4, 1864, Reg. Order/Letter Books, 4th USCI, RG-94, NA.

5. A. S. Boernstein to Solon A. Carter, October 4, 1864, Reg. Order/Letter Books, 4th USCI, RG-94, NA; *Official Army Register: Part VIII,* 172.

6. A. S. Boernstein to Solon A. Carter, October 4, 1864, Reg. Order/Letter Books, 4th USCI, RG-94, NA; *OR,* I, 42, pt. 3: 170.

7. AGO to Christian A. Fleetwood, March 29, 1865, Fleetwood MSS; SO #17, HQ 4th USCI, April 23, 1863, Reg. Order/Letter Books, 4th USCI, RG-94, NA.

8. *The Medal of Honor of the United States Army* (Washington, D.C.: Government Printing Office, 1948), 161; Christian A. Fleetwood, "Alfred B. Hilton," Fleetwood MSS.

9. Blassingame, "Selection of Officers and Non-Commissioned Officers of Negro Troops," 10; "Short Biography of Christian Abraham Fleetwood," 5–6, Fleetwood MSS.

10. Christian A. Fleetwood to James Hall, June 8, 1865, Carter G. Woodson MSS.

11. "Short Biography of Christian Abraham Fleetwood," 6, Fleetwood MSS; Butler, *Butler's Book,* 743.

12. A. S. Boernstein to Edward W. Smith, October 31, 1864, Reg. MSS, 4th USCI, RG-94, NA.

13. SO #54, HQ 4th USCI, October 20, 1864, Reg. Order/Letter Books, 4th USCI, RG-94, NA; A. S. Boernstein to Solon A. Carter, October 24, 1864, Ibid.

14. A. S. Boernstein to Edward W. Smith, October 14, 1864, Reg. MSS, 4th USCI, RG-94, NA.

15. Christian A. Fleetwood diary, September 30–October 2, 1864.

16. Ibid., October 1–3, 6, 7, 9–19, 21–25, 1864; James H. Wickes to Hugh Bond, October 7, 1864, Wickes MSS, MHS.

17. Christian A. Fleetwood diary, October 15, 26, 1864.

18. *OR,* I, 42, pt. 1: 691–93, 695, 697, 704–6, 714–15, 717–18, 722–23, 734–37, 741–43, 750–51, 762–64, 767–77, 795–96; pt. 3: 30, 68, 183–84, 186–90, 193, 215, 218–19, 224, 366–68, 390, 393–98, 686, 690; Butler, *Private and Official Correspondence,* 5: 250–51, 254–56; *New York Herald,* October 23, 31, 1864; Joseph T. Wilson, *The Black Phalanx: A History of the Negro Soldiers of the United States . . .* (Hartford, Conn.: American Publishing Co., 1890), 442–43; Solon A. Carter, "Fourteen Months' Service with Colored Troops," *Civil War Papers* (Massachusetts MOLLUS), 1: 173–74.

19. James H. Wickes to his father, October 29, 1864, Wickes MSS, Boston Pub. Lib.

20. *OR,* I, 40, pt. 3: 111; Christian A. Fleetwood diary, November 7, 1864.

21. James H. Wickes to Hugh Bond, October 20, 1864, Wickes MSS, MHS.

22. Samuel A. Duncan to Julia Jones, November 21, 1864, Duncan MSS, NHHS.

23. Faust, *Historical Times Encyclopedia,* 474–75.

24. Longacre, *Army of Amateurs,* 231–32.

25. *Joint Committee on the Conduct of the War* (3 vols. in 8. Washington, D.C.: Government Printing Office, 1863–68), 1865, pt. 2: 120–21; William Lamb, "The Defense of Fort Fisher," *B&L* 4: 642–43; *OR, I,* 46, pt. 1: 406–8; pt. 2: 90–91, 215–16.

26. *OR, I,* 42, pt. 1: 971–72; pt. 3: 835; *Joint Committee on the War,* 1865, pt. 2: 1, 10–11, 35, 69; Butler, *Butler's Book,* 78; Benjamin F. Butler, *Speech of Maj.-Gen. Benj. F. Butler, upon the Campaign before Richmond, 1864 . . .* (Boston: Wright & Potter, 1865), 21; Rod Gragg, *Confederate Goliath: The Battle of Fort Fisher* (New York: HarperCollins, 1991), 41, 47–53.

27. Christian A. Fleetwood diary, December 6, 1864; SO #372, AGO, October 29, 1864, copy in CSR of George Rogers, RG-94, NA.

28. Christian A. Fleetwood diary, December 6, 7, 1864.

29. *OR, I,* 42, pt. 1: 970; pt. 3: 760, 799; 46, pt. 2: 9–10; *Joint Committee on the War,* 1865, pt. 2: 6–7, 52; Butler, *Butler's Book,* 780; Butler, *Private and Official Correspondence,* 5: 379.

30. Christian A. Fleetwood diary, December 8–10, 1864; SO #2, HQ 4th USCI, January 20, 1865, Reg. Order/Letter Books, 4th USCI, RG-94, NA.

31. Christian A. Fleetwood diary, December 9–12, 1864.

32. Ibid., December 13, 14, 1864; *OR, I,* 42, pt. 1: 964, 966–67, 974, 981, 985; *Joint Committee on the War,* 1865, pt. 2: 15, 69, 95; Butler, *Private and Official Correspondence,* 5: 428, 431, 460–61.

33. *OR, I,* 42, pt. 1: 966, 974, 980–81, 985; *Joint Committee on the War,* 1865, pt. 2: 12–14, 17, 20, 28–29, 69, 73, 82, 89–90, 94–95, 222; Butler, *Private and Official Correspondence,* 5: 388, 398, 460–61; Edwin S. Redkey, ed., "'Rocked in the Cradle of Consternation': A Black Chaplain in the Union Army Reports on the Struggle to Take Fort Fisher . . .," *American Heritage* 31 (October–November 1980): 72–74.

34. Christian A. Fleetwood diary, December 17, 1864.

35. Joseph J. Scroggs diary, December 17, 1864; Edward K. Wightman, *From Antietam to Fort Fisher: The Civil War Letters of Edward King Wightman, 1862–1865,* ed. by Edward G. Longacre (Rutherford, N.J.: Fairleigh Dickinson University Press, 1985), 221.

36. Gragg, *Confederate Goliath,* 45–53.

37. Christian A. Fleetwood diary, December 21–23, 1864.

38. Ibid., December 24, 1864.

39. Butler, *Butler's Book,* 791–92, 815–18; Gragg, *Confederate Goliath,* 77–79.

40. Christian A. Fleetwood diary, December 25, 1864; Wightman, *From Antietam to Fort Fisher,* 222–25; Gragg, *Confederate Goliath,* 88–93.

41. John G. Barrett, *The Civil War in North Carolina* (Chapel Hill: University of North Carolina Press, 1963), 269–70; Gragg, *Confederate Goliath,* 88–95.

42. Christian A. Fleetwood diary, December 26, 1864; *OR,* I, 42, pt. 1: 965–66; pt. 3: 1076, 1085–87; 46, pt. 2: 3–5; Butler, *Private and Official Correspondence,* 5: 442–43, 452–53; Butler, *Butler's Book,* 798–99; Chris E. Fonvielle, Jr., *The Wilmington Campaign: Last Rays of Departing Hope* (Mechanicsburg, Pa.: Stackpole Books, 2001), 183–84.

43. *OR,* I, 42, pt. 1: 659; pt. 3: 216–17, 858; 46, pt. 2: 70–71; Butler, *Private and Official Correspondence,* 5: 247, 263–64, 268, 388, 475–76; *New York Herald,* January 5, 17, 1865; *Richmond Daily Examiner,* January 12, 1865.

CHAPTER 9

1. Warner, *Generals in Blue,* 497–98; Ulysses S. Grant to Alfred H. Terry, January 3, 4, 1865, Terry MSS, Connecticut Hist. Soc., Hartford; Adrian Terry to his wife, January 24, 1865, Terry MSS, Beinecke Rare Book and MSS Lib., Yale Univ., New Haven, Conn.; *OR,* I, 42, pt. 3: 1101; 46, pt. 1: 394; pt. 2: 15, 19–20, 46.

2. James H. Wickes to his father, January 5, 1865, Wickes MSS, Boston Pub. Lib.; Wightman, *From Antietam to Fort Fisher,* 227; *OR,* I, 46, pt. 1: 395.

3. *OR,* I, 46, pt. 1: 395.

4. SO #5, HQ Armies of the U.S., January 7, 1865, copy in Benjamin F. Butler MSS; Butler, *Private and Official Correspondence,* 5: 472–73.

5. *OR,* I, 46, pt. 1: 395–96; pt. 2: 35, 47, 69, 89; Butler, *Private and Official Correspondence,* 5: 466, 473–74; Alfred H. Terry to John A. Rawlins, January 10, 1865, Terry MSS, Beinecke Rare Book and MSS Lib.; Alfred H. Terry to David D. Porter, January 15, 1865, ibid.

6. Gragg, *Confederate Goliath,* 61, 71–72, 94–96, 117.

7. *Joint Committee on the War,* 1865, pt. 2: 102–3; Alfred H. Terry to David D. Porter, January 15, 1865, Terry MSS, Beinecke Rare Book and MSS Lib.; *OR,* I, 46, pt. 2: 90.

8. *OR,* I, 46, pt. 1: 396; Fonvielle, *Wilmington Campaign,* 209–12.

9. *OR,* I, 46, pt. 1: 396–97.

10. Ibid., 397.

11. Ibid., 398; Gragg, *Confederate Goliath,* 175–87; Fonvielle, *Wilmington Campaign,* 232–73.

12. *OR,* I, 46, pt. 1: 399; Gragg, *Confederate Goliath,* 187–89; Fonvielle, *Wilmington Campaign,* 278–79.

13. *OR,* I, 46, pt. 1: 399, 401, 442; pt. 2: 166–67, 176; Alfred H. Terry to John A. Rawlins, January 27, 1865, Terry MSS, Beinecke Rare Book and MSS Lib.; Gragg, *Confederate Goliath,* 188–89.

14. Fonvielle, *Wilmington Campaign,* 278–79.

15. *OR,* I, 46, pt. 1: 399, 410–15, 424, 432–34; pt. 2: 1056, 1059–60; Adrian Terry to his wife, January 24, 1865, Terry MSS, Beinecke Rare Book and MSS Lib.; *Joint Committee on the War,* 1865, pt. 2: 103.

16. *OR,* I, 46, pt. 1: 400.

17. Christian A. Fleetwood to his father, January 21, 1865, Fleetwood MSS.

18. Gragg, *Confederate Goliath,* 232–35.

19. Ibid., 235–36.

20. Barrett, *Civil War in North Carolina,* 281–83; Fonvielle, *Wilmington Campaign,* 380–88.

21. *OR,* I, 46, pt. 1: 424; pt. 2: 167; *New York Herald,* January 24, 1865.

22. *OR,* I, 46, pt. 1: 424, 453–54.

23. Ibid., 47, pt. 2: 111, 154–56, 163, 193, 436–37, 492, 859.

24. Ibid., 163; Fonvielle, *Wilmington Campaign,* 332–33.

25. *OR,* I, 47, pt. 1: 909–10.

26. Ibid., 46, pt. 2: 924–25; Reg. Descriptive Book, 4th USCI, RG-94, E-112/115, NA; John McMurray, *Recollections of a Colored Troop* (Brookville, Pa.: privately issued, 1916), 72.

27. Barrett, *Civil War in North Carolina,* 281–82.

28. *OR,* I, 46, pt. 2: 925.

29. Samuel A. Duncan to Julia Jones, March 15, 23, 1865, Duncan MSS, NHHS.

30. *OR,* I, 46, pt. 2: 925; Washington, *Eagles on Their Buttons,* 71.

31. Barrett, *Civil War in North Carolina,* 283; Samuel A. Duncan to his brother, February 25, 1865, Duncan MSS, DCL.

32. *CR,* April 15, 1865.

33. Samuel A. Duncan to Julia Jones, March 15, 1865, Duncan MSS, NHHS.

34. *CR,* April 15, 1865.

CHAPTER 10

1. Long and Long, *Civil War Day by Day,* 643–46.

 2. Samuel A. Duncan to his brother, February 25, 1865, Duncan MSS, DCL; *OR,* I, 47, pt. 1: 922, 930; Fonvielle, *Wilmington Campaign,* 430.

 3. *OR,* I, 47, pt. 1: 922, 925; Samuel A. Duncan to Julia Jones, March 15, 1865, Duncan MSS, NHHS.

 4. *OR,* I, 47, pt. 2: 1249; Fonvielle, *Wilmington Campaign,* 432–33.

5. *OR,* I, 47, pt. 1: 910–11.
6. Barrett, *Civil War in North Carolina,* 319–43.
7. Samuel A. Duncan to Julia Jones, March 15, 23, 1865, Duncan MSS, NHHS.
8. *OR,* I, 46, pt. 2: 925; Samuel A. Duncan to Julia Jones, March 15, 23, 1865, Duncan MSS, NHHS.
9. Long and Long, *Civil War Day by Day,* 661–65.
10. Ibid., 665–71; *OR,* I, 46, pt. 1: 1232, 1235–36, 1239; pt. 2: 926.
11. *OR,* I, 46, pt. 2: 926; Carded Medical Records of Christian A. Fleetwood, RG-94, E-534, box 3510, NA.
12. Barrett, *Civil War in North Carolina,* 379–89.
13. OR, I, 47, pt. 3: 342.
14. George Rogers to H. I. Campbell, April 16, 1865 (and endorsements thereon), CSR of Rogers, RG-94, NA; *Official Army Register: Part VIII,* 172.
15. Reg. Descriptive Book, 4th USCI, RG-94, E-112/115, NA; *Official Army Register: Part VIII,* 172.
16. SO #27, HQ 4th USCI, May 17, 1865, Reg. Order/Letter Books, 4th USCI, RG-94, NA; SO #34, HQ 4th USCI, June 2, 1865, ibid.; SO #56, HQ 4th USCI, June 28, 1865, ibid.
17. SO #36, HQ 4th USCI, June 7, 1865, Reg. Order/Letter Books, 4th USCI, RG-94, NA; A. S. Boernstein to Charles R. Holcombe, June 20, 1865, ibid.; SO #41, HQ 4th USCI, June 12, 1865, ibid.; SO #54, HQ 4th USCI, June 26, 1865, ibid.; Descriptive Return, August 14, 1865, CSR of John H. Hance, RG-94, NA.
18. Descriptive Book, Co. C, 4th USCI, RG-94, E-112/115, NA; Carded Medical Records of Harry C. Sherriff, RG-94, E-534, box 3508, NA; George W. Allen to John H. McCullough, July 18, 1865, Reg. Order/Letter Books, 4th USCI, RG-94, NA; SO #69, HQ 4th USCI, September 17, 1865, ibid.; SO #78, HQ 4th USCI, August 9, 1865, ibid.; SO #80, HQ 4th USCI, August 14, 1865, ibid.; *Official Army Register: Part VIII,* 172.
19. Samuel A. Duncan to Julia Jones, May 7, 1865, Duncan MSS, NHHS; SO #60, HQ 4th USCI, July 3, 1865, Reg. Order/Letter Books, 4th USCI, RG-94, NA.
20. SO #91, HQ 4th USCI, September 6, 1865, Reg. Order/Letter Books, 4th USCI, RG-94, NA.
21. Deposition of David Dorsey, February 14, 1906, Pension Files of Landin Edmunds, RG-15, NA.
22. SO #67, HQ 4th USCI, July 6, 1865, Reg. Order/Letter Books, 4th USCI, RG-94, NA.

23. James H. Wickes to Lorenzo Thomas, July 9, 1865, CSR of Wickes, RG–94, NA; *Official Army Register: Part VIII,* 172.

24. William H. Hunter to Clinton A. Cilley, July 19, 1865, CSR of Hunter, RG–94, NA.

25. Berlin, Reidy, and Rowland, *Freedom,* II, 1: 654–55.

26. Samuel A. Duncan to Julia Jones, October 13, 22, 1865, Duncan MSS, NHHS.

27. Longacre, *Army of Amateurs,* 319–21.

28. SO #99, HQ 4th USCI, October 15, 1865, Reg. Order/Letter Books, 4th USCI, RG–94, NA; SO #104, HQ 4th USCI, November 9, 1865, ibid.; SO #115, HQ 4th USCI, December 7, 1865, ibid.

29. *Official Army Register: Part VIII,* 172.

30. Carded Medical Records of Christian A. Fleetwood, RG–94, E–534, box 3510, NA.

31. GO #161, HQ Dept. of Washington, December 1, 1865, Letters Recd., 1863–66, 4th USCI, RG–94, NA.

32. Samuel A. Duncan to Julia Jones, October 13, 1865, Duncan MSS, NHHS; Personnel Returns, September–October 1865, CSR of Samuel A. Duncan, RG–94, NA; Charles J. Paine to H. I. Campbell, October 30, 1865, ibid.

33. *Official Army Register: Part VIII,* 172; Samuel A. Duncan to Asst. Adj. Gen., Mil. Div. of the Atlantic, October 3, 1865, CSR of Duncan, RG–94, NA; Personnel Return for November 1865, ibid.; Samuel A. Duncan to Julia Jones, November 11, 24, 1865, Duncan MSS, NHHS.

34. Samuel A. Duncan to C. W. Foster, January 13, 1866, Reg. Order/Letter Books, 4th USCI, RG–94, NA; Samuel A. Duncan to D. W. Van Horne, January 16, 1866, ibid.; SO #12, HQ 4th USCI, January 18, 1866, ibid.; GO #6, HQ 4th USCI, December 27, 1865, ibid.

35. Reg. Descriptive Book, 4th USCI, RG–94, E–112/115, NA; SO #8, HQ 4th USCI, January 11, 1866, Reg. Order/Letter Books, 4th USCI, RG–94, NA.

36. Samuel A. Duncan to J. H. Taylor, March 1, 29, 1866, CSR of Duncan, RG–94, NA; AGO to W. A. LaMotte, March 24, 1866, Reg. MSS, 4th USCI, NA.

37. Circular #7, HQ 4th USCI, March 23, 1866, Reg. Order/Letter Books, 4th USCI, RG–94, NA; GO #5, HQ 4th USCI, May 2, 1866, ibid.; Samuel A. Duncan to Frederick Fuger, April 30, 1866, Reg. MSS, 4th USCI, NA.

38. GO #5, HQ 4th USCI, May 2, 1866, Reg. Order/Letter Books, 4th USCI, RG–94, NA; Allan R. Millett and Peter Maslowski, *For the Common Defense: A Military History of the United States of America* (New York: Free Press, 1984), 233.

39. Pension Files, various enlisted men, 4th USCI, RG–15, NA.
40. Christian A. Fleetwood to James Hall, June 8, 1865, Carter G. Woodson MSS.
41. "A Short Biography of Christian Abraham Fleetwood," 5–10, Fleetwood MSS.

UNPUBLISHED MATERIALS
Regimental Personnel
Birney, William. Letter of August 28, 1863. U.S. Army Military History Institute, Carlisle Barracks, Pa.
————. Papers. Maryland Historical Society, Baltimore.
Brigham, Alfred M. Correspondence. Robert W. Woodruff Library, Emory University, Atlanta, Ga.
Brown, Charles A. Letter of March 30, 1864. Benjamin F. Butler Papers. Library of Congress, Washington, D.C.
Duncan, Samuel A. Letter of April 11, 1866. William Farrar Smith Papers. Vermont Historical Society, Montpelier.
————. Papers. Baker Special Collections Library, Dartmouth College, Hanover, N.H.
————. Papers. New Hampshire Historical Society, Concord.
Eastard, Daniel. Papers. In possession of Ms. Tanya Jones-Sullivan, New York.
Fleetwood, Christian A. Correspondence. Carter G. Woodson Papers. Library of Congress, Washington, D.C.
————. Diaries, 1863–64, and Papers. Library of Congress.
Henry, William. Bounty Documents. Maryland Historical Society.
Hunter, William H. Letter of September 16, 1864. Samuel A. Duncan Papers. Baker Special Collections Library, Dartmouth College.
Maltby, Seth W. Letter of March 14, 1864. Benjamin F. Butler Papers. Library of Congress.
Morgan, Jarrett. Papers. In possession of Mrs. Darlene Dorman, Baltimore.
Price, Solomon. Bounty Documents. Maryland Historical Society.
Various Officers and Enlisted Men. Carded Medical Records. National Archives, Washington, D.C.
————. Compiled Service Records. National Archives.

———. Pension Files. National Archives.

Wickes, James H. Correspondence. Boston Public Library.

———. Correspondence. Maryland Historical Society.

Other

Blassingame, John W. "The Organization and Use of Negro Troops in the Union Army, 1863–1865." Master's thesis, Howard University, 1961.

Bowie, Marilyn Elizabeth. "An Analytical History of the Fourth and Sixth Infantries of the United States Colored Troops in the Civil War." Master's thesis, Howard University, 1969.

Butler, Benjamin F. Papers. Library of Congress.

Churchill, Michael. "A History of the Fourth United States Colored Troops." Internet page, www.ncwa.org/4thUS.html.

Crain, Peter W. Letter of August 9, 1866. Maryland Historical Society.

Department of Virginia and North Carolina. Letters Sent and Received, 1863–65. National Archives.

Fourth United States Colored Infantry. Clothing Records. Moorland–Spingarn Research Center, Howard University, Washington, D.C.

———. Company and Regimental Books. National Archives.

———. Letters Sent and Received, 1863–66. National Archives.

———. Muster Rolls. Maryland State Archives, Annapolis.

———. Record of Events. National Archives.

———. Regimental Papers. National Archives.

Generals' Reports of Service, War of the Rebellion, 1853–65. National Archives.

Hinks, Edward W. Papers. Mugar Memorial Library, Boston University.

Schenck, Robert C. Papers. King Library, Miami University, Oxford, Ohio.

Scroggs, Joseph J. Diaries, 1864–65. U.S. Army Military History Institute.

Smith, William Farrar. Papers. Vermont Historical Society.

Terry, Alfred H. Papers. Beinecke Rare Book and Manuscripts Library, Yale University, New Haven, Conn.

———. Papers. Connecticut Historical Society, Hartford.

———. Papers. Sterling Memorial Library, Yale University.

Wild, Edward A. Papers. U.S. Army Military History Institute.

Wilson, Keith P. "White Officers in Black Units in the Civil War." Ph.D. diss., La Trobe University, Melbourne, Australia, 1985.

NEWSPAPERS

Anglo-African (New York)

Army and Navy Journal (New York)

Baltimore American and Commercial Advertiser
Baltimore Daily Gazette
Baltimore Sun
Cavalier (Williamsburg and Yorktown, Va.)
Christian Recorder (Philadelphia)
National Tribune (Washington, D.C.)
New Regime (Norfolk, Va.)
New York Herald
New York Times
New York Tribune
Petersburg Express
Petersburg Register
Philadelphia Press
Record-Times (Harford County, Md.)
Richmond Daily Examiner
Richmond Dispatch

ARTICLES AND ESSAYS

Abbott, Abial R. "The Negro in the War of the Rebellion." In *Military Essays and Recollections: Papers Read before the Commandery of the State of Illinois, Military Order of the Loyal Legion of the United States.* (4 vols. Chicago: various publishers, 1891–1907), 3: 373–84.

Armstrong, Warren B. "Union Chaplains and the Education of the Freedmen." *Journal of Negro History* 52 (April 1967): 104–15.

Armstrong, William H. "The Negro as a Soldier." In *War Papers: Read before the Indiana Commandery, Military Order of the Loyal Legion of the United States* (Indianapolis: Levey Brothers & Co., 1898), 316–33.

Beauregard, P. G. T. "The Defense of Drewry's Bluff." In *Battles and Leaders of the Civil War,* edited by Robert Underwood Johnson and Clarence Clough Buel. (4 vols. New York: Century Co., 1887–88), 4: 195–205.

———. "Four Days of Battle at Petersburg." In *Battles and Leaders of the Civil War,* edited by Robert Underwood Johnson and Clarence Clough Buel. (4 vols. New York: Century Co., 1887–88), 4: 540–44.

Blassingame, John W. "Negro Chaplains in the Civil War." *Negro History Bulletin* 27 (October 1963): 22–23.

———. "The Recruitment of Colored Troops in Kentucky, Maryland and Missouri, 1863–1865." *Historian* 29 (August 1967): 533–45.

———. "The Recruitment of Negro Troops in Maryland." *Maryland Historical Magazine* 58 (March 1963): 20–29.

———. "The Selection of Officers and Non-commissioned Officers of Negro Troops in the Union Army, 1863–1865." *Negro History Bulletin* 30 (January 1967): 8–11.

————. "The Union Army as an Educational Institution for Negroes, 1862–1865." *Journal of Negro Education* 34 (1965): 152–59.

Bowditch, Charles P. "War Letters of Charles P. Bowditch." *Massachusetts Historical Society Proceedings* 57 (1923–24): 414–95.

Burbank, Horace H. "The Battle of 'The Crater.'" In *War Papers: Read before the Commandery of the State of Maine, Military Order of the Loyal Legion of the United States* (3 vols. Portland: various publishers, 1898–1908), 1: 283–94.

Carter, Solon A. "Fourteen Months' Service with Colored Troops." In *Civil War Papers: Read before the Commandery of the State of Massachusetts, Military Order of the Loyal Legion of the United States* (2 vols. Boston: F. H. Gilson Co., 1900), 1: 155–79.

Connor, Selden. "The Colored Troops." In *War Papers: Read before the Commandery of the State of Maine, Military Order of the Loyal Legion of the United States* (3 vols. Portland: various publishers, 1898–1908), 3: 61–82.

Cornish, Dudley T. "To Be Recognized as Men." *Military Review* 58 (February 1978): 40–55.

————. "The Union Army as a School for Negroes." *Journal of Negro History* 37 (October 1952): 368–82.

Cowdrey, Albert E. "Slave into Soldier: The Enlistment by the North of Runaway Slaves." *History Today* 20 (October 1970): 704–15.

Dyer, Brainerd. "The Treatment of Colored Union Troops by the Confederates, 1861–1865." *Journal of Negro History* 20 (1935): 273–86.

"The Exchange of Prisoners: Reply of Major-General Butler." In *The Rebellion Record: A Diary of American Events,* edited by Frank Moore. (12 vols. New York: various publishers, 1861–68), 11: 159–62.

Fen, Sing-Nan. "Notes on the Education of Negroes at Norfolk and Portsmouth, Virginia, during the Civil War." *Phylon* 28 (Summer 1967): 197–207.

Fleetwood, Christian A. "' . . . To Benefit My Race': A Black Medal of Honor Winner's Bitter Account of Army Treatment." *Civil War Times Illustrated* 16 (July 1977): 18–19.

Fletcher, Marvin E. "The Negro Volunteer in Reconstruction, 1865–1866." *Military Affairs* 32 (1968): 124–31.

Furness, William E. "The Negro as a Soldier." In *Military Essays and Recollections: Papers Read before the Commandery of the State of Illinois, Military Order of the Loyal Legion of the United States* (4 vols. Chicago: various publishers, 1891–1907), 2: 457–88.

Goulding, Joseph H. "The Colored Troops in the War of the Rebellion." *Proceedings of the Reunion Society of Vermont Officers* 2 (1906): 137–54.

"Government of the Contrabands: General Butler's Order." In *The Rebellion Record: A Diary of American Events,* edited by Frank Moore. (12 vols. New York: various publishers, 1861–68), 8: 261–64.

Grant, Ulysses S. "General Grant on the Siege of Petersburg." In *Battles and Leaders of the Civil War,* edited by Robert Underwood Johnson and Clarence Clough Buel. (4 vols. New York: Century Co., 1887–88), 4: 574–79.

Hollandsworth, James G., Jr. "The Execution of White Officers from Black Units by Confederate Forces during the Civil War." *Louisiana History* 35 (Fall 1994): 475–89.

Hubbell, John T. "Abraham Lincoln and the Recruitment of Black Soldiers." *Papers of the Abraham Lincoln Association* 2 (1980): 6–21.

Lamb, William. "The Defense of Fort Fisher." In *Battles and Leaders of the Civil War,* edited by Robert Underwood Johnson and Clarence Clough Buel. (4 vols. New York: Century Co., 1887–88), 4: 642–54.

Levstik, Frank R., ed. "From Slavery to Freedom: Two Wartime Letters of One of the Conflict's Few Black Medal of Honor Winners." *Civil War Times Illustrated* 11 (November 1972): 10–15.

Longacre, Edward G. "Black Troops in the Army of the James, 1863–65." *Military Affairs* 45 (1981): 1–8.

———. "Brave Radical Wild." *Civil War Times Illustrated* 19 (June 1980): 8–19.

Matson, Daniel. "The Colored Man in the Civil War." In *War Sketches and Incidents: As Related by Companions of the Iowa Commandery, Military Order of the Loyal Legion of the United States* (2 vols. Des Moines: P. C. Kenyon Press, 1893–98), 2: 236–54.

Montgomery, Horace. "A Union Officer's Recollections of the Negro as a Soldier." *Pennsylvania History* 28 (1961): 156–86.

Norton, Henry A. "Colored Troops in the War of the Rebellion." In *Glimpses of the Nation's Struggle: Papers Read before the Minnesota Commandery of the Military Order of the Loyal Legion of the United States* (6 vols. Saint Paul: various publishers, 1887–1909), 5: 59–73.

"Notes on the May [1864] Campaign on the James River." *United States Service Magazine* 3 (1865): 22–28, 245–54.

"Operations in Virginia: General Butler's Despatch." In *The Rebellion Record: A Diary of American Events,* edited by Frank Moore. (12 vols. New York: various publishers, 1861–68), 11: 493–504.

Parmet, Robert D. "Schools for the Freedmen." *Negro History Bulletin* 34 (1971): 128–32.

Popchock, Barry. "A Shower of Stars at New Market Heights." *Civil War Magazine* 46 (August 1994): 30–39.

Redkey, Edwin S. "Black Chaplains in the Civil War." *Civil War History* 33 (1987): 331–50.

————, ed. "'Rocked in the Cradle of Consternation': A Black Chaplain in the Union Army Reports on the Struggle to Take Fort Fisher . . ." *American Heritage* 31 (October–November 1980): 70–79.

Reid, Richard. "General Edward A. Wild and Civil War Discrimination." *Historical Journal of Massachusetts* 13 (January 1985): 14–29.

Ritter, E. Jay. "Congressional Medal of Honor Winners." *Negro History Bulletin* 26 (January 1963): 135–36.

Robertson, James I., Jr. "Negro Soldiers in the Civil War." *Civil War Times Illustrated* 7 (October 1968): 21–32.

Shannon, Fred A. "The Federal Government and the Negro Soldier, 1861–1865." *Journal of Negro History* 11 (1926): 563–83.

Simonton, Edward. "The Campaign up the James River to Petersburg." In *Glimpses of the Nation's Struggle: Papers Read before the Minnesota Commandery of the Military Order of the Loyal Legion of the United States* (4 vols. Saint Paul: various publishers, 1887–1909), 5: 481–95.

Simpson, Brooks D. "'The Doom of Slavery': Ulysses S. Grant, War Aims, and Emancipation, 1861–1863." *Civil War History* 36 (March 1990): 36–56.

Slocum, Henry W. "Final Operations of Sherman's Army." In *Battles and Leaders of the Civil War,* edited by Robert Underwood Johnson and Clarence Clough Buel. (4 vols. New York: Century Co., 1887–88), 4: 754–58.

Smith, William Farrar. "Butler's Attack on Drewry's Bluff." In *Battles and Leaders of the Civil War,* edited by Robert Underwood Johnson and Clarence Clough Buel. (4 vols. New York: Century Co., 1887–88), 4: 206–12.

————. "The Movement against Petersburg, June, 1864." In *Papers of the Military Historical Society of Massachusetts* (14 vols. Boston: various publishers, 1895–1918), 5: 75–115.

Sommers, Richard J. "The Dutch Gap Affair: Military Atrocities and the Rights of Negro Soldiers." *Civil War History* 21 (1975): 51–64.

————. "Fury at Fort Harrison." *Civil War Times Illustrated* 19 (October 1980): 12–23.

Sutherland, George E. "The Negro in the Late War." In *War Papers: Read before the Commandery of the State of Wisconsin, Military Order of the Loyal Legion of the United States* (3 vols. Milwaukee: Burdick, Armitage & Allen, 1891–1903), 1: 164–88.

Synnestvedt, Sig, ed. "The Earth Shook and Quivered." *Civil War Times Illustrated* 11 (December 1972): 30–37.

Taylor, Michael W., and Bill H. Hatley. "Fifty Years after the First Battle of Bull Run, Albert Barnes Recalled Drunken Union Colonel Dixon Miles." *America's Civil War* 14 (March 2001): 54, 57–59.

Thomas, Henry Goddard. "The Colored Troops at Petersburg." In *Battles and Leaders of the Civil War*, edited by Robert Underwood Johnson and Clarence Clough Buel. (4 vols. New York: Century Co., 1887–88), 4: 563–67.

"A Visit to General Butler and the Army of the James." *Fraser's Magazine* 71 (1865): 434–48.

Weiss, Nathan. "General Benjamin Franklin Butler and the Negro: The Evolution of the Racial Views of a Practical Politician." *Negro History Bulletin* 29 (January 1965): 3–4, 14–16, 23.

Whyte, James H. "Maryland's Negro Regiments: How, Where They Served." *Civil War Times Illustrated* 1 (July 1962): 41–43.

Wiley, Bell I. "Billy Yank and the Black Folk." *Journal of Negro History* 36 (1951): 35–52.

Wilson, Keith P. "Thomas Webster and the Free Military School for Applicants for Command of Colored Troops." *Civil War History* 29 (1983): 101–22.

BOOKS AND PAMPHLETS

Adams, Charles F., Jr., et al. *A Cycle of Adams Letters, 1861–1865*. Edited by Worthington Chauncey Ford. 2 vols. Boston: Houghton Mifflin Co., 1920.

Addeman, J. M. *Reminiscences of Two Years with the Colored Troops: Personal Narratives of Events in the War of the Rebellion . . .* Providence, R.I.: Snow & Farnham, ca. 1880.

Astor, Gerald. *The Right to Fight: A History of African Americans in the Military.* Novato, Calif.: Presidio Press, 1998.

Barrett, John G. *The Civil War in North Carolina.* Chapel Hill: University of North Carolina Press, 1963.

Berlin, Ira, Joseph P. Reidy, and Leslie S. Rowland, eds. *Freedom: A Documentary History of Emancipation, 1861–1867.* Ser. II, vol. 1, *The Black Military Experience.* New York: Cambridge University Press, 1982.

Berry, Mary F. *Military Necessity and Civil Rights Policy.* Port Washington, N.Y.: National University Publications, 1977.

Bilby, Joseph G. *Civil War Firearms: Their Historical Background, Tactical Use and Modern Collecting and Shooting.* Conshohocken, Pa.: Combined Publishing, 1996.

Birney, William. *General William Birney's Answer to Libels Clandestinely Circulated by James Shaw, Jr. . . .* Washington, D.C.: Stanley Snodgrass, 1878.

Boatner, Mark Mayo. *The Civil War Dictionary.* New York: David McKay Co., 1959.

Brown, William Wells. *The Negro in the American Rebellion: His Heroism and His Fidelity.* Boston: A. G. Brown & Co., 1880.

Browne, Frederick W. *My Service in the U.S. Colored Cavalry . . .* Cincinnati: privately issued, 1908.

Butler, Benjamin F. *Autobiography and Personal Reminiscences of Major-General Benj. F. Butler: Butler's Book.* Boston: A. M. Thayer & Co., 1892.

————. *Character and Results of the War . . .* Philadelphia: privately issued, 1863.

————. *Private and Official Correspondence of Gen. Benjamin F. Butler during the Period of the Civil War.* Compiled by Jessie Ames Marshall. 6 vols. Norwood, Mass.: Plimpton Press, 1917.

————. *Speech of Maj.-Gen. Benj. F. Butler, upon the Campaign before Richmond, 1864 . . .* Boston: Wright & Potter, 1865.

Califf, Joseph M. *Record of the Services of the Seventh Regiment, U.S. Colored Troops.* Providence, R.I.: E. L. Freeman & Co., 1878.

Cavanaugh, Michael A., and William Marvel. *The Battle of the Crater: "The Horrid Pit."* Lynchburg, Va.: H. E. Howard, 1989.

Chase, Salmon P. *Inside Lincoln's Cabinet: The Civil War Diaries of Salmon P. Chase.* Edited by David Donald. New York: Longmans, Green & Co., 1954.

Chester, Thomas M. *Thomas Morris Chester, Black Civil War Correspondent: His Dispatches from the Virginia Front.* Edited by R. J. M. Blackett. Baton Rouge: Louisiana State University Press, 1989.

Clark, Charles B. *Politics in Maryland during the Civil War.* Chestertown, Md.: privately issued, 1952.

Coddington, Edwin B. *The Gettysburg Campaign: A Study in Command.* New York: Charles Scribner's Sons, 1968.

Cornish, Dudley T. *The Sable Arm: Negro Troops in the Union Army, 1861–1865.* New York: Longmans, Green & Co., 1956.

Dennett, George M. *History of the Ninth U.S.C. Troops.* Philadelphia: King & Baird, 1866.

Dyer, Frederick H. *A Compendium of the War of the Rebellion.* Des Moines, Ia.: Dyer Publishing Co., 1908.

Faust, Patricia L., ed. *The Historical Times Illustrated Encyclopedia of the Civil War.* New York: Harper & Row, 1986.

Fladeland, Betty. *James Gillespie Birney: Slaveholder to Abolitionist.* Ithaca, N.Y.: Cornell University Press, 1955.

Fleetwood, Christian A. *The Negro as a Soldier . . .* Washington, D.C.: Howard University Printing Co., 1895.

Foner, Jack D. *Blacks and the Military in American History.* New York: Prager Publishers, 1974.

Fonvielle, Chris E., Jr. *The Wilmington Campaign: Last Rays of Departing Hope.* Mechanicsburg, Pa.: Stackpole Books, 2001.

Franklin, John Hope. *From Slavery to Freedom: A History of American Negroes.* New York: Alfred A. Knopf, 1947.

General Henry Goddard Thomas, 1837–1897 . . . Portland, Me.: Lakeside Press, 1898.

Gerteis, Louis. *From Contraband to Freedmen: Federal Policy Toward Southern Blacks, 1861–1865.* Westport, Conn.: Greenwood Press, 1973.

Gladstone, William A. *Men of Color.* Gettysburg, Pa.: Thomas Publications, 1993.

———. *United States Colored Troops.* Gettysburg, Pa.: Thomas Publications, 1990.

Glatthaar, Joseph T. *Forged in Battle: The Civil War Alliance of Black Soldiers and White Officers.* New York: Free Press, 1990.

Glenn, William Wilkins. *Between North and South: A Maryland Journalist Views the Civil War* . . . Edited by Bayly Ellen Marks and Mark Norton Schatz. Rutherford, N.J.: Fairleigh Dickinson University Press, 1976.

Gragg, Rod. *Confederate Goliath: The Battle of Fort Fisher.* New York: HarperCollins, 1991.

Grant, Ulysses S. *Personal Memoirs of U. S. Grant.* 2 vols. New York: Charles L. Webster & Co., 1885–86.

Green, Alfred M. *Letters and Discussions on the Formation of Colored Regiments* . . . Philadelphia: Ringwalt & Brown, 1862.

Guthrie, James M. *Camp-fires of the Afro-American.* Philadelphia: Afro-American Publishing Co., 1899.

Hargrove, Hondon B. *Black Union Soldiers in the Civil War.* Jefferson, N.C.: McFarland & Co., 1988.

Heitman, Francis B., comp. *Historical Register and Dictionary of the United States Army.* 2 vols. Washington, D.C.: Government Printing Office, 1903.

Henig, Gerald S. *Henry Winter Davis, Antebellum and Civil War Congressman from Maryland.* New York: Twayne Publishers, 1973.

Hewett, Janet, et al., eds. *Supplement to the Official Records of the Union and Confederate Armies.* 3 pts., 95 vols. to date. Wilmington, N.C.: Broadfoot Publishing Co., 1994–.

Holzman, Robert S. *Stormy Ben Butler.* New York: Macmillan Co., 1954.

Horrocks, James. *"My Dear Parents": The Civil War as Seen by an English Union Soldier.* Edited by A. S. Lewis. New York: Harcourt Brace Jovanovich, 1982.

Howe, Thomas J. *The Petersburg Campaign: Wasted Valor, June 15–18, 1864.* Lynchburg, Va.: H. E. Howard, 1988.

Humphreys, Andrew A. *The Virginia Campaign of '64 and '65: The Army of the Potomac and the Army of the James.* New York: Charles Scribner's Sons, 1883.

Johnson, Allen, et al., eds. *Dictionary of American Biography.* 27 vols. to date. New York: Charles Scribner's Sons, 1927–.

Joint Committee on the Conduct of the War. 3 vols. in 8. Washington, D.C.: Government Printing Office, 1863–68.

Kennard, Martin P. *Address of Martin P. Kennard . . . on Presentation to the Town of a Memorial Portrait of the Late Brig.-Gen'l Edward Augustus Wild . . .* Brookline, Mass.: Printed for the Town, 1894.

Lanning, Michael Lee. *The African-American Soldier: From Crispus Attucks to Colin Powell.* Secaucus, N.J.: Birch Lane Press, 1997.

Long, E. B., and Barbara Long. *The Civil War Day by Day: An Almanac, 1861–1865.* Garden City, N.Y.: Doubleday & Co., 1971.

Longacre, Edward G. *Army of Amateurs: General Benjamin F. Butler and the Army of the James, 1863–1865.* Mechanicsburg, Pa.: Stackpole Books, 1997.

Lord, Francis A. *Civil War Sutlers and Their Wares.* New York: Thomas Yoseloff, 1969.

Manakee, Harold. *Maryland in the Civil War.* Baltimore: Maryland Historical Society, 1961.

Mays, Joe H. *Black Americans and Their Contributions Toward Union Victory in the American Civil War, 1861–1865.* Lanham, Md.: University Press of America, 1984.

McMurray, John. *Recollections of a Colored Troop.* Brookville, Pa.: privately issued, 1916.

McPherson, James M. *The Negro's Civil War: How American Negroes Felt and Acted during the War for the Union.* New York: Pantheon Books, 1965.

McWhiney, Grady, and Perry D. Jamieson. *Attack and Die: Civil War Military Tactics and the Southern Heritage.* University: University of Alabama Press, 1982.

The Medal of Honor of the United States Army. Washington, D.C.: Government Printing Office, 1948.

A Memorial of the Great Rebellion: Being a History of the Fourteenth Regiment New Hampshire Volunteers . . . Boston: Rand, Avery, & Co., 1882.

Millett, Allan R., and Peter Maslowski. *For the Common Defense: A Military History of the United States of America.* New York: Free Press, 1984.

Nalty, Bernard C. *Strength for the Fight: A History of Black Americans in the Military.* New York: Free Press, 1986.

Nalty, Bernard C., and Morris J. MacGregor, eds. *Blacks in the Military: Essential Documents.* Wilmington, Del.: Scholarly Resources, 1981.

The Negro in the Military Service of the United States: A Compilation of Official Records, State Papers, Historical Extracts, etc. . . . Washington, D.C.: Adjutant General's Office, 1888.

Negro Population, 1790–1915. Washington, D.C.: Government Printing Office, 1918.

Norton, Oliver Willcox. *Army Letters, 1861–1865: Being Extracts from Private Letters to Relatives and Friends from a Soldier in the Field* . . . Chicago: O. L. Deming, 1903.

Nye, Wilbur S. *Here Come the Rebels!* Baton Rouge: Louisiana State University Press, 1965.

Official Army Register of the Volunteer Force of the United States Army for the Years 1861, '62, '63, '64, '65: Part VIII . . . U.S. Colored Troops. Washington, D.C.: Adjutant General's Office, 1867.

Osborn, Thomas W. *The Fiery Trail: A Union Officer's Account of Sherman's Last Campaigns.* Edited by Richard B. Harwell and Philip N. Racine. Knoxville: University of Tennessee Press, 1986.

Paradis, James M. *Strike the Blow for Freedom: The 6th United States Colored Infantry in the Civil War.* Shippensburg, Pa.: White Mane Books, 1998.

Pleasants, Henry, and George H. Straley. *Inferno at Petersburg.* Philadelphia: Chilton Book Co., 1961.

Pope, Charles Henry, ed. *Paine Ancestry: The Family of Robert Treat Paine, Signer of the Declaration of Independence* . . . Boston: David Clapp & Son, 1912.

Powell, E. Henry. *The Colored Soldier in the War of the Rebellion* . . . Burlington, Vt.: privately issued, 1893.

Quarles, Benjamin. *The Negro in the Civil War.* Boston: Little, Brown & Co., 1953.

Record of the Public Services of Brigadier-General and Brevet Major General Edward W. Hincks . . . Cambridge, Mass.: privately issued, 1888.

Redkey, Edwin S., ed. *A Grand Army of Black Men: Letters from African-American Soldiers in the Union Army, 1861–1865.* New York: Cambridge University Press, 1992.

Robertson, William Glenn. *Back Door to Richmond: The Bermuda Hundred Campaign, April–June 1864.* Newark: University of Delaware Press, 1987.

Robinson, Charles M. *Hurricane of Fire: The Union Assault on Fort Fisher.* Annapolis, Md.: Naval Institute Press, 1998.

Scharf, J. Thomas. *History of Baltimore City and County.* Philadelphia: Louis H. Everts, 1881.

Schiller, Herbert M. *The Bermuda Hundred Campaign: Operations on the South Side of the James River, Virginia—May, 1864.* Dayton: Morningside House, 1988.

Sears, Stephen W. *To the Gates of Richmond: The Peninsula Campaign.* New York: Ticknor & Fields, 1992.

Sefton, James E. *The United States Army and Reconstruction, 1865–1877.* Baton Rouge: Louisiana State University Press, 1967.

Shannon, Fred A. *The Organization and Administration of the Union Army, 1861–1865.* 2 vols. Cleveland: Arthur H. Clark Co., 1928.

Shaw, James, Jr. *Our Last Campaign and Subsequent Service in Texas: Personal Narratives of Events in the War of the Rebellion . . .* Providence, R.I.: Snow & Farnham Co., 1905.

Sherman, George R. *The Negro as a Soldier: Personal Narratives of Events in the War of the Rebellion . . .* Providence, R.I.: Snow & Farnham Co., 1913.

Smith, Lyman A. *Memorial of Adjt. M. W. Smith: A Tribute to a Beloved Son and Brother.* Newark, N.J.: privately issued, 1864.

Smith, William Farrar. *From Chattanooga to Petersburg under Generals Grant and Butler: A Contribution to the History of the War, and a Personal Vindication.* Boston: Houghton, Mifflin & Co., 1893.

Sommers, Richard J. *Richmond Redeemed: The Siege at Petersburg.* Garden City, N.Y.: Doubleday & Co., 1981.

Stein, A. H. *History of the Thirty-seventh Regt. U.S.C. Infantry . . .* Philadelphia: King & Baird, 1866.

Swint, Henry L. *"Dear Ones at Home": Letters from Contraband Camps.* Nashville: Vanderbilt University Press, 1966.

Taggart, John H. *Free Military School for Applicants for Commands of Colored Troops.* Philadelphia: King & Baird, 1863.

Toomey, Daniel Carroll. *Maryland in the Civil War.* Baltimore: privately issued, 1983.

Trefousse, Hans L. *Ben Butler: The South Called Him BEAST!* New York: Twayne Publishers, 1957.

Trudeau, Noah Andre. *The Last Citadel: Petersburg, Virginia, June 1864–April 1865.* Boston: Little, Brown & Co., 1991.

———. *Like Men of War: Black Troops in the Civil War, 1862–1865.* Boston: Little, Brown & Co., 1998.

Tucker, Phillip Thomas. *From Auction Block to Glory: The African American Experience.* New York: MetroBooks, 1998.

Wagandt, Charles. *The Mighty Revolution: Negro Emancipation in Maryland, 1862–1864.* Baltimore: Johns Hopkins University Press, 1964.

War of the Rebellion: A Compilation of the Official Records of the Union and Confederate Armies. 4 ser., 70 vols. in 128. Washington, D.C.: Government Printing Office, 1880–1901.

Warner, Ezra J. *Generals in Blue: Lives of the Union Commanders.* Baton Rouge: Louisiana State University Press, 1964.

Washington, Versalle F. *Eagles on Their Buttons: A Black Infantry Regiment in the Civil War.* Columbia: University of Missouri Press, 1991.

Wert, Jeffry D. *Mosby's Rangers.* New York: Simon & Schuster, 1990.

West, Richard S. *Lincoln's Scapegoat General: A Life of Benjamin F. Butler, 1818–1893.* Boston: Houghton, Mifflin Co., 1965.

Westwood, Howard C. *Black Troops, White Commanders, and Freedmen during the Civil War.* Carbondale and Edwardsville: Southern Illinois University Press, 1992.

Wheat, Thomas Adrian. *A Guide to Civil War Yorktown.* Knoxville, Tenn.: Bohemian Brigade Bookshop & Publishers, 1997.

Wightman, Edward K. *From Antietam to Fort Fisher: The Civil War Letters of Edward King Wightman, 1862–1865.* Edited by Edward G. Longacre. Rutherford, N.J.: Fairleigh Dickinson University Press, 1985.

Wiley, Bell Irvin. *Southern Negroes, 1861–1865.* New Haven, Conn.: Yale University Press, 1938.

Williams, George Washington. *A History of the Negro Troops in the War of the Rebellion, 1861–65.* New York: Harper & Brothers, 1888.

Wilmer, L. Allison, J. H. Jarrett, and George W. F. Vernon, comps. *History and Roster of Maryland Volunteers, War of 1861–5.* 2 vols. Baltimore: Guggenheimer, Weil & Co., 1899.

Wilson, Joseph T. *The Black Phalanx: A History of the Negro Soldiers of the United States . . .* Hartford, Conn.: American Publishing Co., 1890.

Wistar, Isaac J. *Autobiography of Isaac Jones Wistar, 1827–1905: Half a Century in War and Peace.* Philadelphia: Wistar Institute, 1937.

Woodson, Carter G. *The Negro in Our History.* Washington, D.C.: Associated Publishers, 1922.

Wright, James M. *The Free Negro in Maryland, 1634–1860.* New York: Columbia University Press, 1921.

INDEX

A

abatis, 117, 149
Abbott, Joseph C., 149, 151–54, 161
Adams Express Company, 102
Adams, John, 93
African-Americans, recruiting of, 7–11
Aiken's Landing, 115
Alexandria, Va., 155, 170
Ames, John W., 35, 60, 79–80, 121, 151, 153–57
Anderson, Battery, 147
Anderson, Fort, 135, 153, 155–56
Anglo-African, 42, 93, 95–96, 102
Antietam, Battle of, 4
Appleton, William H., 26, 120, 124, 127, 165
Appomattox Court House, Va., 164
Appomattox River, 69, 72–74, 77, 79, 81, 85, 98–99, 108–10, 144
Armstrong Rifle, 136
Army of Northern Virginia, 4, 37, 39, 73, 97, 149, 164
Army of Tennessee, 39, 98, 162
Army of the Cumberland, 39
Army of the Gulf, 10
Army of the James, 63, 74, 77, 84, 95–97, 99, 103–4, 107, 130, 132, 136, 141, 145, 152–53, 163–64, 170
Army of the Potomac, 4, 7, 29, 33, 39, 46, 63, 68, 73, 78, 83–84, 94–95, 97, 103–4, 107, 115, 132–33, 163
Arnold, Michael G., 35
  as hospital steward, 35,
  messes with Fleetwood, 41

on plight of black POWs, 64–65
on capture of City Point, 71
hopes for active service, 74
on defense of Spring Hill, 75–77
on June 15 attack on Petersburg, 93
on visit of Grant and Lincoln, 97
on sharpshooter fire, 99, 108
on army postal service, 102
views Crater Mine attack, 105
ponders capture of Wilmington, 158
enters Wilmington, 158–59
on Hunter's sermon in Wilmington, 159–60
postwar life of, 176
Articles of War, 173–74
Ash, Elijah, 93, 174
Ashmun Institute, 3
Atlanta, Ga., 63, 98, 115. 155
Averasboro, N.C., 162
Avondale, Md., 25

B

Bailey, Marcellus, 19, 32
Baker, Joseph, 93, 125
Baltimore & Ohio R. R., 6, 13
Baltimore, Md., 1, 3–7, 12–15, 19, 21, 29, 68, 82, 103, 113–14, 137, 169, 172, 175
Banks, Nathaniel P., 10
Banks, William, 32
Barnes, Alfred P., 19–20, 25, 165
Bass, Frederick, 47, 118–20, 122
Battalions
  43rd Va., 66

Battalions, *continued*
    Richmond Howitzers, 117, 122
Batteries
    8th N.Y., 36
    "B," 2nd U.S., 74, 77
    "E," 1st Pa., 36
    Rockbridge Arty., 117
Baylor's Farm, Battle of, 85–87
Beaufort, N.C., 138, 140, 145–46
Beauregard, P. G. T., 72, 76–77, 81, 83,
    94, 96, 110, 112
Belger, Camp, 14–15, 19–21, 27
Belle Isle, 54–55
Bell, Louis, 85, 88
Ben de Ford, 138
Bentonville, Battle of, 162
Bentonville, N.C., 162, 164
Bermuda, 134
Bermuda Hundred, 69, 71–74, 76–78,
    81, 83, 94, 102–3, 108, 110, 112–
    13, 136, 142, 144–45
Bethel A. M. E. Church, 6
Birney, David B., 83, 94, 115–16, 118,
    121
Birney, James G., 11
Birney, William, 11–12
    reports to Baltimore, 12
    recruits 4th U.S.C.I., 12–18, 24–25,
        128
    liberates slaves, 14–16
    appointed brigadier general, 22
    joins X Corps, 83
    in attack on New Market Heights,
        116–17
    leads U.S.C.T. division, 132
    helps force Lee's surrender, 164
Blue Ridge Mountains, 5
Boernstein, Augustus, 19, 25–27, 120
    funds regimental band, 19
    commands regiment, 52, 165
    on Wistar's Raid, 55
    reinforces Spring Hill, 79–81
    in June 15 attack on Petersburg,
        86–87, 90–91
    and ill officers, 100
    praised by regiment, 101
    leads regiment to Bermuda Hundred,
        108
    on sick leave, 113

    doubts quality of recruits, 114
    selects candidates for commendation,
        125–28
    replaces battle losses, 130–31
    on Fort Fisher expeditions, 147
    as martinet, 166–69, 175
    as provost marshal of New Bern, 168
    occupies Fort Slocum, 171
    court-martial and dismissal of, 172–74
Boley, Cyrus, 124
Bond, Hugh, 16, 112
Booth, John Wilkes, 165
Boston, Mass., 26
Bottom's Bridge, 54–55
Bowdin, Reverdy J., 40–41
Bowman, S. M., 114
Bradford, Augustus W., 16
Bradley, James M., 165
Bragg, Braxton, 39–40, 43, 136, 146–
    47, 149, 151, 153, 156–57, 161–
    62, 178
Brandy Station, 29
Brigham, Alfred M., 26, 34, 59, 65, 68,
    81, 83, 87
Broadway Landing, 84
Brooks, William T. H., 85, 88
Brown, Charles R., 53–54
Brown, William H., 7
Bruce, William Cabell, 177
Brune, John C., 1–3
Brune, Mrs. John C., 1–2
Buchanan, J. C., 125
Buie, Elhawan, 125
Buie, W. G., 125
Bull Run, First Battle of, 72
Burgee, Isaac E., 93
Burnham, Fort, 117, 124, 131–32
Burnside, Ambrose E., 104–5, 108, 114
Butler, Benjamin F.
    shelters runaway slaves, 8–9
    relieved in Louisiana, 10
    replaces J. G. Foster, 36
    reinstated to field command, 46
    and African-American troops, 46–48
    condemns drunkenness on duty, 52–54
    takes field, 68–69
    captures City Point, 71
    fortifies Bermuda Hundred, 72
    moves to attack Petersburg, 73

moves to attack Richmond, 73
secures Spring Hill, 74
in Battle of Drewry's Bluff, 76
"bottled up" at Bermuda Hundred, 77
reinforces Army of the Potomac, 78
reinforces Spring Hill, 79, 81
attacks Petersburg, 81–83, 85
political hopes of, 82
breaks out of "bottle," 94
extends Petersburg lines, 97
boosts morale of army, 102–3
trades white regiments for U.S.C.T., 123
reviews candidates for commendation, 127
issues medals to U.S.C.T., 129
launches final offensive of 1864, 132
on Fort Fisher expedition, 136–42, 147
explains failure to Grant, 142
relieved of command, 145
Butterfield, Daniel, 33

C

Camlin's Slave Pen, 14
Campbell, Fort, 153
Cape Fear River, 135, 147, 153, 156, 161, 178
Cape Hatteras, 145
Cape Henry, 138
Carroll County, Md., 14
Carroll, Joseph, 175
Casey, Silas, 24
Cassell, Alex, 137
Caswell, Fort, 135, 153
Caulk, Isaac, 125
Cavalier, 48
Cedar Creek, Battle of, 138
Chaffin's Bluff, 110, 115, 117
Chaffin's Farm, 122, 124, 132
Chancellorsville, Battle of, 4
Charleston, S.C., 22, 72, 134, 161
Chattanooga, Tenn., 40, 43
Chesapeake Bay, 14, 29, 65, 138
chevaux-de-frise, 117, 119–21
Chew, Josiah, 125
Chickahominy River, 54, 81, 83
Chickamauga, Battle of, 40
Christian Recorder, 35, 42

City Point, Va., 69, 71–73, 78, 80–81, 83–85, 87, 96, 137
Clayton, William, 175
Cleveland, Ohio, 82
Clifton, Fort, 73, 98
Clingman, Thomas L., 151
Cobb's Hill, 81, 83, 96
Cold Harbor, Battle of, 78, 81, 84, 98
Cold Harbor, Va., 78, 82–84, 94
Colored Troops, Bureau of, 10, 12–13
Columbiad Rifle, 136
Columbus, Ohio, 176
Confederate Point, 135, 138–39, 141, 144, 146–47
Congress, Confederate, 11
Converse, Fort, 74, 77, 79
Convoy, 60
Cooper, Thomas, 93
Cooper, W. C., 41, 102, 174
Cornwallis, Lord, 30–31
Corps, Army
II, 84, 94–95, 97
V, 95
VI, 95–97
VIII, 4
IX, 95, 103–4, 108
X, 68, 73, 78, 81, 85, 112, 116–17
X (Provisional), 115, 168
XVIII, 63, 71, 73, 78, 81, 83, 85, 94, 104, 110, 115
XXIII, 155–56, 162, 168
XXIV, 141, 149, 170
XXV, 103, 136, 170
Cosley, Grafton, 25, 125
Cox's Bridge, 163
Crater Mine, Battle of the, 105–7
Craven Street Prison, 168
Creager, J. P., 15
Crimean War, 136
Culpeper Court House, Va., 29
Curtis, N. Martin, 141, 147, 149–50

D

Dahlgren, Ulric, 59–60, 71
Darbytown Road, 116, 132
Dartmouth College, 23
Davis, Jefferson, 72, 134
Dawsen, James, 125
DeCoursey, Joshua, 33–34

Deep Bottom, 97, 113, 115–17, 132

Deer Creek, Md., 17, 66

Democratic Party, 82

Dillenback, John W., 45, 93, 131

Dodson, Thomas, 175

Dorchester County, Md., 14

Dorsey, Nathaniel W., 124

Douglass, Frederick, 78, 177

Draper, Alonzo G., 117, 119, 121–22

Drewry's Bluff, 73, 110

Drewry's Bluff, Battle of, 76, 82, 104, 150

Dublin, Md., 17

DuBose, Dudley, 117

Dunbar, Paul Lawrence, 177

Duncan, Samuel A., 22–24, 37, 94, 96
  joins regiment, 21–22
  first impressions of regiment, 24–27
  attitudes toward U.S.C.T., 24
  leads regiment to Yorktown, 28–29
  describes Yorktown, 31
  rebuilds fortifications, 34
  on Mathews County expedition, 36–38
  anticipates campaign, 39
  life in winter quarters, 41
  reads dispatches to regiment, 43–44
  fights fire at Yorktown, 49–50
  enjoys Christmas meal and hunt, 50
  commands brigade, 52
  condemns drunkenness on duty, 52–53
  on Wistar's Raid, 54–55
  on punative expedition, 59
  moves up James River, 69, 71
  captures City Point, 71
  attacks Fort Clifton, 73
  secures Spring Hill, 74
  attacks Petersburg, 83–92
  moves to Bermuda Hundred, 96
  reoccupies Petersburg works, 97
  supports Crater Mine attack, 105, 107
  returns to Bermuda Hundred, 108
  helps dig Dutch Gap Canal, 111
  seeks recruits for 4th U.S.C.I., 113–14
  in attack on New Market Heights, 117–19, 121
  wounded, 121, 124
  praises troops, 125
  berates McClellan, 133–34
  returns to duty, 157
  as brevet brigadier general, 157
  advances on Wilmington, 157
  enters Wilmington, 158–59
  attacks McRee's Ferry, 162
  advances to Goldsboro, 163
  deplores slavery, 163
  on return to Goldsboro, 165
  anticipates long postwar duty, 168, 170
  returns to command of 4th U.S.C.I., 174
  as brevet major general, 174
  final months in command, 174–75

Durham Station, 164

Dutch Gap, 110–14, 116, 131–32, 167

Dyson, John H., 125

E

Early, Jubal A., 115, 138, 161

Eastern Shore of Maryland., 11, 14

East Washington, N.H., 23

Eberhardt, John J., 165

Edmunds, Landin, 168

Edwards, William, 93

Elliott's Salient, 104–6

Elzey, Arnold, 55

Emancipation Proclamation, 9–10

Enfield Rifle, 21, 33, 73, 78, 116, 131, 150, 168

F

Faison's Depot, 163

Farrar's Island, 110, 112, 143

Federal Point, 135, 155, 157

Ferrero, Edward, 104, 107–8

Fisher, Fort, 135–38, 140–42, 144, 146–47, 149–55, 163

Fisher, Fort, Expeditions to, 136–41, 144–52, 178

Fisher's Hill, Battle of, 115

Five Forks, Battle of, 163

Flag Pond Battery, 147

Fleetwood, Charles, 1, 13

Fleetwood, Christian Abraham
  prewar life, 1–4
  flees Baltimore mob, 4–7
  joins 4th U.S.C.I., 13–14, 20
  parades through Baltimore, 21
  moves to Yorktown, 29, 31

on health of regiment, 31
and army friendships, 35
assists chaplain, 35–36
on Mathews County expeditions, 37–38, 60
eating habits of, 40, 95, 102
health of, 40
life in winter quarters, 41–42
on hunt for guerrillas, 46
enjoys Christmas meal, 50
on expedition to Gloucester Point, 51
on Wistar's Raid, 54–55
felled by exhaustion, 59
on punative expedition, 60
reads books, 62–63, 102
at Point Lookout, 65
returns from Fort Clifton, 73
helps defend Spring Hill, 74–75
on aborted attack on Petersburg, 78
in June 9 attack on Petersburg, 82
in June 15 attack on Petersburg, 91
on move to rear, 94
defends regiment in print, 95
returns to Fort Clifton, 98
wounded, 99
feuds with comrades, 101
chronicles social functions, 101
visits Army of the Potomac, 103
views Crater Mine attack, 105, 107
helps erect regimental headquarters, 109
assigned to recruiting party, 113
in attack on New Market Heights, 120–21, 126
selected for commendation, 125
receives Medal of Honor, 127
denied commission, 128–29
on new officers, 130
hopes for peace and quiet, 132
on Fort Fisher expeditions, 137–38, 140–42, 150
observes effects of explosion, 152–53
hospitalized, 164, 171
listed as deserter, 171, 174
postwar life of, 176–78
rejects postwar military career, 176
Fleetwood, Sarah Iredell, 177
Ford's Theater, 164
Foster, Charles W., 10

Foster, John G., 11, 27–28, 30, 46
Foster, Robert S., 117
Four-Mile Creek, 118
Frazer, Peter, 108, 110
Fredericksburg, Va., 4
Free Military School of Philadelphia, 18
Freedmen's Bureau, 176
Freedmen's Savings and Trust Company, 177

G
Galbraith Lyceum, 3
Gary, Martin, 117–19
General Hospital for Colored Troops, 164
George Leary, 66–67
Getty, George W., 59
Gettysburg Campaign, 4–7, 28
Getty's Station, 59
Gibson, William E., 130
Giles, Charles H., 125
Gillingham, W. Watson, 124
Gillmore, Quincy A., 63, 68, 72–74, 76, 82–83
Gloucester Court House, Va., 37
Gloucester Point, Va., 34, 51, 60, 68
Goldsboro, N.C., 155, 162–63, 165–66, 168
Governors Island, N.Y., 80
Grant, Ulysses S., 10, 39–40, 43–44, 62–63, 71, 73, 77–78, 81, 83–84, 90, 94, 96–98, 104–6, 110–11, 114–16, 134, 136–37, 141–42, 144–45, 155, 161, 164–65
Gray, James, 93
Greene, William H., 165
Gregg, John, 117, 122, 124
Grover House Road, 116

H
Hall, James, 3, 6, 128, 176
Hall, William, 175
Halleck, Henry W., 27
Hamilton, Camp, 30, 47, 68, 83
Hampton Roads, 28–29, 59, 63, 67–68, 80, 133, 137–38, 141, 145
Hampton, Va., 28
Hance, John H., 35, 100–101
Hancock, Winfield S., 84, 94
Handy, A. Ward, 3, 14, 20, 41, 43, 113

Harford County, Md., 17, 66, 127
Harpers Ferry, W. Va., 100
Harrison, Fort, 117
Harrold, Isaac, 124
Harvard College, 26
Hawkins, Thomas R., 35, 121
Haynes, Joseph, 125
Henry, William, 33
Herman Livingston, 137, 140
Hill, Wareham C., 68, 99–100, 124, 165, 168, 171
Hilton, Alfred B., 120, 125–27
Hilton, Mrs. Harriet, 127
Hinks, Edward W., 67–68, 94, 99
    takes field, 68
    attacks City Point, 71
    guards City Point, 73–74
    secures Spring Hill, 74
    withdraws to City Point, 77
    in aborted attack on Petersburg, 78
    returns to Spring Hill, 78
    reinforces Spring Hill, 79
    in June 9 attack on Petersburg, 81–82
    in June 15 attack on Petersburg, 83–86, 88–90, 92
    praises his division, 92
    command reduced, 96
    returns to Fort Clifton, 98
    retires from field, 109–10
Hoag, J. Murray, 124–27, 130, 165
Hoke, Robert F., 146, 149–53, 155–58
Holcombe, Charles R., 62, 68, 100, 166
Holman, John H., 12, 57, 84–86, 89, 92, 94, 96, 117, 119, 121–22
Holmes, Fort, 153
Holt, Joseph, 16
Hooker, Joseph, 4
Hooper, Philip C., 125
Hudson River, 80
Hunter, David, 9
Hunter, Rev. William, 19, 25, 27, 35–36
    joins 4th U.S.C.I., 35
    begins religious services, 35
    teaches soldiers and civilians, 35–36, 40
    Thanksgiving sermon and speech, 43–44
    in June 15 attack on Petersburg, 88
    feuds with Fleetwood, 101
    holds services at Petersburg, 102
    gains schoolhouse, 102

visits Army of the Potomac, 103
accompanies recruiting party, 113–14
on Fort Fisher expedition, 140
preaches sermon in Wilmington, 159–60
resigns commission, 169
Hutchins, George A., 125
Hutchins, William H., 25

I
Island Creek, 163

J
James River, 63, 69, 71, 73, 78, 82–84, 97, 101, 112, 115–16
Jenkins, J. W., 125
Jerusalem Plank Road, 97
Johnson, Andrew, 164–65
Johnson, Henry, 125
Johnston, Fort, 153
Johnston, Joseph E., 30, 98, 162, 164–65
Jones, James, 93
Jones, Julia, 23, 69
Jones's Landing, 61, 116, 141
Jordan, James, 1, 3
Jordan's Point Road, 89

K
Kane, Josiah F., 93
Kautz, August V., 81–87, 115–16
Kelly, Thomas S., 120
Kenansville, N.C., 163
Kennesaw Mountain, Battle of, 98
Key, Cornelius, 125
Key, Francis Scott, 5
Keyes, Fort, 51–52
Kiddoo, Joseph B., 57, 59, 83, 91, 96
Kilpatrick, H. Judson, 58–59, 71
Kilpatrick-Dahlgren Raid, 58–60, 71
King and Queen Court House, Va., 59
King, William V., 68, 86–87
Kingsland Road, 116–18
Kinston, N.C., 162
Kirkland, William W., 151
"Knights of Saint Main," 41–42, 50

L
Lamb, William, 135–36, 140–41, 146, 150, 152
Laurel Hill Church, 124

Lavinia, 102
Ledlie, James H., 105–6, 108
Lee, Robert E., 4–5, 7, 9, 30, 55, 63, 73, 78, 81–82, 94, 96, 98, 117, 132, 134, 161, 163–64, 175
Lee, S. Phillips, 69, 110, 112, 136
Les Miserables, 54, 62
Libby Prison, 54–55
Liberia, 3
Lincoln, Abraham, 4, 7, 9, 11, 23, 46, 54, 62–63, 71, 97–98, 104, 115, 133–34, 159, 164, 171
Lincoln, Fort, 171
Lincoln University, 3
Linghams, Charles, 125, 175
Liverpool, England, 3, 134
Louisiana, 136, 139
Lyceum Observer, 3–4, 7, 20

M
Magruder, John B., 29, 30
Malakoff Tower, 136
Maltby, Seth W., 52–53
Martindale, John H., 85, 88–89
Maryland General Assembly, 13, 42
Masonboro Inlet, 138, 140
Mathews County, Va., 36–39, 44, 59–60
Mathews Court House, Va., 60–61
Mattaponi River, 59
Matthews, W. E., 125, 175
Matthias Point, 138
McClellan, George B., 23, 28, 30, 33, 133
McCullough, John H., 165, 168
McHenry, Fort, 5
McRee's Ferry, 161
Meade, George G., 39–40, 62–63, 68, 73, 77–78, 81, 83–84, 94–97, 103–4, 106, 112, 114–15, 132, 134, 161, 163
Medal of Honor, 127, 164
Mendall, Sidney J., 86–87, 93, 99, 165
Mexican-American War, 62
Mexico City, 170
Middle Military Department, 4
Middle Peninsula, 36, 59, 61, 68
Military Division of the Mississippi, 63
Mill Creek, 162
Millie Penty, 29
Mine Run, 39

Mississippi River, 39
Mitchell, Dr. John W., 19, 35, 88, 126, 131, 165
Mohler, Henry G., 156
Monroe Doctrine, 170
Monroe, Fort, 8, 12, 27–30, 36, 46, 49, 55, 57, 63, 67–68, 83, 102, 137, 141, 145
Montauk, 137, 140–41
Morehead City, N.C., 162
Morgan, Jarrett, 17, 34, 65–66, 80, 85
Murdock, Isaiah, 56
Myrtle Sound, 147, 150, 154

N
Nassau, 134
National Union Party, 82, 115
Negro Affairs, Department of, 47
Neuse River, 162–63, 170
Newark, N.J., 80
New Bern, District of, 168, 174
New Bern, N.C., 100, 162, 166–69, 174
New Kent Court House, Va., 55
Newman, Moses, 25
Newman, Rider, 93
New Market Heights, Battle of, 116–27, 130–31, 178
New Market Heights, 116–18, 121–22, 132
New Market Road, 116, 124
New Market, Md., 25
New Market, Va., 61
New Orleans, La., 9, 46
Newport News, Va., 28
Newtown, Va., 138
New York City, 80
New York Times, 99
Nicholls, Garrison, 125
Nichols, Andrew, 125
Noble, Jacques, 156
Norfolk, Va., 12, 100
North Anna River, Campaign of, 78
North Atlantic Blockading Squadron, 69, 134
North Carolina, Department of, 155
North Carolina, District of, 46
North River, 37, 61
Northeast River, 161
Northeast Station, 161–62
Norton, Augustus A., 125

O

Oak Island, 135
Odiorne, Dr. George G., 19
Ohio River, 4
Old Point Comfort, 67, 138
Orange Court House, Va., 61
Ord, Edward O. C., 104–5, 107, 115–
    17, 163
Osgood, Charles, 102
Owens, Nathan, 32

P

Paine, Charles J.
    replaces Hinks, 109
    background of, 110
    helps dig Dutch Gap Canal, 111
    in attack on New Market Heights,
        116, 118–19, 121–22
    advances to Laurel Hill Church, 124
    assigns 4th U.S.C.I. reserve role, 132
    on Fort Fisher expeditions, 137, 141,
        146–47, 149–51, 153
    advances on Sugar Loaf, 154, 156
    advances on Wilmington, 157–58
    advances to Cape Fear River, 161
    advances to Goldsboro, 163
    advances to Raleigh, 164
    returns to Goldsboro, 165
Pamunkey River, 78, 84
Parker, Joseph, 66
Parker, Robert, 125
Parker, Will, 66
Parrington, John W., 68, 86–87, 93, 100,
    165
Patapsco River, 7, 29
Peace Democrats, 82, 98
Pender, Fort, 135, 153
Peninsula Campaign, 23, 28, 57
Petersburg & Weldon R. R., 97
Petersburg, Attack on (June 9, 1864),
    82–83
Petersburg, Attack on (June 15, 1864),
    88–92, 178
Petersburg, Va., 71–73, 77–78, 81–85,
    88, 94–98, 103, 105, 108, 113,
    124, 127, 134, 136, 140, 146, 155,
    163, 178
Philadelphia, Pa., 3, 12, 18, 34
Piankatank River, 37, 60–61

Pickett, George E., 72–73, 94
Pickett's Charge, 33
Piper, Horace L., 165
Point Lookout, Md., 65–67
Point of Rocks, 74, 78–79, 84, 96, 100,
    108, 110, 137
Porter, David D., 136–41, 146, 149–56
Porteus, Dr. J. G., 31
Port Hudson, La., 10
Port Royal, S.C., 9
Portsmouth, Va., 59, 80
Potomac River, 5, 65, 138, 144, 155
Powell, Edward H., 57
Powhatan, Fort, 69, 77
Price, Thomas N., 124
Pulitzer Prize, 177

Q

Quincy, Mass., 23

R

Radical Republicans, 82
Raleigh, N.C., 164
Rapidan River, 39, 68, 73
Rappahannock River, 39
Regiments
    1st N.Y. Mtd. Rifles, 36, 51
    1st S.C. Vols., 9
    1st U.S.C. Inf., 12, 57, 86, 90
    2nd N.H. Inf., 65
    2nd U.S.C. Cav., 74, 96, 119
    2nd U.S.C. Inf., 24
    3rd U.S.C. Inf., 12
    4th U.S.C. Inf.
        formation of, 12–20
        pay of, 13, 41–42, 101–2
        bounty of, 13, 47
        band of, 14, 19, 21, 43
        recruits of, 16–17, 25
        officers of, 17–19, 21
        surgeons of, 19
        uniforms of, 20
        parades through Baltimore, 21
        arms of, 21, 33
        demographics of, 25
        transfer to Yorktown, 28–32
        camp routine, 32–34, 40, 42–43
        artillery practice, 34
        relations with 6th U.S.C.I., 34, 50

on Mathews County expeditions, 36–39, 60–62
sutlers of, 40–41, 102
builds winter quarters, 41
Thanksgiving Day activities, 43–44
hunts guerrillas, 45–46
fights fire at Yorktown, 48–50
expedition to Gloucester Point, 50–52
officer vacancies in, 52
on Wistar's Raid, 54–56
covers retreat of cavalry raiders, 58–59
on mission to Portsmouth, 59
on punative expedition, 59–60
duty at Point Lookout, 65–67
prepares for field campaign, 68
moves up James River, 69
lands at City Point, 71–73
attacks Fort Clifton, 73
secures Spring Hill, 74
withdraws to City Point, 77
in aborted attack on Petersburg, 77–78
returns to Spring Hill, 78
greets army visitors, 78
reinforces Spring Hill, 79–80
returns to City Point, 81
occupies Bermuda Hundred, 81
in June 15 attack on Petersburg, 83–92
losses in battle, 93, 124–25
rests at Petersburg, 94–95
moves closer to captured works, 95
returns to Bermuda Hundred, 96
returns to Spring Hill, 96–97
reoccupies Petersburg works, 97
returns to Fort Clifton, 98
losses to sniper and artillery fire, 99
suffers in trenches, 99
loses officers, 100–101
social functions of, 101–3
supports Crater Mine attack, 104–7
returns to Bermuda Hundred, 108
moves to Dutch Gap, 110
helps dig Dutch Gap Canal, 111–13
tries to recruit in Maryland, 113
gains recruits from Ohio, 114

in attack on New Market Heights, 116–23
men selected for commendation, 125–28
reduced to 200 effectives, 131
digs in near Fort Burnham, 131–32
spends two weeks under arms, 131
assigned reserve role, 132–33
denied right to vote, 133
on Fort Fisher expeditions, 136–41, 144–52
advances on Sugar Loaf, 153–56
advances on Wilmington, 157–58
enters Wilmington, 158–59
attacks McRee's Ferry, 162
advances to Goldsboro, 163
advances to Raleigh, 163–64
returns to Goldsboro, 165
occupies New Bern, 166–70
on garrison duty in Washington, D.C., 170–75
mustered out, 175–76
veterans' postwar lives, 176–78
summary of service of, 178–79
5th Mass. Cav., 84–87, 90, 95–96, 119
5th Pa. Cav., 45
5th U.S.C. Inf., 52, 77, 79, 83, 86–87, 91, 96, 114, 139, 157
5th Va. Cav., 61
6th U.S.C. Inf., 34, 50, 60, 74, 79, 83, 87, 91, 96–97, 117, 121–22, 153
7th Conn. Inf., 130
10th U.S.C. Inf., 57
11th Conn. Inf., 51
11th Pa. Cav., 36–37, 60
14th N.H. Inf., 23
27th U.S.C. Inf., 152–53
29th U.S.C. Inf., 103
30th U.S.C. Inf., 103, 153
39th U.S.C. Inf., 103, 154
54th Mass. Inf., 10–11, 128
55th Mass. Inf., 128
148th N.Y. Inf., 48
188th Pa. Inf., 130
Reno, Fort, 171
Republican Party, 82, 104
Revolutionary War, 28–30
Reynolds, Stephen W., 99, 165

Richmond & Petersburg R. R., 72, 82, 94
Richmond, Frank, 168
Richmond, Va., 28–29, 33, 54–55, 58–59, 63–65, 69, 71–73, 77–78, 81, 83, 97, 110, 115–17, 122, 131–32, 134, 136, 155, 163
Rio Grande, 170
Roberts, Alfred B., 125
Rochambeau, Jean-Baptiste, 30
Rogers, George, 18, 25–26
    commands 4th U.S.C.I., 18–19
    on leave in Ohio, 52
    berates subordinate, 53–54
    on mission to Portsmouth, 59
    on Mathews County expedition, 60–62
    on trip to Point Lookout, 65
    seeks return of officers, 68
    reinforces Spring Hill, 79, 81
    in June 15 attack on Petersburg, 86–87, 91
    opens recruiting office, 100–101
    approves recruiting party, 113, 136–37
    on Fort Fisher expeditions, 136, 147, 150–151
    advances on Sugar Loaf, 153, 156
    resigns commission, 165
Rosecrans, William S., 39
Ross, John R., 25
Rust, Norman M. 101

S
Saint Mary's, District of, 65
Savannah, Ga., 134, 155
Schenck, Robert C., 4–5, 7, 11–14
Schofield, John M., 155–56, 162–63, 165
Schofield, Reuben A., 165
Scott, Winfield, 62
Sells, George, 171
Sharpsburg, Md., 4
Shaw, John, 93
Shenandoah Valley, 5, 63, 115, 138, 161
Sheridan, Philip H., 115, 138, 161
Sherman, Thomas W., 9
Sherman, William T., 62–63, 68, 98, 115, 134, 155, 161–65, 169
Sherriff, Harry C., 168

Sierra Leone, 3
Simmons, Arthur, 175
Skiff, G. W., 41
"Slabtown," 30–31, 35, 41, 47–48
Slocum, Fort, 171–72
Smith's Creek, 161
Smithville, N.C., 135, 162
Smith, William F., 63, 68, 72–74, 76, 78, 81, 83–86, 88, 90, 93–94, 104–5
Soldiers' Aid Society of Baltimore, 19
Soldiers' Home (Washington, D.C.), 173, 175
Soldier's Wife, The, 102
South Carolina, Georgia, and Florida, Department of, 72
South, Department of the, 22
Southside R. R., 97, 115, 163
South Washington, N.C., 163
Spanish-American War, 178
Spear, Samuel P., 37–38, 55–56, 59–60
Spicer, Daniel W., 93, 124
Spotsylvania Court House, Battles of, 78
Spring Hill, 74–75, 77–81, 96–97, 108
Stanton, Edwin M., 9, 12, 28, 42, 46, 101, 128, 164–65, 169–70
Stanton, Fort, 171
Stevens, Fort, 171
Steward, John, 175
Stuart, J. E. B., 4–5, 7, 61
Suffolk, Va., 59
Sugar Loaf, 136, 146–47, 150, 153–56
Sumner, Fort, 171
Sumter, Fort, 8
Supreme Court, U.S., 176

T
"Taps", 33
Terry, Alfred H., 117, 121–22, 132, 144–47, 149–50, 152–56, 158, 162–64
Thompson, John, 93
Tim Cringle, 102
Timson, Calvin, 93
Torp, Allan, 125
Torp, Dennis, 125
Totten, Fort, 171
Town Creek, 156
Traverse, William H., 125
Trent's Reach, 110, 112

U

Underground Railroad, 17

V

Vail, Melissa,, 31
Vannings, Samuel W., 124
Veal, Charles, 120–21, 125–28
Vicksburg, Miss., 10
Virginia and North Carolina, Department of, 11, 47, 57, 100
Virginia Gazette, 48
Volunteer Coast Guard, 36

W

Wagner, Battery, 11
Walrath, George H., 87–88
Ward, Andrew, 25, 125
War Democrats, 82
Warner, John, 93
Warren, John H., 125
Washington Cadet Corps, 178
Washington County, Md., 5, 14, 17, 19, 23–24, 78, 83, 97, 114, 144
Washington, D.C., 164, 168, 170–72, 174, 176–77
Washington, District of, 175
Washington, George, 30, 62
Weitzel, Godfrey, 136, 140–42
Western Shore of Maryland, 65
West, Robert M., 45, 54–55
Wharry, Dr. Kenneth, 19, 169
Wheeler, Edward J., 17, 35, 42
White, Eben, 16
White House, 175
Whiting, William H. C., 150
Wickes, James H., 26, 68, 99, 110–13, 124, 132–33, 169

Wilber, Zenas F., 165
Wild, Edward A., 57, 69, 77, 82, 89
Wilderness, Battle of the, 78
Williamsburg, Va., 28, 45, 54–56, 58
Wilmington & Weldon R. R., 158–59, 161, 163
Wilmington, N.C., 134–36, 138, 142, 144, 146, 151, 153, 155–58, 161–62, 164, 178
Wilson, Isaac, 66
Wilson's Wharf, 69, 77
Winchester, Battle of, 115
Wistar, Isaac J., 30, 34, 49, 65
    commands at Yorktown, 30
    leads Mathews County expedition, 36–38
    praises black troops, 38
    proposes cheers for Grant, 43–44
    confers with Butler, 46
    promotes Duncan, 52
    leads raid on Richmond, 54–56, 71
    condemns black troops, 62
Wolfe, Joseph D., 52
Wormley, James, 78
Worrall, William P., 52–54
Wright, Elias, 90, 149, 152, 157

Y

York River, 29, 34, 36–37, 65
Yorktown, Va., 28–41, 43, 46, 48–52, 54–55, 57, 59–60, 62, 64, 66, 68

Z

Zion Hill A. M. E. Church, 159